1927:

The Picture Story of a Wonderful Year

1927:

The Picture Story

of a Wonderful Year

by

CARL H. GILES

ARLINGTON HOUSE

New Rochelle, New York

SECOND PRINTING, FEBRUARY 1972

Library of Congress Catalog Card Number 70-154414

ISBN 0-87000-129-9

MANUFACTURED IN THE UNITED STATES OF AMERICA

This one is for my mother, Thelma, who aided immeasurably in research, and for my father, W. C., who probably will regard it as my best book.

ACKNOWLEDGMENTS TO:

Earl L. Shaub who graciously granted permission to use excerpts from his auto-biography, *All in a Day's Work*, 1961, G. S. Rand Publications, Inc., New York City, one of the most outstanding compilations of editorial experiences published in this century.

Col. Clarence D. Chamberlin who also graciously granted permission to quote from his book, *Record Flights*, 1942, Beechwood Press, New York City, one of the most notable accounts of aviation history.

Frank Reyson who was instrumental in finding some of the photos in this book, a Bronx man who remembers the beer, pizza, and sub sandwiches of the graduate school months at the West Virginia University School of Journalism as only a friend can savor such recollections.

Peggy Davis, my alert and attractive secretary, who wields a fast dictionary, an understanding of life and communication, and evidently some insight into a writer, and to Iris Riggs who knows much about this book from her manuscript knowledge.

Publisher Charles L. Gould of the San Francisco *Examiner* who very cooperatively proved the press can still exercise excellent public relations by furnishing much information and several photos of aviation of the era, and to the newspaper's librarian, Mr. L. Lieurance.

Vice President George W. Healy, Jr., who contributed quotes and photos concerning the high waters that year, under the auspices of his great newspaper, the *Times-Picayune* in New Orleans.

Publisher Harold F. Grumhaus and his assistant, William N. Clark, of the Chicago *Tribune*, who contributed art of the era's crime in the Windy City.

FBI Director J. Edgar Hoover who furnished photos of criminals.

All those who contributed art and information including Librarian John Redding of the National Baseball Library at the National Baseball Hall of fame, Pro Football's Hall of Fame, the American Railroad Association and the Canadian Pacific, and the American Red Cross.

And, to my wife, Shelby, who keeps track of contracts, and to Sheldon, my 4-year-old son, who now knows his Daddy writes books.

Contents

1927:

The Picture Story of a Wonderful Year

1 9 2 7

The Marines Land in Nicaragua

THE Twenties have more trademarks than any other decade in history. It was an era of vaudeville and violence, Americana and atmosphere. Somehow the sayings—like "speakeasy" and "Joe sent me"—aren't clichés. They're inscriptions on—perhaps for—life.

No other ten-year period of man has been so monumental. It was an evolution and revolution, an uninhibited indoctrination of society to itself. People ushered in modern technology and amalgamated it with merriment and madness. It was an almost undisciplined physical and mental transition, a time of extremes. The only years ever considered audible themselves, they roared with fury and finesse, chattered with machine-gun fire, and blew the purity of jazz music.

They screamed in a cacophony of progress and hedonism. The climax came in '27. Man contributed more significance to that one year than to any other. His achievements are still resounding, and his errors still echo in his conscience.

The almanac is gorged with the great people and events of '27. But the essence and synthesis are in all the stories of that triumphal, and somehow terminal, year. They concocted the catalyst that dominates

the calendar of time. Resurrecting those 365 days is a graphic tour, an excursion and insight into the saturation of millions of people living to their fullness for a year, and leaves one to ponder the big "Why?" it happened.

America had been waking up with homemade hangovers for seven years. Prohibition booze never left a stereotyped headache. Sometimes it didn't leave a head. Each imbiber had his own individual agony. And the tumultuous decade was entering its most magnificent and most noisy year.

Although it was going to be the most audible of all years—the whirring of the 200-horsepower motor of the *Spirit of St. Louis,* the leather duet of Dempsey and Tunney, the impact of the Babe's bat on the 60th homer, the marines landing in Nicaragua—the first day came to the nation congenially. President Calvin Coolidge literally extended his hand to all citizens for a couple of hours, and 3,185 clasped it. From 1:00–3:00 P.M. he accepted visitors in the Blue Room of the White House. People entered the front door, peered at the mistletoe delicately lashed to the chandelier over the entrance, and proceeded to the receiving room. Each shook the hand of the popular and somewhat stocky Chief Executive and left in a state of Republican grace.

But more than 100 million other Americans didn't attend the Washington reception. Some loafed. Family outings ranked high in activities. Many of the 22 million automobiles in the country were on the roads. Car connoisseurs flaunted their barge-like Lincolns and Duesenbergs. Franklins, Whippets, and Hupmobiles were among the more than fifty makes competing to motorize America. Over half the vehicles in the nation were Fords. Tin Lizzies waved dust from the many unpaved roads. The hearty, guttural chugging of motors dropped a decibel as they crossed the innumerable covered bridges. Bad roads and tire construction combined to produce the usual proliferation of flats, holidays not excepted. Many of the six million radios in homes were only a week old. The Christmas gifts were tuned to the new medium, which had already garnered its share of critics.

"If anything could kill radio," Federal Radio Commissioner H. A. Bellows said, "it is the nature of the programs that have been broadcast."

Loafers and armchair analysts of the news scene found more time on the holiday to criticize the biggest story opening the new year. The nation's intervention in Nicaragua was of international consequence, and some fatalists were forecasting a second global war. Latin American temperature and temperament were backdrops for the drama. U.S. troops, gorgeously uniformed revolutionary leaders, and peasant armies added a little continental color to the dialogue of the decade.

The conflict became physical when the tiny jungle country came up with two presidents. Adolfo Diaz was recognized by the United States. Unfortunately, Nicaraguan Liberals did not. They considered him a reactionary puppet elected by the Nicaraguan Congress, which in turn was pressured by America. His opposition mobilized and proclaimed Dr. Juan Sacasa as the rival president. Mexico promptly recognized Sacasa as the one and only president.

On January 6, 1927, combat-ready marines were put ashore by the U.S.S. *Rochester* on Nicaragua's "Mosquito" Coast. President Coolidge gave Congress a list of justifications for entering the internal war. He said the Diaz government needed military support. America had to protect her business interests there, including a lease on a proposed canal sight. And Mexico was supplying arms to the rebels.

Rear Admiral Julian L. Latimer, commander of the *Rochester*, and the top American military spokesman, ordered President Sacasa to disarm his troops or to pull them out of the Puerto Cabezas area. Local mahogany growers were ordered to pay taxes only to the Diaz regime. But the rebels ignored the demands and fought.

Anti-war sentiment in the United States ranged from no-holds-barred congressional debate to editorial protests. Senator William Edgar Borah, chairman of the Foreign Relations Committee in Congress, said the administration was looking for grounds to start "a shameless, cowardly little war with Mexico."

"We are simply bullying the Nicaraguan people," Senator Burton K. Wheeler of Montana said, "because it is a small nation, and we are doing it to protect men who obtained concessions from the Diaz government that was set up there at the point of the bayonet. Should we have landed American marines in Italy when Mussolini overthrew the government and set up a dictatorship? Should we land marines in Russia to protect American property and lives in Russia?"

FIRST ASHORE—These marines just leaving the U.S.S. *Rochester* were among the initial expeditionary force that landed on December 22, 1926. *Marine Corps*

SWIMMING SUPPLIES—Rivers like the San Juan here were among the many barriers confronting the marines, but this column of pack mules crossed more formidable water and terrain on its mission. *Marine Corps*

PORTRAIT IN THE JUNGLE—Major Victor F. Bleasdale dwarfs his little mount during a pause in the Nueva Segovia Campaign from July through August. *Marine Corps*

TOP HATS AND TOP BRASS—General Dion Williams, center, inspects the Aviation Field at Managua. *Marine Corps*

SANDINO'S COLORS—Major Gilbert Hatfield's men display the flag they captured after defeating the Liberal troops at Ocotal. *Marine Corps*

BIG STICK POLICY OF U.S. versus ICE CREAM STICK—Marines entertain innocent children, who are the inevitable victims of war, with ice cream. *Marine Corps*

BANDIT RAIDERS—Bands of rebel Liberals, like these led by General Manual Maria Jiron giving a sword salute, continued to plague the Conservative government after the civil war officially ended. *Marine Corps*

REIN UP—These serious-looking Liberal troops decided to surrender rather than fight the marine detachment, which halted them on one of the interior roads. *Marine Corps*

TROOP SHIPS—White-suited sailors contrast with the khaki uniforms of the marines on the ship in the foreground as these American ships make their way through canal locks. *Marine Corps*

HEROES WHO REFUSED TO RETREAT—When attacked by 600 Liberal troops, Major Gilbert Hatfield and his men were among the few dozen defenders at the Ocotal battle. *Marine Corps*

IPLOMATIC PROTOCOL ON THE PORCH—Palm fronds frame President-elect Herbert Hoover while he was in Corinto on a tour of Nicaragua during the civil war. *Marine Corps*

PATROL PAUSES—This squad rests while the mounts graze during one of the many treks into the jungle in pursuit of bandits, Liberals who refused to surrender when the conflict was over. *Marine Corps*

Secretary of State Frank B. Kellogg replied to the critics that the Communists were trying to take over Nicaragua through Mexico. He also noted that high-ranking Reds were working in the U.S. against its interests in Central America. But Kellogg did not sway the public with his explanation.

International objections to American marines taking sides in the attempted coup included parades and demonstrations. Students and trade unionists marched in the streets of Guatemala and Salvador with anti-American banners and chanted versions of "Yankee, go home." American business was involved, even to granting loans to Diaz. He borrowed one million dollars from a Manhattan bank so he could pay his soldiers 50 cents per day.

Within two weeks of the first landing there were 15 U.S. Navy warships in Nicaraguan waters. And the civil war was getting more brutal. But American casualties were miraculously low. During the last week of July, 39 marines and 48 Nicaraguan militiamen were attacked by 600 rebels in the northwestern town of Ocotal, near the Honduras border. One of the local natives, the *alcade,* or mayor, recorded the battle:

> The hour is 1 a.m. I hear shouts of "death to the Americans" in the streets. Six hundred or maybe 1,000 strong, the forces of General Augusto Calderon Sandino surround the Americans under Major Gilbert Hatfield and attack from all sides. American sharpshooters keep the corners clear. A Browning and two Lewis guns rake the yard. Anyone so imprudent as to cross meets death.
>
> The hosts of Sandino sweep on, attempting to capture the park, to use the stone wall for protection. It is now daylight—the Americans have not retreated an inch. The American sharpshooters are piling up the dead.
>
> Sandino sends a note to the heroic Major Hatfield, intimating that as he—Hatfield—has no water, he will eventually have to surrender. Hatfield replies, ". . . a marine never surrenders."
>
> Five airplanes are seen at 3 p.m. They approach in battle formation. They get in line, flying low, and open fire with their machine guns. They drop bombs on Sandino's army, which now is beginning to retreat.
>
> On the floor I see a marine dead—the only casualty among the

Americans. In the park and inside the houses are Sandino's dead. In one place I count 21.

The rebels were outtrained and outgunned. Of the 600 troops, the marines reported 300 were killed and 100 were wounded. The bombs accounted for the majority of the casualties because of direct hits. Many men died from minor wounds in the tropical heat, since no medical aid was available.

One Mexico City newspaper said of the battle, "May President Coolidge sleep peacefully after the assassination of 300 Nicaraguans who committed the error of defending their country, violated by an invader." Mexico was more than peeved that its support had not been enough to depose Diaz.

Officially, the war had been over for two months, and President Diaz had proposed a treaty with the U.S. in March. Over 5,000 marines then occupied most of the major cities except Granada and Matagalpa. The treaty, which provided for the U.S. to keep the peace in the country and to preserve the continuity of his government, gave America the right of intervention, and asked for an American financial adviser to restore the economy of the country. Moreover, it asked for a $20 million loan for rebuilding.

President Coolidge sent former Secretary of War Henry L. Stimson to Nicaragua as his personal representative. Stimson talked to both factions and gave out peace terms. The practicing New York City lawyer and top Washington troubleshooter became the supreme umpire in solving the civil war. He reported directly to President Coolidge. In May he supervised the disarmament of both armies. Over 6,000 rifles, 270 machine guns, and millions of rounds of ammunition were turned over to the marines. Stimson wired Coolidge, "The civil war in Nicaragua is now definitely ended." It took Stimson less than six weeks to settle affairs.

The following morning 300 rebels still bearing arms attacked a marine unit in the village of La Paz Central. The platoon leader, Captain Richard B. Buchanan, was killed along with Private Marvin Andrew Jackson. Fourteen rebels died.

The Ocotal battle was the last major incident, but the U.S. remained in Nicaragua until 1933. Sandino of Nicaragua, hero of the Commu-

nists and pet of gullible souls in the U.S., retreated into the hills. Even while he was burning villages and killing his fellow countrymen, magazines like the *Nation* praised his patriotism. (Sandino called his army the Army of Central America—a not very patriotic name.) In China, the Communists named a division after him.

If he had won, Nicaragua could have become the first Communist satellite in Central America and Sandino a very early Fidel Castro. As it was, the marines licked him. When they left Nicaragua, he came out of hiding and was promptly ambushed by political opponents and killed.

1 9 2 7

Prohibition's Wildest and Wettest Year

PROHIBITION was a 14-year alcoholic orgy that gave birth to long cars, pure jazz, Chicago typewriters. It also saw bosoms give way to legs in flapper fashions. On January 16, 1919, Congress passed the 18th Amendment, and Al Capone was elected the president of Prohibition.

The two organizations that were responsible for the Noble Experiment were the Women's Christian Temperance Union and the Anti-Saloon League. Some of the members of the Dry societies worked so hard for the abolishment of beer and booze that they became alcoholics!

Dissension started at the turn of the century. But when World War I began in 1914, the Prohibition promoters really began a sober drive. They proclaimed that the grain used to make spirits was needed to help feed the friendly Allied nations.

Three years later, when America entered the conflict, the Drys launched a distillery-closing campaign of epic proportions. That grain was needed in many countries was evident. Germany had banned schnapps. Russia had stopped vodka production. Canada went dry except for highly independent Quebec.

Getting rid of booze when we didn't have to was causing some commotion. There was clearly no grain shortage. But the fanatical Drys kept hammering away, trying to nail the casks closed forever. Some Dry congressmen years later confessed that, when the amendment was passed, they had bought votes and in some cases had resorted to blackmail to get Wet congressmen to change their votes.

The war ended in November of 1918, but the Prohibitionists had already persuaded and pressured 30 states to ratify the amendment. Thirteen months later the amendment was law.

Legal whiskey went away at midnight on Saturday, January 16, 1919. The first two years of the drought saw whiskey triple in price. But it was still good booze. The bootleggers had laid in stores of the stuff. Then it was gone. Freelance fermenting started, and the speakeasy became the faucet for the nation's thirst, the funnel down the throat of an already tipsy decade.

There was economic prosperity in America, and the public wanted to toast to it. Al Capone became the leading illegal-booze boss of America. Rotgut poured from poisonous stills, and people went insane, went blind, and had their insides eaten up. Prohibition was suddenly a sick joke.

Citizens became disgusted with life. Corruption was a stench stifling the nose of the public. Government Prohibition agents and everyone from cops to congressmen were flagrantly being paid off.

Prohibition made people drink more! It was a natural reaction. Take away a privilege and watch people who have never abused it do so with doubled motivation. More drunks were jailed on weekends than had been before booze was outlawed.

And two new types of drinkers emerged from this era. Men and women in their sixties began to sop up more sauce, and the teenagers found they could stand any kind of music. While their parents were out in the speakeasies, boys and girls in their teens began to swing to the horrible hootch.

Champagne was one of the safest drinks available during Prohibition. The syndicates weren't concerned with faking any of the more exotic drinks. They were too busy keeping the white lightning flowing. Rum was another drink you could down with reasonable assurance it didn't have carbide, snake heads, and cigarette butts in it.

Riding the choppy waters off the Eastern coast were the rumrunners. Fleets of boats—some of them small launches—brought rum ashore at night. The rumrunners operating out of Cuba and the Bahamas carried on naval warfare with the Coast Guard. Some ferocious sea battles took place just off the coasts of New York and Florida.

Some of the most monumental flings in history took place during Prohibition. The stock market was a good place for a handout. Some of the financial wizards rented clubs for private two- and three-day parties. No Capone rotgut around these functions! Only the best imported stuff that could be smuggled in was served.

But the average Jack Armstrong had to keep swilling the bad booze. New Jersey stills ran off some of the foulest fluids ever produced by man. It took a man with drive to find a good drink.

The Noble Experiment piled up startling statistics, most of them in money. The federal government lost over one billion dollars in taxes and in trying to enforce the farce. Around 90 federal agents were victims of hoodlum guns.

Politics brought about Prohibition. Politics ended it. Al Smith, New York governor, was the Democratic presidential candidate in 1928. He fought for Repeal. But Herbert Hoover defeated him at the polls with the help of the Dry vote.

In 1932, New York City Mayor Jimmy Walker clamored for Repeal. His fellow-Democrat, Franklin D. Roosevelt, agreed with him. After FDR was elected, one of his first acts was the enactment of a law legalizing the manufacture of 3.2 beer. By the end of December, 3.2 had its stout brother back. Prohibition was repealed.

Mr. Earl L. Shaub is a retired journalist in Nashville, Tennessee. The following reflection from his 27-year newspaper career, which included the 20s and 30s, is taken from his book *All in a Day's Work*:

> One cannot think of newspaper work in the Roaring Twenties without recalling hundreds of stories involving the farce of prohibition. It was estimated that 30,000 speakeasies and hundreds of night clubs flourished in New York because the State and City declined to enforce the Volstead Act. Of course, the few Federal agents who were there couldn't do much in the face of such odds.
>
> Naturally that many illegal establishments turned up a lot of good stories since some of them were ideal hangouts for crooks,

gangsters and killers. Every week prohibition produced columns and columns of news about rumrunners, beer barons, liquid czars and others who were involved in graft, feuds, fights and murders over concessions and territories. Al Capone, for instance, got more white space and bigger headlines than the President of the United States.

Prohibition officers also came up with a lot of news stories. One of my best friends—a former Chicago reporter—was a prohibition officer in New York and he supplied several good stories we used and at least two that I suppressed until now.

One of these pertained to my acquisition of about forty bottles of the finest assorted alcoholic beverages which he brought to my apartment after raiding a French restaurant. We never had so many friends before or since as during the short time that liquor was on the premises.

I invited this agent to share our apartment during Margaret's absence on an extended trip to the coast. He frequently took me to swank restaurants where drinks were sold but cordial proprietors would not let him pay for anything other than tips.

One time my friend came in long after midnight and tossed ten grand in long green on the bed.

"Want any of it? Help yourself." he asked.

"Thanks," I said, "I can't buy anything tonight."

He put the money in his pocket and told me a week later he used it as a down payment on a home for his widowed mother and younger sister in Chicago.

Two months after that we were sitting in an East 56th Street speakeasy and he dozed off with his head on the table. Soon the owner of the speak walked in, looked at my sleeping buddy.

"You little son-of-a-bitch," he said, "if you ever want anything just let me know. I mean that."

Then he turned to me. "Is he a friend of yours?" I acknowledged that he was.

"I like that bastard because he is a man of his word," he related. "He raided my brewery about two months ago. The night watchman telephoned me and I took two or three gunmen and hurried down there. When I walked in my office this fellow was seated at my desk. He arose, met me half way across the floor, extended his right hand and we shook hands. Then we sat down

and talked turkey. I gave him ten thousand dollars and he promised never to molest the brewery again. He kept his word. Tell him I said to let me know if he ever needs anything."

The brewer beamed when I told him our friend had used the money to buy a home for his widowed mother.

"Thank God," he exclaimed. "For once I did the right thing."

I often wonder what became of my companion who, in addition to being a prohibition officer and a newspaper reporter, was a student of philosophy and literature and had an excellent academic education.

He was also an adventurer. Shortly after the speakeasy conversation, he went back to newspaper reporting and was assigned to cover the New York headquarters of a Mexican Revolution. He became convinced the rebels would win and got interested in the prospect and the profit of marching with a victorious army into Mexico City.

"You know I love adventure," he said when he told me goodbye.

Next day he and another recruit took off in a plane for Sonora. Soon after that I read that the rebels had been disastrously defeated. A month went by and I got a card from my friend saying he had managed to make his way to Arizona. I never heard from him again.

One of my annual assignments was the Miss America Beauty Contest at Atlantic City. I covered this so many seasons I became able to pick winners two or three days before the judges did. This was not because I was intuitive or knew much about beauty but because, in those days, the amount of money a girl's sponsor put up was a factor.

One year I wrote a story on Thursday saying, "Miss (Name of City) will win this year's beauty contest next Saturday night if the (Name of City) Booster Club can raise another ten thousand dollars." The club raised it and the girl won. I understand money has been eliminated as a factor since the beauty contests have been revived in recent years.

I was also able to pick some winners in advance because I usually knew some contest judges. Friendship with judges had other advantages, too, as I recall in the following incident.

One afternoon Earl Carroll, one of the judges and producer of

SUAVE SALUTE—This Greyhound driver courteously tips his hat to the pretty flapper as he takes her bag; and note the streamlined conveyance, a '27 model.

HAYING IN THE SOUTH—The muted lighting of the speakeasies in the cities was another world while the farmers pitched hay in the summer sun.

FARM MECHANIZATION—Reapers had been around for some years, but more of them were being used in the late 20s.

the Earl Carroll Vanities, bolted into my room and said, "I hope you have a drink. I need one."

As we sipped the liquor, I told him, "I'm having troubles. Several of our client newspapers are sponsoring girls in this contest and want me to get special interviews with them. I do not have time to visit their hotels along four miles up and down the boardwalk to see all of them."

"That's no problem," Carroll said after another drink. "I will telephone all those girls to come up here right now and you can interview them without ever leaving the room."

I gave him the list, he got on the 'phone and in less than an hour we had seven of the most beautiful girls in the United States in my hotel room. They didn't think they could ignore Carroll's summons because he was a judge of the contest and also producer of The Vanities, rival of the famous Ziegfeld Follies.

I not only got the interviews but Carroll insisted on putting on a private beauty contest right there. He and I sat far back on my bed and leaned against the wall after he lined the girls up across the room. Then he criticized them brutally. He told one her neck was too long, he told another her hips were out of line and he told another her smile was insipid. He had something uncomplimentary to say about each of them.

"The trouble with most of you girls is you have not suffered enough," then Carroll launched into a dissertation on beauty. "Frankly, a woman is not beautiful unless she shows a trace of tragedy in her face to indicate she has lived a balanced life.

"Another important factor in computing a woman's beauty is her hands." He paused and then elaborated, "The hands were made for loving. The average man unconsciously looks at a woman's hands and instinctively imagines the type of caressing they might apply. The shape of a woman's hands, the texture of their skin, the manicure of the nails often have a deciding effect on a man's imagination and on a beauty contest." Then Carroll told us that styles in beauty change from year to year.

"Sometimes the tall girl wins and sometimes it's the plump girl," he explained. "Sometimes the athletic girl has the edge and sometimes the trend is toward the girl in the rocking chair. Also remember: talents, accomplishments and brains add to a girl's beauty. After all, beauty is more than skin deep." He rambled on but those were the high spots of his talk on beauty.

I not only wrote my interview with the girls without leaving the room but I wrote what Carroll said about beauty and wired it to New York under his byline.

I don't know whether Carroll remembered saying those things, but when he saw "his" article in the New York *American* next morning he went up and down the boardwalk showing it to his friends. No wonder he was proud of it. That was a marvelous free ad for any Broadway producer.

Carroll was a good guy and I was sorry when he was indicted for stupidly perjuring himself. It was during the prohibition era and I covered his trial on a charge of possessing a bathtub full of champagne. The charge was brought when newspapers reported a naked girl took a bath in the sparkling liquid at a backstage party. Prohibition officers wanted to know where Carroll got the champagne.

Carroll's attorneys had practically proved the liquid was gingerale instead of champagne. The girl herself testified she didn't know what she bathed in because she didn't taste it. It looked as though the case was about over when the prosecution called Carroll to the stand and asked, "Did anybody take a bath in anything backstage that night?"

Carroll foolishly said, "No."

That was bad. Two years. I think.

One of the humorous lines of testimony came when attorneys asked the girl who attended the party and she replied, "I don't know. Just a lot of old men about forty."

One of those "old men" was Irvin Cobb who was summoned as a witness and testified he thought the liquid was gingerale.

1 9 2 7

CHAPTER 3

Crime's Most Notorious Cast

CRIME was an art form in the 1920s. There was an unexplainable criminal camaraderie during the decade. The hoodlum world seemed to be bonded by some mystical lawless force, abiding by some strange code of honor formulated by the times. Gangsterdom reached its most dramatic heights with a cast unapproachable by any era.

All the color wasn't blood. Flowers bloomed after the bullets. There were more elaborate funerals during the 20s than in all the history of interment. Gangsters would murder their rivals in the most inhumane ways, as they would anyone else who bothered them. But they buried them with all the gaudiness and finesse at their command. And their money could buy a lot of the former. They bought ornate coffins costing $10,000–15,000 and up. Flower deliveries were made by convoys of trucks. Ranking hoods rated at least $10,000 worth of flowers. The elite got $50,000–75,000 worth of colorful blooms.

Dion O'Banion, a lame Chicago mobster-politician, helped establish the tradition of the overly flowery underworld funeral. He was one of the first big gang leaders murdered in the intramural hoodlum war. Three men entered his floral shop, a front for his bootlegging rackets,

on November 11, 1924. He extended his hand to greet them, thinking they were there to pick up $750 worth of flowers for the funeral of a president of the Unione Siciliana, who had miraculously died of natural causes. One grasped his hand while the others shot him six times and left him dying among the chrysanthemums. Generally, he was more wary and carried two guns in shoulder holsters under his coat.

Funerals were not only swank; they were ceremonial outings for the killers. The gangsters wore their finest suits and drove their luxury barge cars. They wanted only "nice" funerals for their deceased "friends." And the flashy homages made good copy in the press instead of a clichéd death story. The public found them entertaining, also. Thousands of people attended many of them. The public almost seemed to understand the rituals, and the most notorious criminals received some sort of objective admiration or exaltedness from the masses. The years were overpoweringly blunt and dramatic, and the criminals who could profit from and survive against them got a certain public recognition.

Al Capone was the boss of the biggest criminal empire. The King of Gangland took over Chicago and a good bit of the world in 1925. He inherited his throne from Johnny Torrio, who abdicated to return to his native New York City and later formed the national crime syndicate.

Chicago did an annual liquor business of over $100 million during Prohibition. The gangsters paid some $30 million of it for protection. Almost every law-enforcement official in the city seemed to be on the hoodlum payrolls. Congress had provided some 4,000 agents under the supervision of the Treasury Department to enforce Prohibition. They were deployed from 105 cities. Federal agents were almost no threat, and they were bought off as easily as local police personnel.

"Bribery is rampant," Assistant Secretary of the Treasury Seymour Lowman said in '27. "Some days my arm gets tired signing orders dismissing crooks and incompetents." Prohibition agents were bought off en masse in some cities. A chief agent in New Jersey said all his agents except three were being bribed. Another reported he had been offered over $250,000 per week if his agents would ignore a big beer-ring operation.

But not all the Prohibition agents accepted bribes, and the crooks

didn't have all of the good times. Two of the most dreaded booze sleuths were Moe Smith and Izzy Einstein. They closed speakeasies in New York and New Jersey as though they were booking shows. Izzy was five-five, fat, and comical. Moe was five feet seven inches tall, fat, and comical. Club owners didn't know whether the duo was doing a comedy skit or raiding them. Their gimmick was weird disguises.

Moe might walk in a speak dressed like a farmer, and Izzy might enter wearing a white tie and tails. They confiscated over five million bottles of liquor and made 4,392 arrests during their careers. And they did all of it with a smile. Some of their fans contended the speak bosses were among Izzy and Moe's closest friends. But even their jovial and dedicated persistence didn't really make it any harder to get drunk in the uproariously wild Northeast.

"Prohibition looked like a good opening for a lot of smart young men," Capone said.

Although booze and beer were the biggest rackets during Prohibition, they weren't the sole sources of income for the gangs. They bought liquor—some of it only minutes old—for around $15 a barrel wholesale and sold it for $70. The mark-up on beer was even bigger. They purchased it for $3 a barrel and sold it for $60. But gambling, prostitution, and narcotics accounted for vast revenues.

Capone's apprenticeship began in a bawdyhouse. He was an errand boy who was impressed by the dandies of the underworld. The husky Italian was in his middle twenties when he began his reign. His front was the Malt Maid Company, a Chicago brewery. The dapper bootlegger was sensational in appearance but conservative in preserving his welfare. He slept only in steel-shuttered rooms to insure that no bombs would be tossed through his windows.

He said he had no desire to die in the street punctured by machine-gun fire, and the easy-smiling, cigar-smoking 200-pounder kept five to fifteen bodyguards with him. His concern over his safety kept him in seclusion when gang wars were particularly rampant. His automobiles were actually tanks. One of his cars, a steel-plated and supercharged Cadillac, cost $30,000. Although most of the big, boxy touring cars were open, the thugs preferred them. They usually installed some armor and bulletproof windows as essential modifications.

And there was always the staccato coughing of machine-gun and

rifle fire. Chicago thoroughfares were shooting galleries for the gangs. Once after a gun battle that killed two north side beer runners and wounded three others, Capone told the press he was "abhorred by the butchery." There were over 12,000 homicides in the nation in '26. Just how many were gang war casualties is not known.

But some shooting statistics can be tallied. During one week Chicago had 12 murders, 14 burglaries, and 31 robberies. One crime expert says there were 92 intergang murders in Chicago during 1924-26. Over 100 Chicago policemen died from gang guns during Prohibition. Over 12,000 people were charged with felonies in the city in '27, but only some 600 were convicted. Witnesses who dared to take their information to court were not noted for their longevity, and the courts were generally not renowned for their efficiency in convicting cases.

But there were some federal courts that took justice quite seriously. Judges George T. Page and Albert B. Anderson of the U.S. Circuit Court of Appeals in Chicago ruled that "nose evidence" was sufficient evidence for illegal-liquor convictions. They said if agents could sniff alcohol in a restaurant, they could padlock it for a year. At first, agents tried to search clubs or tried to buy whiskey on the sneak. Some law-abiding restaurateurs began employing detective-waiters to frisk customers for hip flasks and hidden bottles before serving them ice or chasers.

The intramural liquor wars were fought with some heavy armament, including a private air force, on occasion. A rural downstate Illinois roadhouse, the Shady Rest, which headquartered one gang, had machine guns mounted in the windows and cases of dynamite in the cellar. It was a boozing encampment under siege by a rival gang. In November of '26 an airplane made some bombing runs over it, but the besieged gang considered it a minor disturbance since the house didn't get any direct hits.

But one cold January night in 1927, the Shady Rest fell and was burned. Four charred bodies pocked with bullets were found in the ashes.

Finally, Charles Birger, one of the gang chieftains, was nabbed and convicted of being an accessory to murder in the killing of the mayor of West City, Illinois. He wasn't ready to give up. He informed on his rival chieftain, Carl Shelton. The police didn't take a chance on losing

their star witness. While he was on the stand, he wore a bulletproof vest, courtesy of the police department.

Every gang greedily envisioned a monopoly. The thugs began raiding rival warehouses, hijacking trucks, and encroaching on the other's territory. Revenge started to get more nasty. As crime began to organize more and mature, it got more callous.

"Diamond Joe" Esposito, reportedly a gang leader and a politician of some scope, was caught by his crooked competition with his back turned. When he was taken to the morgue, the attendant thought it had been a very neat assassination. He couldn't find any wounds in the front of the body, but when he turned the corpse over he found 58 bullet holes in the back.

One night in New York City, some sadistic syndicate killers shot a man, tied the corpse to the rear bumper of their car, and dragged it out in the country. The abused-body story in the newspapers upset the mob leader who had ordered the murder. His hired killers explained they didn't want blood stains on their new car so they thought of the tow job. In Chicago, triggermen would sometimes douse their dead victims with gasoline and cremate them. George "Machine Gun" Kelly's victims were usually pretty well shot up, but the slightly built killer wasn't much of a marksman. Unfortunately, for several people, he accidentally discovered, due to his lousy shooting, that if he aimed at the sidewalk the ricochets would spray anything in front of him. The slugs flattened when they hit and made much nastier holes when they slammed into someone.

"Don't shoot, G-men! Don't shoot, G-men!" Kelly pleaded during the early morning hours of September 26, 1934, coining the nickname of FBI agents, when his Memphis hideaway was raided. He and 20 other hoods were convicted in the kidnapping of an Oklahoma City oil millionaire.

John Dillinger was in the Indiana State Prison during half the 20s. He started serving joint sentences of two to fourteen years and ten to twenty years for conspiracy to commit a felony and for assault and battery with the intent to rob. He went to jail in '25 and was released on parole eight and a half years later in May of '33. Four months later, he launched a crime trail through the Midwest that made him the most wanted man in the nation. Between September 1933 and July 1934 he

FROM BOUNCER TO BOSS—Scarface Al Capone made hundreds of millions of dollars from his various rackets and once boasted he owned Chicago, including City Hall. Chicago *Tribune*

TOO AMBITIOUS—Racketeer-politician Dion O'Banion died because his aspirations of enlarging his Chicago operations upset rival gang leaders. Chicago *Tribune*

738 NORTH STATE ST.—This is part of the crowd that assembled outside O'Banion's florist shop on the morning he was murdered. Chicago *Tribune*

ESCAPED SLAUGHTER—George "Bugs" Moran, shown here with his wife, escaped the St. Valentine's Day Massacre because he was late. Chicago *Tribune*

MOTHER OF DEATH—Ma Barker used a machine gun like a combat veteran, and she always looked after her four sons, making sure they had on clean bulletproof vests.

"OLD CREEPY"—Alvin Karpis liked this nickname better than "Rat," which FBI Director J. Edgar Hoover gave him.

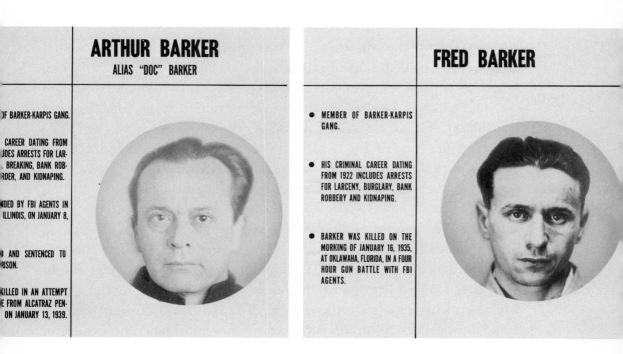

ARTHUR BARKER
ALIAS "DOC" BARKER

• OF BARKER-KARPIS GANG.

• CAREER DATING FROM UDES ARRESTS FOR LAR- BREAKING, BANK ROB- RDER, AND KIDNAPING.

• NDED BY FBI AGENTS IN ILLINOIS, ON JANUARY 8,

• AND SENTENCED TO RISON.

• KILLED IN AN ATTEMPT E FROM ALCATRAZ PEN- ON JANUARY 13, 1939.

FRED BARKER

• MEMBER OF BARKER-KARPIS GANG.

• HIS CRIMINAL CAREER DATING FROM 1922 INCLUDES ARRESTS FOR LARCENY, BURGLARY, BANK ROBBERY AND KIDNAPING.

• BARKER WAS KILLED ON THE MORKING OF JANUARY 16, 1935, AT OKLAWAHA, FLORIDA, IN A FOUR HOUR GUN BATTLE WITH FBI AGENTS.

and his gang robbed four banks, raided three police arsenals for weapons, raided three city jails and freed the prisoners, killed ten men, and wounded seven. On July 22, 1934, Dillinger told a dark-haired attractive acquaintance, Anna Sage, who ran a whorehouse in Gary, Indiana, that he would like to take her and his friend, Polly Hamilton, to a theater in Chicago. Sage made a deal with the FBI, because she was an alien about to be deported because of her brothel business. She wore a red dress so that the agents would recognize she was the one leading the renowned robber-murderer into a trap. The trio saw Clark Gable playing in *Manhattan Melodrama*. When they left the movie at the Biograph, the mustached, rather handsome Dillinger sensed something was wrong. He ran down an alley, trying to pull his pistol from his pocket. Before he could draw it, he was shot down by the agents. The FBI was unable to help Sage with her immigration problems, and she was forced to leave the country, but she did get half of the $10,000 reward money.

Some of Dillinger's gang were among the criminal legions looting and shooting up society in '27. Lester J. Gillis, alias "Baby Face" Nelson, was one of the most notorious. He just happened to be between prisons that year. Auto theft in '22 got him two years in a boys' reformatory. He was in and out of jails until July 1926. From then until late in '34, when he was killed, he was mostly out with his guns aimed at police or bank tellers. Ironically, he partially fulfilled a revenge threat of getting the agents who killed his friend Dillinger. He killed two of them just before he was fatally wounded on a highway near Barrington, Illinois, by other FBI men.

Nelson died in his car, which also contained his wife and another gang member. They put his body in a ditch and drove away. The drama of their careers ended in the stark reality of a gutter and an alley.

Millions of people evidently did regard Dillinger and Nelson as heroes. The FBI was condemned by many for winning these dramas. Thousands of people filed past Dillinger's corpse when it was exhibited in a Chicago morgue only hours after his death. Letters from young and old citizens criticized the FBI for being the real villains. Some newspapers editorially attacked the bureau. They didn't consider a trap as fair play. Psychologists said the worship was due partially to

the respect for the outnumbered. And, the sympathetic public recalled with glee some of the well-known antics of the deadly duo, especially some of their escapes. One of the most notorious exploits was Dillinger's escape from the Cook County Jail at Crown Point. He whittled a wooden gun out of a scrap piece of board. With the fake firearm, he locked up eight guards and a dozen trustees before escaping.

One of New York's most vicious killers was branded for his appearance. Vincent Coll was nicknamed "Baby Face" by his girl friends and the warped women who idolized him. In the underworld, his cohorts called him, more appropriately, "Mad Dog." He worked with Dutch Schultz and Jack "Legs" Diamond before turning against them. In the 1930s he publicly announced he was going to kill Diamond. Coll was a flamboyant killer who refused to keep bodyguards or use a chauffeur and special cars. His daring disregard for his safety ended when he was machine-gunned to death while in a telephone booth.

The six-foot plus, emaciated-looking Diamond was typical of the flashy, hedonist racketeer during Prohibition. The thin killer, like many of the wealthy New York City gangsters, had a hideout in the Catskill Mountains. The Diamond retreat was a mansion with much traffic coming and going. Beautiful showgirls wiggled in and out, escorted by representatives of the top echelons of crime.

Although "Legs" liked fancy houses, cars, and luxuries, he shunned personal protection. He was one of the hardest-drinking mob leaders. And he had enough wounds to know better. Bullets had been dug out of his bony body over a dozen times. The press called him "the Clay Pigeon." But, like many of the hoods who led charmed lives during the 20s, the 30s saw his demise. He seemed to think he was superior to rival gangs' guns. But while slipping out to see one of his mistresses one night, he was killed by a fusillade of slugs from a pump shotgun at close range.

One of the most continental criminals, and probably the most famous confidence man of the decade, was Dapper Don Collins. An ex-circus assistant lion tamer, who handled the whips and props, he found the boudoir more profitable than the cage. He set up a "shake" racket. Posing as a hotel detective—generally with the cooperation of the desk man—Collins would walk in on philandering couples engaged in sexual intercourse. He would charge them with registering under

false names or with violating the Mann Act—crossing a state line with a woman for immoral purposes—or with breaking some other law. Naturally, he would accept blackmail money instead of pursuing his duty.

"Dapper Don"—also nicknamed "Rat" because of one of his names, Robert Arthur Tourbillion, which was undoubtedly another of his good-natured put-downs—printed and sold fraudulent stocks. An accomplished crooked gambler, he played on the transatlantic ships. He frequented London and the Riviera in quest of rich gullible people whom he bilked. And, he was indeed dapper enough to keep pretty showgirls with him constantly. Some of the most famous beauties of the stage were among his intimate friends. He was arrested some 36 times, served five short terms in prison, and always retained his sophistication. His admirers said he could con judges and juries as easily as he could his victims.

Sporting tailored suits, frilly shirts, and expensive topcoats, he looked wealthy, and was. At times, anyway. Reportedly, he had over a million dollars cash in his possession on one occasion. He needed a lot of money, for he frequently tipped pretty waitresses or accommodating waiters $200 after an elegant meal. The likable rake always worked alone and was disgusted by violence. He never carried a weapon except his conning charm. During the 30s the Secret Service, the FBI, and the police in Los Angeles, Chicago, Milwaukee, and Miami Beach were after him. He was turned in by a friend at the end of the decade. Age and tuberculosis had slowed him considerably. When two detectives picked him up in a Manhattan hotel, he had 84 cents. He put on his best, now frayed and with a few buttons missing.

"Have to look good for the photographers, gentlemen," Dapper Don said as he left with the officers. He died of tuberculosis in Attica Prison in New York State. No mourners attended his funeral. One unsigned flower delivery arrived.

"From a friend who wanted you to die in peace," the card on the floral tribute said.

One of the most brilliant criminals in history was serving his apprenticeship during 1927. Willie "The Actor" Sutton was Public Enemy Number One several times. The 150-pound, slightly built, mild

man with myopic eyes was a genius, as prison psychologists discovered after tests. His IQ figures and his ingenuity proved he was a superior mental being. He considered robbing banks and jewelry shops to be intellectual challenges.

He stole over two million dollars from some sixty banks and jewelry stores. When circumstances put him in prison on a few occasions, he always escaped. Once he directed the construction of an escape tunnel from a prison. The soft-spoken Sutton stole enough equipment to install electric lights in the hole that freed him and some other prisoners. He got out of Sing Sing in '25 and teamed up with one of his boyhood Brooklyn friends, Eddie Wilson.

Wilson was also an intellectual. He always spent his time in the library while he was in prison, while Sutton generally worked in the prison library or hospital where his brilliant mind could best be utilized. Wilson was also an accomplished thespian. He not only was almost as much a master of disguise as his friend but also was a serious student of poetry and loved to recite it. Neither ever resorted to violence, but they did carry firearms on some of their burglaries and robberies, though they never struck or shot at anyone.

Willie—the name the press always used, but his friends called him Bill—always cooperated fully with the authorities when he was arrested. He confessed in minute detail all the places he had robbed and how. He would even reveal places where he had not finished the job, in case other suspects were being held for the attempts.

"I'm coming clean," he used to say, "just in case you're holding anyone for those jobs."

At times during his career, Willie would work at honest employment for as long as two years or more before succumbing to the temptation of robbing a bank. Once he worked as an attendant at a hospital on Staten Island for almost two years while New York City's finest hunted him. And, he didn't wear any disguises except while committing a crime. He had every conceivable type of uniform, including a fireman's and a policeman's, in his wardrobe. As a makeup artist, occasionally he changed his features with cosmetic masks. The fabled "Actor" wasn't one of the most notorious names of the decade. His fame was to come later. Probably no other criminal of the 40s,

50s, and early 60s captured the interest of the public so intensely. His name continues to be mentioned by the media almost daily in some capacity. Even comedians often refer to him in their routines.

Kate "Ma" Barker and her murdering brood of four sons terrorized the country for over fifteen years. The hefty, dark-haired, hard-eyed, matronly Ma could have passed for an innocuous mother if she hadn't always been killing, kidnapping, and robbing banks. Born in the Missouri Ozarks, she raised her sons there, teaching them from infancy how to become professional criminals. She taught them stealth, how to plan robberies, and how to shoot.

She set up a rifle and pistol range for her boys where she would put tin cans on fence posts and supervise their marksmanship. Ma was a sharpshooter. Actually, only two of her offspring were in the gang during the 30s. The oldest boy, Herman, committed suicide in '27 rather than surrender on murder charges to police who surrounded his hideout. Lloyd went to Leavenworth in '32 on a 25-year mail-robbery conviction. Like all the rest of the family, he died from gunshots. But his death was domestic rather than public. After his parole from prison, Lloyd was killed by his wife in 1949 in Colorado.

Arthur, alias "Doc," was killed in '39 trying to escape from Alcatraz, where he was serving a life sentence. Fred died with Ma in '35, after several FBI agents fought a four-hour gun battle with the deadly pair in their central Florida hideaway.

The trunk of their car had steel practice targets in it, since Ma believed in accuracy outside the law. Dominating her sons as few mothers have ever done, she was always the uncontested leader and did all the planning. She always made her boys wear their bulletproof vests when the occasion called.

Just when Alvin Karpis, who also became Public Enemy Number One, formed a gang partnership with Ma is not known. But during one five-year period the Barker-Karpis crime combine killed ten people, wounded four, and stole over one million dollars. Karpis was branded "Old Creepy" and so conformed to the concept of the underworld rat that FBI Director J. Edgar Hoover referred to him simply as the "Rat."

Karpis didn't appreciate the name and informed Hoover he was going to kill him for being responsible for the deaths of Ma and Fred.

The bureau chief took a personal interest in the case. He and a squad of agents had flown from Washington when they learned of his hide-out in New Orleans. Before "Old Creepy" was able to reach for a rifle in the back seat of his car, Hoover personally grabbed him. As the G-men were flying Karpis to St. Paul to stand trial on a kidnaping charge, they landed en route in Kansas City. At the airport an agent picked up a newspaper with a headline that read, "Karpis Robs Bank in Michigan." "Old Creepy" laughed, since he had the top lawman in the country to testify that he had not robbed any bank that day. (The fact is, some lesser thieves and murderers found it helpful to imitate the modus operandi of well-known criminals, who were blamed for every crime everywhere.)

A week before Christmas in '27, Capone held a press reception, which offers an intense insight into the understanding of the year and the decade. One news magazine indicated he was glum over his appraisal of Prohibition. But he did not take away anything from his stature or reputation during the news conference in Chicago.

"I'm going to St. Petersburg, Florida, tomorrow," Scarface Al said. "Let the worthy citizens of Chicago get their liquor the best they can. I'm sick of the job. It's a thankless one and full of grief. I don't know when I'll get back, if ever.

"I've been spending the best years of my life as a public benefactor. I've given people the light pleasures, shown them a good time. And all I get is abuse.

"Well, tell the folks I'm going away now. I guess murder will stop. There won't be any more booze. You won't be able to find a crap game, let alone a roulette wheel or a faro game.

"Public service is my motto. But I'm not appreciated. My wife and my mother hear so much about what a terrible criminal I am. It's getting too much for them and I'm just sick of it all myself. Today I got a letter from a woman in England. Even over there I'm known as a gorilla. She offered to pay my passage if I'd kill some neighbors she's been having a quarrel with.

"I wish all my friends and enemies a Merry Christmas and a Happy New Year. That's all they'll get from me this year. I hope I don't spoil anybody's Christmas by not sticking around."

Police and his underworld enemies hardly wept at his oration. He

did go to Florida and made it a point to pose for photographers while sunning and fishing. But back in cold Chicago, his mobsters kept their guns hot and their liquor as explosive as usual.

Crime, like all of life, in '27 was unexplainable. Why gangsterism achieved so much significance during the decade is still disputed. Moral breakdowns usually follow wars; and there also was the impetus of Prohibition. But this unholy alliance doesn't explain the nonstop, decade-long activity, nor the fine, flowery funerals.

1 9 2 7

CHAPTER 4

Sacco and Vanzetti: Anarchists or Martyrs?

SACCO and Vanzetti. Sacco-Vanzetti. Whether they are coupled with a conjunction or a hyphen, they are inseparable in American history. And no other criminal case has been more controversial. It was much more than two men tried and executed for murder. The nation and the times were on trial. Many people say the decade was put to death. Racism, pathetic politics, unethical people, crooks, and a maze of prejudices were among the sordid circumstances.

On April 15, 1920, in South Braintree, Mass., a paymaster, Frederick A. Parmenter, and a guard, Alessandro Berardelli, were shot to death and robbed of a $15,000 shoe-factory payroll by two men who "looked like Italians." Two Italians—Nicola Sacco, a shoemaker in a factory, and Bartolomeo Vanzetti, a fish peddler—were arrested on May 5, 1920, as suspicious characters. The nation was in the throes of a radical hunt. The heavy influx of aliens into the country bothered much of the public. There was much concern over communism in the heavily populated Northeast. Both men were on the Red list, as were thousands and thousands of others, not all of them aliens.

There were supposedly numerous eyewitnesses to the murder and

robbery since the street was crowded, and the crimes were within sight of the factory. Several workers watched through windows from inside the building. As always when there is more than one spectator, there were scores of conflicting statements from the many who supposedly watched the murder-robbery. Agreement was pretty unanimous that the killers were four in number and that they sped away from the scene in a big black automobile. A similar vehicle was found several miles away. The tracks of a car with a smaller wheelbase led away from the abandoned auto. Ten miles from Braintree in Bridgewater a garage owner said four men had come to his business to pick up a small car which one of the men had left to be repaired. Two of the men bore some resemblance to Sacco and Vanzetti who had not yet been picked up. But the range of witnesses' descriptions included half the population of Massachusetts, as some testimony later showed. That same day the two were arrested. They were picked up on a streetcar. The 29-year-old Sacco was carrying a loaded .32-caliber pistol, and the guard had been killed with the same size slug. The 32-year-old Vanzetti was armed with a .38 and had several 12-gauge shotgun shells in his pockets.

A 12-gauge shotgun had been used by one member of a gang that attempted a payroll robbery in Bridgewater on December 24, 1919. Vanzetti was quickly tried for the attempted robbery, primarily on the evidence of having had the shells in his possession when he was arrested. Some of the descriptions given by eyewitnesses to the attempted robbery were similar to the face and build of Vanzetti. He was convicted and sentenced to 12–15 years. Then both he and Sacco were indicted for the Braintree murders and brought to trial before Judge Webster Thayer in July 1921.

The case was focused purely on identification, and there was a mass of contradictory testimonials and conflicting interpretations. Pro and con contests concerning the trial were highly emotional and bitter. Both were anarchists and atheists. Sentiment against radical foreigners was growing anyway, due to the boils of Communist sympathy and support festering on the working ranks of the cities.

Although some factory-window witnesses who had previously identified other Italians as the killers swore that the subjects in the court-

room were the guilty ones, 20 Italians said they had bought eels from Vanzetti who was pushing his fish cart at the time of the robbery. The Italian consul in Boston attested that he had been with Sacco at the hour of the crime. The arresting officers stated the pair had drawn their guns when they approached them.

The judge instructed the jury to do its duty as "did our boys in France." Many law authorities still say that the judge made some prejudicial statements in and out of court during the trial. His war remembrance plea was particularly effective, perhaps, since both were pacifists, despite their guns, as well as radicals. Both had failed to register for the draft in 1917. Sacco went to Mexico for four months to avoid the draft. But he became homesick for his wife and his son, Dante, and returned home. They were also well aware they were classified as radical aliens and were not in the best standing with their government.

Their radical activities included, they maintained, raising funds for the defense of a radical leader named Andrea Salsedo who was being held without warrant in New York City by the Department of Justice. Just hours before their arrest they said they had learned he had jumped or been pushed from the 14th floor of a building. They did note they had been looking for an automobile so they could collect some radical literature that was in the hands of their friends, which literature they had decided to destroy because it was too inflammatory.

The court was always filled to capacity during the trial. Armed guards circled the building and were inside the court. Spectators were searched before being permitted to enter. Secret Service agents posing as Reds were seated at various points. On July 14, the jury found both defendants guilty of murder, after five hours of deliberation. Old Judge Thayer entered the courtroom for the sentencing. His stern paleness was intensified by the black robe. Policemen seemed to sense the climax and lightly rested their fingers on their shotgun triggers. Men tried to swallow unnoticed that mysterious congestion of concern in their throats.

"Nicola Sacco," the clerk droned, "have you anything to say why sentence of death should not be passed upon you?"

"Yes, sir," the clean-shaven, somewhat delicate-featured Italian said.

"I am not an orator. It is not very familiar with me, the English language. I never know, never heard, even read in history anything so cruel as this court."

"Bartolomeo Vanzetti, have you anything to say?"

"Yes," the eloquent fish peddler said, "what I say is that I am innocent . . . I have never stole, never killed, never spilled blood . . . but I have struggled all my life, since I began to reason, to eliminate crime from the earth . . . I am suffering because I am a radical; I have suffered because I am an Italian . . . but I am so convinced to be right that you could execute me two times, and if I could be re-born two other times, I would live again to do what I have done already. I have finished; thank you."

Judge Thayer, whom Sacco had called a "gowned cobra," passed sentence. The death date was set during the week of July 10, 1927, and the court adjourned. Later, Governor Fuller granted a one-month respite to permit further investigation of the case, the fervor of which was increasing internationally.

As the electric-chair date got closer the lives of the two men merged more and more with their ideals. Sacco came to America when he was 17 years old. He went to work as a shoe cutter and became known as one of the fastest in all New England factories. After his return from Mexico, he again took up his trade in nearby Stoughton. He was working there at the time of his arrest. His employer gave him a good character reference.

Away from work, Sacco seemed to be equally admirable. He was a steady, quiet, peaceable man who was apparently arrested carrying a gun. His home garden was of great interest in his life. Patiently and frugally, he had saved $15,000 and intended to use some of it to take his family for a visit to his homeland. But he did have his philosophy that the upper class took advantage of the lower. Against the advice of his counsel, he blurted out some of his beliefs, which probably were quite detrimental.

During the first few months of his seven-year imprisonment, his wife gave birth to his daughter, Inez. She grew up while Sacco waited to be put to death. He saw her over the years, but his love for her could not be fulfilled from his cell. Although he was not fluent in

English, he was capable of communicating his depression and bitterness for the plight of the aliens of those years.

Vanzetti was an authentic intellectual with the radical leanings of many foreigners during the era. He was a good writer and speaker. His articles appeared in several Italian publications, and he gave speeches at the radical meetings. If the highly literate fish peddler had obtained more formal education, he would probably have been an outstanding scholar, maintained some who knew him well.

One of the most inflammatory incidents during the years of court debate and investigation was a confession by Celestino Madeiros. He was under conviction for murder when he met Sacco in the Dedham jail. On November 18, 1927, he proclaimed he had been one of the four who committed the robbery-murder. Neither Sacco nor Vanzetti was involved, he said. A year before, a pioneer ballistics expert proved with photographs that the bullet that killed the guard was not fired from Sacco's gun.

Between 1921 and 1927 new trial motions were repeatedly turned down. And the reactions came. Such renowned people as Fritz Kreisler and Anatole France raised their voices in protest. Sacco, who was less outspoken than Vanzetti, went on a month-long hunger strike. Louise Dembitz Brandeis, the wife of the U.S. Supreme Court Justice, turned over her nearby Dedham home to Mrs. Sacco so she could be near her husband and cook his meals when she was permitted to do so.

The men had been symbols of martyrdom for seven years before their actual execution order came. And the nation split deeper into factions over the case. Many famous artists, writers, intellectuals, even the highest-ranking government authorities, state and federal, protested the fate of the fish peddler and the shoe edger. Massachusetts Governor Alvan T. Fuller could have commuted the sentences. He constantly claimed the trial had been just and fair. And there were those who agreed with him, too. But others disagreed—violently. One radical mailed him a box of dynamite. Postal inspectors opened the suspicious-looking parcel before taking it to him, fortunately. Fiorello LaGuardia, then a congressman and later the mayor of New York, flew to Boston to plead with the governor for clemency. Telegrams asking for presidential intervention arrived at the White House. But

President Coolidge was vacationing in North Dakota. Several celebrities wanted to fly out to see him, but White House personnel said they would not be received. Silent Cal intended to stay that way.

Edna St. Vincent Millay was one of those near the doors of the Charlestown State Prison, just outside Boston. Her willowy and frail figure seemed—and perhaps, always was—incapable of housing her concern for the two men. The New York *Times* had published Millay's poem, *Justice Denied in Massachusetts*. And there were John Dos Passos, Dorothy Parker, Heywood Broun, and Walter Lippman. Katherine Ann Porter came. And Zona Gale and H. G. Wells.

But neither poetry nor the pleas of many of the most respected people in the world could stop Massachusetts from throwing the switch. On August 22, tens of thousands of people came to metropolitan Boston. Buses from New York trailing red paper streamers bore cards on their sides: "Sacco and Vanzetti Must Not Die!" The ominous-looking travelers were Communists singing "The Red Flag" into the still heat of that Monday. Machine guns, searchlights, and fire hoses supplemented the usual weapons at Charlestown Prison. People were allowed to come only within 300 yards of the death house.

Vanzetti was allowed out of his cell to embrace his sister who had just arrived from Italy only hours before. Sacco talked to his wife and 14-year-old son before dying. Later in the evening he wrote his boy a last letter, telling him to comfort his mother and to fight the rich and help the weak.

As the pair walked to the electric chair, millions, mostly women, wept. They died in the first hour of the morning seven minutes apart, first Sacco, then Vanzetti. Their brains and hearts were removed for examination at the request of Harvard University doctors. Massachusetts gave the remains to the families. The friends and sympathizers wanted to hold a funeral and sought a public hall that would accommodate a big crowd. But no Bostonian would permit them the use of a big building. The coffins were carried to a small chapel in Boston's North End.

After brief ceremony, the bodies were cremated. The death smoke wisped into the sky from the high chimney of the crematorium. Mrs. Sacco, her son, Dante, and Miss Luigia Vanzetti sat inside a curtained limousine parked outside. Their friends, curiosity seekers, and the

police stayed until the smoke blended with the night.

The following account of the execution of Sacco and Vanzetti was written by Earl L. Shaub in his book *All in a Day's Work*. He was one of the reporters who covered the death story.

Another memorable double execution I covered was the Sacco-Vanzetti electrocution at Boston in August, 1927.

There is still some doubt as to whether those two insignificant men were guilty of killing a shoe company paymaster and guard during a holdup in South Braintree in 1921, but I have no opinions on that since I did not cover the trial which preceded the execution by years.

The electrocution of Nicola Sacco and Bartolomeo Vanzetti was not big news because the principals were prominent. They were not. The fact is they were about as inconspicuous as two individuals can be. Vanzetti was a poor fish peddler and Sacco was a shoe worker. In spite of their station in life, however, the Sacco-Vanzetti case was inflated far beyond its news value by a small group of men who, through sensational publicity, raised a huge sum of money to defend the suspects who were pictured as innocent martyrs because of their radical political beliefs. Some estimates hold they raised more than five million dollars and retained most of it as their fees. Some observers referred to this as a money raising racket. Anyway, they made a successful appeal to rich old ladies as well as thousands of other people. When I visited defense headquarters in Boston a few days before the end, I saw several dowagers from Back Bay and Park Avenue shelling out the long green to finance an attempted last minute stay by the Supreme Court. Although that effort failed, it was lucrative as considerable money was raised to make the gesture.

Many poor rabble rousers and radicals across the country and in some foreign lands were also shouting for the release of the two men. This reached a climax, so far as my observations went, the Sunday I arrived in Boston to cover the execution scheduled later in the week.

I was accompanied by an assistant, Ray Miller, a former Chicago newspaper man who had recently joined our New York staff. I had to file a story before 6 p.m. and, not knowing which way to turn in a strange city on a dull Sunday afternoon, we walked over to Boston Commons hoping to think up some kind of lead.

On the Commons, we found a score of soap box orators whooping it up for Sacco and Vanzetti. Each one was surrounded by a group of zealous, applauding sympathizers. Some had walked over from Cape Cod and some came from Greenwich Village and other places. As we wondered what would happen if someone heckled the orators, we spied a girl wearing a red raincoat though the weather was fair. I offered her ten dollars to walk across the Commons with a sign on her back. She agreed and we repaired to a nearby drug store where we bought white shoe polish and printed an inflammatory remark about Sacco and Vanzetti on the back of her red coat.

We followed at a discreet distance as she started walking across the Commons. Then bedlam broke loose in the noisiest and roughest riot I ever saw. Somebody called the police and, in nothing flat, dozens of mounted cops and patrol wagons swooped down on the tangled mob. They jailed over two hundred of the rioters including our girl in the red coat. That provided my story for the day and it got an eight column head in The New York *American* next morning. While I was batting out the riot yarn in a nearby Western Union office, Ray went to police headquarters and bailed out our girl in the red coat. Many of the others were fined and some of the leaders were sent to a psychopathic ward until after the execution.

This is the first time I have confessed publicly to inciting that riot to get a story and I hope the statute of limitations for such an act in Massachusetts has expired.

The next two or three days were hectic as the defense committee made one futile attempt after another to get a court stay or executive reprieve and this gave reporters plenty of developments and speculation to write about. Late each afternoon, I borrowed a typewriter in the Boston *American* office where I wrote and filed stories overhead to New York.

As Ray and I were leaving *The American* office the evening before the execution, we met a Greenwich Village character I happened to know who called himself Lew Ney (Looney). He was accompanied by two unwashed girls in dusty, ruffed up dresses.

"Boy, I'm glad to see you here," Lew said. "These ladies and I hitchhiked from New York today. After paying our subway fare

to the end of the line, we only had 25 cents left, but people were good about picking us up—so here we are."

After telling us they only had 25 cents, Lew suggested, "Let's all go somewhere and get something to eat."

Hearst reporters had good expense accounts in those days so we went to a basement dive where the girls found a wash room while we ordered drinks and supper. During the meal, I asked why they had come to Boston.

"Just couldn't stay away," one of the girls replied. "Everybody is coming up on account of Sacco-Vanzetti."

After I finished eating, I said, "I know Ray has a little money left so why don't you have another drink. I must excuse myself now and turn in for a good night's sleep because I will be locked in the penitentiary nearly all tomorrow night to cover the execution."

As I arose to go, one of the girls seized my arm and asked, "You mean you will be inside the prison walls."

"Yes," I replied.

"You must take me with you," she exclaimed, clutching my arm tighter. "I must go as your secretary. Anything."

"I only have one pass," I told her. "I can't take anybody."

"You must take me," she insisted. "You must. I'll do anything you ask. Anything. I'll be your mistress for life if you will only take me inside the prison walls tomorrow night."

"Why?" I asked. "Why must you go? You can't possibly witness the execution."

Then she told me, "The nearer I get to that chair the greater the thrill."

I think that explains why so many fanatics converged on Boston at that time. That explains why 5,000 sadists milled outside the prison walls in combat with 700 policemen who tried to keep them two blocks back at the hour of the executions. It also explains why 3,000 others stormed Bunker Hill at the same time.

"Mass hysteria," the papers said. "Mass perversion" is a better word when applied to the multitudes who sought a thrill by getting as near as possible to the death chair.

Incidentally, I read in the papers two weeks later that the girl who begged me to take her inside the prison walls had shot a man in Greenwich Village. I couldn't restrain this whimsical

thought. Maybe he took her as a mistress for life and she shot him for the sadistic thrill.

For readers who may be interested in the death chamber scenes during the execution of Sacco and Vanzetti, I am reprinting the lead and some other excerpts of the story I wrote for the Hearst morning papers at that time.

State Prison, Boston, Mass., Aug. 23—Sacco and Vanzetti died game. Both made speeches in the death chamber before they were electrocuted just after midnight this morning.

"Long live Anarchy," shouted Sacco in Italian after he entered the chamber. Then without any instructions he sat down in the chair and said in broken English, "Farewell to my wife and children and all my friends."

As the straps were being applied he added, "Good evening, Gentlemen." He was speaking to the officials. Then, "Farewell, Mother."

That was his last.

Vanzetti made a longer talk in which he protested his innocence. He was cool and collected. As he entered the death chamber he shook hands with his guards. Then he sat down in the chair and said, "I wish to tell you I am innocent and never committed a crime, but sometimes a sin. I thank you for everything you have done for me. I am innocent of all crime—not only this one, but of all crimes. I am an innocent man."

Here he paused. The straps were being applied. Then he added, "I wish to forgive some people for what they are doing to me now."

Thus Vanzetti's last words were those of forgiveness to those he had considered his enemies.

There was no chaplain present. Neither man wanted spiritual consolation. They wanted to die as they had lived—outside the pale—to use their own words.

They wore blue shirts, gray trousers and black slippers. They had no coats . . .

1 9 2 7

CHAPTER 5

The Great Mississippi River Valley Flood

APRIL was wet. In the North, winter snow melted into the maze of creeks and streams that help make the Mississippi one of the world's great rivers. And it rained. Some of the elderly who knew the river said it was going to be much more than the annual spring flood. They were right. The water would inundate a half-dozen states, kill thousands, and do a billion dollars' damage. No other high water in American history can compare to the 1927 flood.

During the first few days of the month, many residents along the river sensed the ominous power of the river building up to an unprecedented wrath. The Mississippi moved with more speed for a couple of weeks as it took on the cold waters from the North. Then it began to slow, getting more awesome in its swelling. In Memphis, people stood on the bluff and watched houses bob down the river toward the Gulf. Farm animals, debris of every description, and huge barns and buildings swirled toward the ocean on the terrifying current. From Cairo, Illinois, where the mighty waterway bends sharply and takes on the mammoth Ohio River, to the Gulf of Mexico the rain-swollen, high-rising Mississippi was aflood.

Levees were washed out. Those still standing during the first few weeks were crocheted with snakes that had been forced out of their marshy havens. By the middle of the month, hundreds of thousands of acres of lowlands were lakes, scores of people had died, and 25,000 refugees were homeless and seeking aid from the Red Cross. But the flood was just starting to pick up momentum. Levees would crumble during the night and take towns into the river. The terror-ridden and obstinate were made to leave their homes for their own safety by the authorities.

Secretary of Commerce Herbert Hoover, who had just returned from a trip to Nicaragua where he had been checking on U.S. intervention in a civil war there, was notified by President Coolidge to direct flood relief operations. Hoover had been resting in California following his Central America mission. He set up emergency headquarters in Memphis. And the river continued to drown the Southland.

"You better leave," neighbors told three families living on a plantation near Little Rock, Arkansas.

"We think we'll stay," the three big families said. "The river won't get near us." The sprawling waters were several miles away. The families could not comprehend that the river could sweep across the countryside in a quick wave. They died. People watched from a bank during the night. Lights dashed wildly around the houses for a few minutes. Then they were extinguished as the river lashed through, smashing the houses and covering them with several feet of water.

Pestilence ravaged the lower South. Typhoid killed thousands. Scarlet fever, dysentery, and measles plagued the refugees. Drenched, depressed, and beaten by the water, they succumbed easily to the diseases. Much of the property flooded was owned by the rich, particularly rich cotton planters. But most of the victims were small farmers and sharecroppers, those who farmed a patch of poverty with a couple of horses, pigs, a few cows and chickens.

By the first week of May, the Mississippi flood crest was moving like an amoebic blob, crawling southward at a mile an hour. Arkansas, Mississippi, Missouri, Louisiana, Western Kentucky, and Western Tennessee were battered by the waters. Over 300,000 were homeless and thousands of square miles were flooded. People kept drowning and dying in disaster-related accidents and from diseases. Some 50

million grains of quinine were dispensed by the Red Cross and other relief agencies. Over a half-million people were inoculated against diseases, many of them against their will. The Red Cross used trainloads of oil to burn the bloated bodies of farm animals, which numbered in the tens of thousands in some of the seven states that were partially under water.

At first amazed and appalled by the deaths and widespread suffering, the nation began to aid the area, which encompassed over one-eighth of the nation. The country was aware of the great rains that had hit 31 states and two Canadian provinces, all drained to some extent by the Mississippi. People contributed food, clothing, and household items to the refugees.

Hoover sailed up and down the navigable sections of the river, inspecting and directing rescue work. The Gulf began to darken with the prodigious discharge of rich silt from the continent. New Orleans' commercial fishermen said fish were going to the sea in great schools to avoid the suffocating dirt. The bayous were glutted with dead cattle. Buzzards circled over the floating graveyards of livestock. Wolves preyed on the levees, eating deer and other animals that had washed ashore or were tired from swimming.

Rescue boats and steamers churned the muddy tide hauling loads of people to emergency camps. Scout planes helped direct the craft to where they were needed. Pilots learned that straight lanes of water coursing through forests usually meant that somewhere below the water was a highway. Navy tugs, barges, and fishing boats were among the rather motley mobile fleet that saved thousands of lives.

Tornadoes added to the disaster. They sliced through Arkansas, Texas, Illinois, Missouri, and Kansas killing 250 and injuring a thousand. Over one hundred were killed in Poplar Bluff, Missouri.

"We are humble before such an outburst of the forces of Nature and the futility of man in their control," Hoover said of the mounting flood drama. "It is the greatest peace-time calamity in America."

Knowledgeable observers agreed, including the press. And there were the many human-interest stories, ranging from human misery and pathos to humor. A Negro baby born in a boxcar was named Refugee Jones.

Hoover's popularity continued to crest as the water dropped. Some

of the refugees arranged a Hoover celebration and presented him with
a loving cup inscribed:

PRESENTED TO
Hon. Herbert Hoover
In Token of appreciation and gratitude
for his wonderful work and sympathy
during
Flood of 1927
By The Colored People of
Arkansas

"Sho' would have had a hard time didn't Mr. Hoover come to fetch
us to high ground," one admirer said.

The following story about the flood was written by George W.
Healy, Jr., a newsman who covered the drama for the New Orleans
Times-Picayune. It appeared in *Dixie Roto Magazine,* Sunday supple-
ment to the New Orleans *Times-Picayune*.

. . . And for the Crescent City, it wasn't only the river. Two
weeks before the height of the Mississippi at New Orleans became a serious threat, the city had what seemed to some an
ominous dress rehearsal. New Orleans got its worst dunking—
from rainfall. Between the morning of April 15, Good Friday,
and 4 a.m. on Saturday, April 16, precipitation was 14.01 inches,
more rainfall than New Orleans had in any two months in 1961
and twice as much as Phoenix, Ariz., had in the entire year.

The deluge put a substantial part of the city under water with
depths ranging from 6 inches to 7 feet. Tens of thousands of residents were marooned on the upper floors of their homes on
Easter Sunday.

The drainage system of the Sewerage and Water Board was
hampered by power and pump failure. The pumps that did work
simply couldn't move the great volume of water that fell.

Before New Orleans had come out from under that Good Friday rainwater, word arrived from Greenville, Miss., that 9000
square miles of rich farm lands, cities and towns were being
flooded by the collapse, on April 22, of the Mississippi river levee

at Stops Landing, about 10 miles upstream from Greenville.

The day following the Stops Landing crevasse, the molasses tanker *Inspector* rammed the levee at Junior Plantation, 40 miles downstream from the city. This event brought the first break in the levee line south of the Red river and added nothing to New Orleans' peace of mind.

On Sunday, April 24, when the Mississippi river rose to 20.9 feet on the Carrollton gauge (with the Junior Plantation crevasse obviously providing no relief at New Orleans), many residents of the city were having obvious cases of jitters. At least one bank brought in sandbags to protect its vaults in the event a New Orleans levee should give way. Many residents placed skiffs and bateaux in their yards or on their porches. Others stocked their upper floors with groceries, utensils and canned fuel to boil water. Some even left the city for higher ground.

It doesn't sound reasonable today, but there was a growing fear that the city's progress—if not its actual survival—was in jeopardy.

New Orleans' business leadership met the challenge. A citizens' committee, headed by the late James P. Butler and advised by competent engineers, recognized that something drastic had to be done.

Barring the experimental Bohemia Spillway, far downstream, the only flood control plan followed in those days by the various levee boards was to build levees higher and higher. There were no effective reservoirs, no cut-offs, no effective spillways, no floodways.

The New Orleans committee realized that it was too late to do anything about adding substantially to the city's levees. A few sandbags, yes, but that only meant raising the levees a foot or two. The committee convinced the late Gov. O. H. Simpson that a levee near New Orleans had to be breached to release water from the river and thereby relieve pressure at the toe of levees protecting the city. Arrangements were made for the Orleans levee board to guarantee compensation for residents of the area that would be flooded by such a man-made crevasse.

Caernarvon, on the east bank of the river between Poydras and Braithwaite, was selected as the site of the levee dynamiting. The first blast, on Friday, April 29, was a flop, literally and figura-

PADDLE WHEELER PUSHING—This large load of flood victims getting ready to go ashore at Vicksburg, Mississippi, was a scene repeated hundreds of times up and down the river. *American Red Cross*

GRAZING ON THE LEVEE—Tens of thousands of heads of livestock sought refuge and forage on the levees that still stood along the Mississippi. *American Red Cross*

ISLANDS IN COTTON SAND—Thousands of horses and cattle were marooned on little mounds like these near Greenville, Mississippi, during the inland sea. *American Red Cross*

FOR FIELD KITCHENS—This large load of food is being unloaded and put on trucks; it was sent to the flood relief camps, which fed some 20,000 for several weeks at Greenville. *American Red Cross*

PADDLING TO TOWN—This is Greenville, Mississippi, soon after the levees broke, and the water stayed for over a month. *American Red Cross*

HELP THE FLOOD VICT...

The Nation is Facing the Greatest Relief Problem
IN IT'S HISTORY

SEND OR BRING MONEY

AMERICAN RED CROSS
312 WEST 9TH

CINCINNATI CHARITY—The Queen City of Ohio raised $75,000 for the '27 flood sufferers.
American Red Cross

RHODE ISLAND CHAPTER—Red Cross nurses like these helped raise money and went to the Mississippi Valley states to give medical aid during the flood. *American Red Cross*

FOOD DURING FLOOD—These workers were among those who fed three meals a day to the 10,000 refugees in the Red Cross camp on a still-standing stretch of the Greenville levee. *American Red Cross*

FLOOD RELIEF CONFERENCE—On April 22 (seated l. to r.) Rear Admiral E. R. Stitt, Secretary of War Dwight F. Davis, Secretary of Navy Curtis D. Wilbur, Acting Chairman James L. Fieser, Secretary of Commerce Herbert Hoover, Assistant Secretary of Treasury Charles S. Dewey, Secretary of Treasury Andrew W. Mellon, Miss Mabel T. Boardman met officially to act upon the disaster. *American Red Cross*

WATER IN GREENVILLE—The Mississippi town was surrounded by miles of water and was completely cut off from the world for months except for boat and seaplane transportation. *American Red Cross*

tively. Soil blown out of the levee went straight up in the air and then flopped down into the holes in the levee's crown whence it had been blown. Twelve hours after the first blast there was only a trickle of water through the Caernarvon openings.

There was no torrent until 48 hours later, when a diver placed a heavy charge of explosives under the batture in front of the levee. When this charge blew up the batture, the levee collapsed. Hundreds of thousands of cubic feet of water began flowing out of the river every second into a shortcut to Breton Sound. The Carrollton gauge started registering declines in the river stage. New Orleans breathed easier.

New Orleans' troubles with high water in 1927 were minor compared with the troubles of her neighbors.

Fifteen lives were lost when a residence was washed away in the village of Winterville, Miss., northeast of Greenville. Officials estimated that the flood was the direct cause of 100 deaths in Arkansas and Mississippi.

Louisiana, feeling the brunt of the high water later than Arkansas and Mississippi, was more fortunate. Only three deaths in the state were attributed directly to the flood. This was a tribute to thorough warning and to carefully planned rescue work by an emergency organization headed by the late Gov. John M. Parker.

The run-off of flood waters in Louisiana was rapid compared with the run-off in Mississippi. Many thousands of homes in the Mississippi Delta, between Stops Landing and Vicksburg, were under water or had water in them from late April until early September.

This report of what happened 35 years ago is more than a matter of historical fact to the writer. It also is a matter of memory—vivid memory.

Oscar Valeton, now the senior photographer of The *Times-Picayune* Publishing Company, and I spent most of Easter Sunday, 1927, wading and swimming in the area roughly bounded by Freret Street, Napoleon Avenue, Washington Avenue and Carrollton Avenue. That, however, wasn't real flood experience.

My first connection with the major flood was as a boatman-reporter. When word reached The *Times-Picayune* of the Junior Plantation crevasse, three reporters were assigned to get to the

scene. The late Ken Knobloch was assigned to try to make it by automobile on the east bank of the river. Another reporter was told to go down the west bank. I was told to charter a motorboat and go down the middle of the river at night.

The tough part of that assignment was getting to Junior Plantation without getting shot. Guards armed with shotguns and rifles patrolled every foot of levee. They patrolled both banks, and any boat or other object coming too close to either bank got, at best, a warning blast.

After getting shot at, or at least warned several times, we steered the last 20 miles by ear. Lying on deck, under the wheel, I'd put the wheel to the right when there was gunfire on the port side. I knew I was too close to the left bank. When shots started coming from the starboard side, I'd put the wheel to the left.

When I stepped from the motorboat to the levee about 100 feet from the crevasse, I knew I "had it made"; the first person I saw was Nolan Bruce, engineer in charge of levees in that district and a classmate of mine in college. He not only told me almost everything I needed to know about the crevasse, but he got me to a telephone that was working. Some time later Bill Wiegand of The *Morning Tribune* staff arrived, but the two reporters for The *Times-Picayune* who were trying to travel to the levee break by automobile never got there. I never asked Bill Wiegand how he made it.

My second flood assignment was to meet a boatload of refugees moved from flooded Greenville to dry Vicksburg. The passenger list, if that phrase may be applied to a deck full of bedraggled men, women and children, included my bride-to-be.

My third connection with the flood was as a rewrite man. Working in The *Times-Picayune* news room, I made news copy of the reports telephoned from Caernarvon when the levee was dynamited. The toughest part of that job was trying to convince visiting newspapermen who swarmed the next room that the Carrollton gauge really wasn't registering an immediate fall in the river.

After Caernarvon, my contact with the flood was continuous for more than a month.

I was riding with the driver of a Bunkie bread truck behind

the Bayou des Glaises levee when it blew out—about 100 feet from us.

Thanks to the foresight of the late Dr. I. M. Cline, a truly great weather forecaster, to the assistance of an innkeeper at Melville and to the cooperation of the American Red Cross and the Texas and Pacific railroad, I managed to be the first outsider to reach Melville just after the Atchafalaya river levee crevassed just below the railroad bridge at that town.

Dr. Cline advised me to stay near Melville after the Bayou des Glaises levees collapsed. The Melville innkeeper, a Mr. Able, telephoned me at Opelousas late at night, almost the instant that the Atchafalaya river started flooding his town. The Red Cross and the railroad provided, respectively, a scow with two outboard motors and a switch engine and flatcar. The switch engine pushed the flatcar from Opelousas toward Melville until water from the new crevasse was deep enough to launch the scow.

About six hours after we outboarded into Melville from the west, Herbert Hoover, then secretary of commerce and flood relief director, and his special train arrived at the Melville levee from the east. Knowing the only active telephone in town was operable from a scaffold in the local exchange building, I had the late George Akerson, Mr. Hoover's secretary, watch most of my clothes while I swam down the town's main street to telephone the story of the relief party's arrival to The *Times-Picayune*. (My scow had been borrowed by a local resident to pluck other local residents from treetops and rooftops.)

Thanks again to Dr. Cline, I was in New Iberia the night flood waters spilled out of Spanish lake and covered the highest spot in that city. An engineer retained by the city had given assurances that it would not be flooded. Dr. Cline telegraphed me that it would. As usual, Dr. Cline was right.

The Red Cross wasn't exactly everybody's mother in that disaster, but it certainly was a hotel or restaurant to many people. I slept in Red Cross refugee camps at Mansura, at Marksville, at Lafayette and elsewhere. I ate in Red Cross shelters at Breaux Bridge and Opelousas. There just wasn't any other place to eat when the waters were rising.

I also rode with cowhands from the Gray ranch, near Lake

Charles, when they responded to a Red Cross appeal to save thousands of heads of cattle in Lafayette, St. Martin, Iberia and St. Mary parishes.

At the peak of the flood Will Rogers came to New Orleans to give a benefit performance for the Red Cross at the Saenger Theater. It was a sellout. Ironically, that then brand-new theater had been flooded by the rainfall of Good Friday.

The 1927 flood was an object lesson. It taught the rest of the nation that the half-dozen states which touch the lower Mississippi River couldn't control all the water originating in two-thirds of the Union. The result: The Flood Control Act of May, 1928.

Under this act, federal responsibility for control of the Mississippi River was acknowledged. Under it, the Bonnet Carre Spillway and the Morganza Floodway were built. Under it, the length of the river was reduced by a series of cut-offs. Under it, many reservoirs, locks and dams were put to work.

Ol' Man River still should not be described as tame, but he's far from the wild stream he was a third of a century ago.

In the year of the flood, one of Broadway's most resounding successes opened—*Show Boat*. The power and blind force of the river were epitomized in a classic song from that show, "Ol' Man River."

1 9 2 7

CHAPTER 6

Ocean *Fliers* and *Barnstormers*

GOGGLES and gas seemed to be the ingredients of aeronautics during the first years of the decade. Aviation was as uninhibited as anything on the ground. They were dancing in the clouds, too. Barnstormers shuffled along wings, dangled from struts, and whipped through space doing acrobatics from ropes. Flying was just as informal as the aerial circuses. Navigation was a matter of following rivers and swooping low over railroad depots to read the signs. Landing was the ability to choose level pastures.

Barnstormers worked rural areas usually. They would land on a farm and charge the curious who gathered for short rides. According to one story, barnstorming was named for those devious pilots who needed fuel money. They would buzz a barn and drop ice on the roof. Then they would land and bet the farmer it was going to hail soon. The farmer would survey a hot, clear sky and tell them they were lousy judges of weather. The pilots would go for a short flight and then return. They would examine the barn, find the cold evidence, and leave with their winnings to carry on their confidence game in the sky. They literally stormed barns.

These Bohemian pilots were an assortment of adventurers and World War I aviators who had been christened over the clouds of France and Germany. They constituted a strange confraternity of fliers. Some lost their joust with death in their stunts, and scattered bits of themselves and their Jennys over fairgrounds, airports, and farm fields. Crashing was common, and it was not unusual to see a freshly cracked-up pilot hitchhiking to the nearest general store to get materials to repair his plane. Nails, lumber, canvas, glue, and pigmented dope fixed almost all damages. The airmen of the era had to be more carpenter than mechanic. Wired-together wings and propellers were common.

Most barnstormers flew obsolete World War I crafts. The Curtiss J.N.4—the Jenny—was the most popular airship. Standards, D.H.4's, and Canucks were among the most-used makes. Most of the fragile planes could be bought used for modest prices. Some used models sold for $300–$500. A few of the more successful flying circuses could make more than that in one day.

Wing-walking was the featured attraction. The performer rode in the front cockpit of the two-place planes. He—and sometimes a she— would crawl out of his seat and walk along the lower wing, holding onto the bracing wires against the great wind pressure. Gingerly, he would climb onto the upper wing. Then he would fasten bracing wires —which were invisible from the ground—to a leather and steel harness girdling his chest. With this security, he became an incredible athlete. He cavorted in a variety of positions while the pilot executed intricate maneuvers. Wing-walkers added some drama to their already great appeal. They would often fall intentionally, letting their emergency ropes save them. Then they would climb back on the wing and act as if they were taking off their safety cables.

Some of the top wing-walking acts included the very dangerous plane transfer. Two planes would fly only a couple of feet apart— sometimes inches—and the performer would crawl across a ladder from one plane's wing to the other one. Precision flying, agility, and courage were necessary to perform the amazing stunt.

In the bigger cities, the circuses sometimes held night shows. They would light up their planes with an array of lights and fireworks. Parachute jumps were novel and impressed spectators. By 1927 though,

barnstorming was dying. It had helped personalize aviation. Dare-devils and flying fiends had swooped air travel into the mainstream of American life. Airmail planes had proven their efficiency in speeding up postal deliveries. But there was still some of the pioneer spirit even in flying letters due to the infancy of the medium. But it was quickly maturing.

Flying became meaningful in 1927. The year's record flights officially initiated the mode of air travel. The decade turned the props on the immortal trips, to some extent, but the fantastic year was the climax, as with everything else happening. It just had to be that way.

In May 1919, Raymond Orteig, a Frenchman who owned the Lafayette Hotel in Greenwich Village, offered $25,000 to "the first aviator who shall cross the Atlantic in a land or water craft [he meant a seaplane] from Paris or the shores of France to New York, or from New York to Paris or the shores of France, without stop." But the cash went unclaimed for eight years because of inefficient engines. There were no motors capable of such long distance.

Then in '26 the Wright company produced a 220-horsepower air-cooled powerplant. Three of them carried U.S. Commander Richard E. Byrd on his North Pole flight that year. Pilots began to consider an Atlantic flight. The polar flight hero was the first choice to win the Orteig prize. Clarence D. Chamberlin, one of the most-famed gypsy flyers, was the second favorite candidate to span the ocean. There was no third name really in contention. Certainly, Charles Augustus Lindbergh was not prominent. The 25-year-old was the son of a Populist congressman, who had been born in Sweden and died when Charles was 21. His mother, Mrs. Evangeline Lodge Lindbergh, was teaching at the Cass Technical High School in Detroit when her son made his immortal trip. His parents had been separated for several years.

Lindbergh began flying when he was 20. He dropped out of the University of Wisconsin during the middle of his sophomore year and enrolled in a flying school in Lincoln, Nebraska. A year later, he bought his first plane, a $500 ship. After four years in the Army Air Service, he got a job as an airmail pilot for a tiny airline. He had to ditch planes four times when he became lost in fog and ran out of fuel. But parachuting was tame to the onetime barnstormer who had also walked wings.

The young knockabout pilot figured he might as well fly the Atlantic as anyone else. He saved much of the money he made working for the airline. By May of '27 he had picked up a new single-engine—a Wright Whirlwind—monoplane in St. Louis for $14,000. He had to borrow some of the money, but he also attracted attention. But he wasn't the only one getting ready. Others were preparing to take off from Roosevelt Field on Long Island. A week-long storm had already delayed some plans. On the morning of May 19 the weather cleared, and Lindbergh happened to be the only man ready. He had gone to bed around midnight, but couldn't sleep. A few minutes after 2:00 A.M. he arose and started gassing up *The Spirit of St. Louis*.

With four sandwiches, emergency army rations, two canteens of water, and 451 gallons of gas, Lindbergh started down the water-logged runway at Roosevelt at 7:52 A.M. Several men grasped the struts and helped the heavily loaded plane get started. The winded pushers and several hundred people watched him taxi to the end of the strip and into the safety zone. Then he was out of it. The monoplane lurched on the soft uneven field. It bounced in the air and then down. He was winding full throttle toward a tractor and a gully when he got the *Spirit* in the air, missing the tractor by 15 feet and some telephone wires by 20.

His route was the shortest to Paris. Called the great circle, it cut across Long Island Sound, Cape Cod, Nova Scotia, then skirted the Newfoundland coast. The handsome six-foot-one adventurer had a few challenges on the trip. But staying awake was his biggest problem. He dozed several times but somehow kept flying. Near the European mainland, he sighted some fishing vessels. Circling low, he yelled, asking if Ireland was just ahead. No answer came. But Ireland was just ahead, then southern England and the Channel.

He followed the Seine River to Paris and circled the city before spotting the field at Le Bourget. He was not prepared for the 25,000 people who swept toward the *Spirit of St. Louis* as he tried to taxi up to the front of the hangars. He had to chop his engine to keep his propeller from slicing into the crowd. In 33 hours and 29 minutes he had connected the continents, a 3,600-mile conquest of the Atlantic at an average speed of 107½ miles per hour.

"Well, here we are," the gawky, smiling country boy told the people who opened the cabin door. "I am very happy."

"I am proud to be the mother of such a boy," his mother said in Detroit, when she was informed her son had made a successful flight.

The immediate aftermath of the trip included a cordon of police stopping the spectators from stripping souvenirs from the *Spirit*. Official congratulations started with U.S. Ambassador Myron Herrick and French dignitaries. Then a relaxing massage for cramped muscles. And some coffee, although he had refused to take any on the flight. A motor trip through congested streets to Paris and ten hours of sleep in the U.S. Embassy.

Lindbergh became immortal and a millionaire almost instantaneously, although he refused million-dollar movie and vaudeville contracts and an assortment of other lucrative offers. Raymond Orteig, the Manhattan hotelman, paid him the $25,000 prize. After the compliments of Europe, he returned, along with his beloved plane, to America on a ship. Between banquets and festivities, where he accumulated rows of medals, he flew the *Spirit* to every state in the union, promoting the future of aviation. Two airlines made him a consultant. Stock options in the corporations made him rich.

While Lindbergh was being bestowed with honors, other pilots, most notably Clarence Chamberlin, were getting ready to duplicate his feat. Chamberlin, a 29-year-old barnstormer, was born in Denison, Iowa, the son of a jeweler. He had been flying almost ten years and had set flying records, including that of staying aloft longer—51 hours —than anyone else ever had during that time. The tall, reedy Chamberlin had been planning to fly over the ocean longer than probably anyone.

"The idea of a transatlantic flight had been in my mind since my first association with Mr. Bellanca [Guiseppe Bellanca, an Italian plane designer] in 1920," Chamberlin said. "Bellanca was convinced he could build a plane that would do the job. It was my dream to fly it. In the years that followed I tried again and again to get someone to finance construction of such a ship, our plan being first to gain recognition and demonstrate the plane's ability to fly to Paris by establishing a new world record for duration, and then go after Mr. Orteig's money."

But it was June 4, 1927, before Chamberlin could get airborne en route to Germany. Circumstances and technicalities kept him from taking off before Lindbergh. Finally, the slim pilot got a Bellanca plane, the *Columbia*. Charles A. Levine, a wealthy businessman, bought the plane. After some negotiating on who would be the pilot, Chamberlin was chosen. Levine decided to accompany him. He matched the Orteig money, $25,000, for a successful flight. All this dissension was months before Lindbergh left the runway.

"Yet the days dragged on, and the Bellanca did not start for Paris," Chamberlin said. While Lindbergh was on his way, the *Columbia* was fueled and ready. Bellanca preferred to wait and see whether Lindbergh made it before taking off.

"Some people may wonder why I ever considered going at a time when Lindbergh had just landed in Paris," Chamberlin said hours after "Lucky Lindy" landed, "and the goal for which we had been aiming no longer existed. I think I can tell them. I had been trying to promote a flight of this sort for years, had been telling skeptical people what the Bellanca plane could do, and I had been living with the idea that at last I was going to have a chance to prove some of my 'crazy' claims. A thing like that isn't given up easily.

"Bellanca and I had offered the Chicago *Tribune* a New York–Paris flight back in 1924 and 1925 if they would back us to the extent of $10,000. Harry Baker, manager of the Pacific and Atlantic news picture agency in New York [a *Tribune* subsidiary], had laid the proposition before that paper and it had been turned down. No one had listened to me in the past, and I wasn't going to let slip an opportunity to vindicate myself and the plane. I wanted to be able to say 'I told you so' to those who had refused to finance me when they had a chance.

"Bellanca was opposed to making the flight if anyone else made it first; I preferred, of course, to make it first, but after I had been cheated of that, through no fault of my own, I was determined to go on and make a better showing than the man who had beaten me to the first non-stop flight from New York to Europe. It was with no idea of trying to 'crash in on Lindbergh's glory,' as some people suggested, or of attempting in any way to detract from or belittle what he had done —nothing ever could do that—that I planned to hop off on the day of his triumph. But I knew that the Bellanca could beat Lindbergh's

record unless she met with mishap, and in this event I, at least, would have demonstrated that all my talk about flying to Europe was not—just talk. Our tests had shown the plane could fly to Berlin easily, and perhaps to Warsaw. Bellanca might be out but the plane was ready, and it was my idea to finish the job I had started.

"So, when I called it off on the day of Lindbergh's triumph, it was with no idea of abandoning the transatlantic flight but solely because our arrangements for that particular time had gone awry . . .

"Except for short test flights the *Columbia* bided her time for the next two weeks while we scanned the weather maps daily, and nightly, too, for that matter. We had made up our minds to go at the first favorable opportunity, although Levine had announced he was through with 'announcements' and would say nothing more of his plans until the *Columbia* was ready to fly. There was no reason to hurry now and Levine turned the delay to good use by coming down to Curtiss Field and going along with me on every instrument testing flight I made. He had a great flair for 'joy riding' anyway, so those who saw him never questioned his explanation that he went up 'just for the fun of it.' "

Chamberlin was at Roosevelt Field at 5:00 on the morning of June 4. He had almost as many problems on the runway as had confronted him for years in his attempt to cross the Atlantic. Still the world did not know who would go with him. The following excerpt is from Chamberlin's book, *Record Flights*:

Back on the field again, I was besieged by photographers insistent on last-minute flashlight pictures, and by friends and would-be friends who wanted to shake hands and wish me well, or get me to autograph a card for them. Several thrust "good luck" pieces into my hands and pockets. One man forged his way through the crowd, dragging a woman after him and demanding that I "shake hands with the wife" because she had been the last to shake Lindbergh's hand "and he got there safe." All of which was kindly meant, but didn't help a great deal when I needed to give all my attention to warming up the motor properly, watching the oil pressure gauge and doing the other little things that assure continued performance from an airplane engine.

Still no one knew who would accompany me. It was almost full daylight now, and part of the crowd, taking their cue from the

photographers, who had gone down the runway for "shots" of the take-off, began spreading over the field. There were not enough police to handle the situation and the few there were, believing this to be "another false alarm," tried only half-heartedly to clear the crowd out of the way. Mr. Levine had driven up a few moments before, his wife unexpectedly with him, and the reporters swarmed about him to ask who would be "Chamberlin's navigator." He put them off with assurances that the second man would "climb in just before she goes." His flying clothes were already in the back of the cabin with mine.

Levine came over and talked to me, the bystanders thinking he was saying farewell. I told him everything was ready to go. The police by this time had driven the crowd back from the runway, but they still formed a lane on either side of it. I thought we could get through. Levine, bareheaded and in an ordinary business suit, climbed into the cabin and sat as though conversing with me while I tried the motor at full throttle. It was "sweet" and I nodded for the blocks to be pulled from in front of the wheels. Once more the throttle crept open under my hand.

For a moment the heavily loaded ship stood trembling as though she would never move while the Whirlwind roared at full throttle. Then, slowly, she began to lumber down the field. Forgotten now was Levine, sitting at my side, and everything else save the job in hand and the curious crowd pressing in ahead. A motorcycle cop was speeding down the runway in front of the *Columbia*, warning them back, but they paid no attention; I knew they would stand and look and never move, fatuously confident the plane would roar down the narrow lane they had formed, until some little chance obstruction sent it swerving among them and it would be too late.

Because her wheels were set far forward and her center of gravity was far behind them, the Bellanca had a tendency to swing, pendulum-wise, right and left, and to buck in the same manner as she started to leave the ground. She was almost unmanageable and I was "fighting" the rudder back and forth for all I was worth to keep her under control. It was no use trying to get through that narrowing lane of people. I pulled the throttle back, turned the Columbia when she had lost enough speed and taxied back up the field.

I made no effort to conceal from the police and everybody else that I was sore. I'm afraid I made it painfully and profanely clear that I knew what I wanted when I wanted it and that my immediate desire was for them to do their stuff and get the crowd out of my way. Naturally the crowd closed in to see what was wrong and this added to the confusion.

Mrs. Levine had been a little worried when she saw her husband climb into the *Columbia* beside me, and start down the field, but someone standing by assured her we were only going to "test" the plane. This explanation satisfied her, particularly after the *Columbia* turned and taxied back. She hadn't the slightest notion of Levine's determination to go; he had mentioned the idea jokingly to her long before and she vowed then she would burn the plane if she thought he meant it. So he kept his plans to himself.

The police managed to drive all the crowd over to the right side of the runway . . .

As we gathered speed the Bellanca resumed her bronco antics, and I had all I could do to keep her under control. I was afraid to try to hold her on the runway because of the crowd at the right, so I played safe and swung off onto the sodded field at the other side. The going was not quite so good here but at least I had more room. Disaster loomed for a breathless split-second as the Bellanca's wheels forsook the runway. There, straight ahead of her whirling wooden propeller, was one of the three-foot stakes, topped by a star, with which the Wanamaker crew had marked the runway boundaries. I expected the propeller to strike it and splinter into a thousand pieces, but there was no stopping or turning aside. On we roared, and as if by a miracle the stake passed through the blades of the propeller untouched! It had slipped past between revolutions, and I was breathing again.

But I was breathing hard and deep. The Bellanca was giving me all I could do, and for about thirty seconds after I opened the throttle I was the busiest man in Nassau County. By this time the plane was beginning to lift into the air, and as it did so, the up and down bucking motion commenced—wheels touching first and then tail skidding in a quick rocking action. I got it away from the ground as quickly as possible (a 2,000-foot run) and in the moment of taking to the element for which she was designed, the

Bellanca became a perfect flying machine and my troubles were over.

We were climbing well, and as the motor had a tendency to labor when wide open under this condition, I throttled it from 1,750 revolutions a minute to 1,700 while we were still over Roosevelt Field and just passing Commander Byrd's *America* on her starting platform at the other end of the runway from which we had started. It was a few minutes after six and we were on our way.

Even before the *Columbia* was 200 miles away, the compass quit. Both men were concerned. They debated going back.

"Go ahead," said Levine when Chamberlin put the decision up to him, "I'd rather be in Davy Jones' locker than go back and face those newspapermen. They didn't think I wanted to fly to Europe anyway."

As the little Bellanca left the mainland, the two were jubilant. "Europe the next stop," Levine said.

"What are two men, more or less?" Chamberlin said in his dry humor.

Over the ocean, the *Columbia* was forced to fly above 20,000 feet. Fog and bad weather were almost fatal. If they had left while Lindbergh was in flight, they would have had much better flying conditions. The plane did not have the instruments for blind flying. Temperature added to the plight of the fliers. Fatigue and the weather almost caused them to crash. Chamberlin chronicles the ordeal over the ocean and how the *Columbia* almost crashed, in the following account from *Record Flights*:

> Exhaustion, cold, the strain of unending labor over flabby controls at high altitude where oxygen is scarce—all these had got in their work. My mental state was that of a man who is desperately seasick, although, of course, I suffered no nausea. If I had been trying to fly by instruments I would have sat there and looked at them and not cared what they read; it was the physical and mental apathy of a man who thinks that nothing matters any more and does not care particularly what happens. Above the clouds, flying was more or less instinctive; their tops furnished a definite horizon and it was only necessary to keep the

Columbia's wings and nose level in relation to that, and to re-member how far we wandered each way from the course we could not follow until day broke. Levine was in better shape than I but he was of little help. In daylight and fair weather I could turn the plane over to him without fear, but with thick weather and night to combat, I dared not trust the controls to him.

Dawn came a last, and a welcome sight it was. Fatigue had made me light-headed by this time. I still knew what I was doing, but a feeling of unreality was creeping over me and I knew that unless I rested for a moment or two there was danger of my passing out. It was light enough for Levine to handle the ship.

"See what you can do with her for a while," I said. "I've got to have some rest." And I shoved back on the gas tank "shelf" in blissful relaxation.

We were still at an altitude of 20,000 feet or more, and Levine was following my example of killing time until it was full day-light. All went well for ten or fifteen minutes. Just what hap-pened then is hard to say, but flying in the thin air at this height required more skill than Mr. Levine ever had been called on to exert and it is probable he lost some altitude. Or he may have started down one of the promising cloud "valleys" only to find his progress blocked at the end. Either this, or in trying to lift the Bellanca over a ridge of fog after losing a little altitude, he got us into the mist. It was a matter of seconds then until he was hopelessly bewildered and utterly without sense of direction. In-evitably he pulled the *Columbia* up into a stall.

If she had been an ordinary airplane then, she would have gone tail-spinning down through the fog. Being a Bellanca, she did the nearest thing she could to a spin. Off on her left wing she went, nose down, in a steep and dizzy spiral. The blinding mists, sweeping by, gave no hint of what was going on; some-thing was wrong but Levine had no idea what.

My lethargy dissolved before the disaster facing us. Even in the time it took me to slide down off the tank into my seat, the Bellanca's wings had started shuddering and shimmying as if they would be ripped away from the fuselage of the sturdy little ship at any instant. Her balanced rudder, oscillating in the terrific dive, was whipping the rudder bar back and forth with leg-

breaking force and shaking the rear end of the plane with such violence that I expected the whole tail to be torn off.

Never in my life have I felt that death was so close or been so badly scared. Levine, on the contrary (with the odd failure to realize that flying has its hazards, which is so characteristic of him), was enjoying the experience hugely. When the ship got beyond his control he had shut off the motor and then taken his hands and feet off the unmanageable controls entirely. He was sitting there laughing and told me afterward he had been amused because the *Columbia* was behaving "like a bucking bronco." It evidently never occurred to him that the next "buck" might take us both into eternity.

So violent was the action of the rudder bar that it would have been utterly foolhardy to try to stop it all at once. Instead, I pushed my feet down cautiously to catch it at the end of its vicious arc and "dampen" out the terrible vibration that seemed about to carry away the tail. I was as much at a loss about direction and what was going on in that fog as was Mr. Levine, but the plane's behavior and the frightful rush of air told me we were going down at tremendous speed.

The altimeter needle swept past the hundred-foot marks like the indicator of a swift elevator clicking off the floors in a great office building. It was the bank and turn indicator that told me what the plane really was doing—a diving, banking turn to the left, which was taking us down, down, down. . . . Our air speed indicator had calibrations only as far as 160 miles an hour but the hand had passed this mark and was jammed up against a dial post as if it were going to push it out of the way.

It is hard enough to take a plane in normal flying position, go into a cloud and keep an even keel when you have the proper instruments for "blind" flying. It is so much harder if your instruments aren't all they might be, that I had been wandering about all night in zero cold above the clouds rather than try it. But to take a plane that is out of control in the fog and ready to fall apart from vibration, and make it tractable again is one of those jobs that just can't be done until you have to do it.

The first thing I did was to "smother" the rudder with my feet in a progressive choking-down maneuver that stopped its wild oscillations. Then I ruddered out of the weird spiral dive into

which we had fallen, my eyes on the bank and turn indicator until it told me we were going straight ahead. After that it was a relatively simple matter to pull up the Bellanca's nose until she lost her comet speed and the inclinometer and air speed indicators showed she was reasonably near level flight again. Writing about it now, I can see that this all sounds easy, but in actual accomplishment it was a difficult matter; probably the hardest job I ever faced in my life. Certainly I never want to meet such a situation again.

We had fallen into trouble at approximately 21,000 feet, and by the time I had the Bellanca under control again, the arrested needle of the altimeter stood at 4,000 feet! In the brief space since the plane had started her wild plunge we had dropped more than three miles toward the earth!

There had been one factor in our favor—it had started to get light. We were still in thick fog when I got the *Columbia* under control again, but it was light enough for me to tell when—and if —we came through the bottom of the clouds. I knew we were somewhere over Germany, unless my calculations were all wrong, and I knew also that the Harz Mountains in Germany pushed up to 3,000 or 4,000 feet in many places. It would be too bad to meet one of these peaks in the fog after having just pulled out of one nasty mess. I wiped the cold perspiration off my face, cleared the motor, and stuck the Bellanca's nose down again. Ceiling or no ceiling underneath, we had started down and we had to go on through.

Would we come out all right or were we about to smear ourselves and the *Columbia* all over a rugged and unyielding landscape? If we hit a valley there was little likelihood the fog would extend all the way to the ground, but there was every possibility that some of the mountain tops were shrouded by the mist through which we were flying. Thus I had succeeded from one worry to another. Mr. Levine was as unperturbed as ever.

The clouds grew thinner and began to be broken during the last 2,000 to 3,000 feet, but it was still too near dawn to distinguish anything below. Between 500 and 1,000 feet we came through the ceiling altogether and found ourselves flying in rain and mist over a body of water. The visibility was poor and we thought at first we might be over the North Sea as only one

LUCKY LINDY AND WILL—Charles Lindbergh, left, stands beside the fuselage of a plane with Will Rogers.

PORTABLE PLANE—Col. Chamberlin points to his new plane with folding wings.

AND IT QUIT—Chamberlin, in the dark suit, watches while the compass of the *Columbia* gets a final check before the flight to Germany.

BOXY FOKKER—This flat-bellied Army tri-motor made the first flight over the Pacific.

FIRST NONSTOP TO HAWAII—Lt. Albert Hegenberger is the "Lindbergh of the Pacific."

San Francisco Examiner
Monarch of the Dailies

AN AMERICAN PAPER · AMERICA FIRST · AMERICAN PEOPLE

THEY'RE OFF TODAY!

CXXVII. NO. 47. THE WEATHER—Fair, For in Evening Tuesday CC — SAN FRANCISCO, TUESDAY, AUGUST 16, 1927—THIRTY-FOUR PAGES — DAILY 5 CENTS. SUNDAY 10 CENTS: DAILY AND SUNDAY PER MONTH, $1.15.

NINE DOLE FLYERS READY FOR NOON HOP

S. F. BOULEVARD BONDS URGED

Today

(column notes)

...of a Ship.
n Would Wonder.
erfume Ladies.
One Star.

hur Brisbane
1927, by Star Company.)

a ship in the midst
changed since Solo-
of David, wrote his
the hardy Phoenician.
hous freight for Solo-
would wonder at the
American
General Grant-Mark
would wonder at the

ten on the Aquitania,
, floating cities that
au, as free from ro-
moving pictures on
ever has crossed in
his eyes, like Rip

eck, much wider than
sidewalk, and almost
ses a wheezy, short,
ling a small dog to
all its owner's quali-
lisposition to snap at
They turn at the
s allowed forward of

ears a beautiful rib-
, possibly a grand-
a brilliant pink silk
such high visibil-
d time captain might
in rious. Much gold
and on her cheeks,
ead the rouge that
in Kachina's descrip-
orrer, dry era, cere-

nefarting lady passes,
mes another, forty
, forty times worse
in bright red, she
perfumes of Arabia,
worst, tickiest per-
and smokes an cig-
rette.

is used as a word,
hasize a speech that
deeply appreciated
with black, sleek,
stomach caving lu-
gan accent, and no
read than a Russian

woman's father prob-

spend a week in this
not realizing that
he ocean until the fog
en some say. "I don't
d." The more nervous
horn with two more

nternal wealth has
into cocktail and
emporiums. There
ds of menus, wine
listed as cocktails
room program, and
rkers on their own
ough a list of Ameri-
foods that amazes
hem.

mut comes a radio
National News Service:
on, Edrard and Frisch,
machine, beat Cham-
ance record, flying 53
inutes." You thank
oon we shall fly to
the dog and per-
Rain bops. They will
liane, promenading a
n Page 6, Column 2.)

RICH FISHER'S MURDER AT SEA LAID TO TWO OF KIN

Federal Authorities Arrest Son-in-Law and Daughter of Mica-lizzi, Killed in Open Boat

The murder of Frank Micalizzi, wealthy Italian fisherman, was laid directly at the door of his son-in-law, Beverlo Auteri, and Auteri's wife, in a murder complaint issued yesterday by United States Commissioner Thomas U. Hayden.

Bitter family hatreds, intensified by fear of losing a $100,000 fortune, led to the shooting of Micalizzi, whose bullet-riddled body was found drifting off Monterey Bay on July 25, according to Mrs. Centra Micalizzi, the widow, who swore out the complaint.

Auteri did the actual shooting, it is charged, while Silvia Micalizzi-Auteri, the step-daughter, conspired in the murder and was an accessory. Both Auteri and his wife are under arrest, and are being held without bail. They will probably be ar-raigned before Commissioner Hay-den today.

Auteri has been under question-ing at intervals since the discovery of his father-in-law's body, but has denied any knowledge of the cir-cumstances surrounding Micalizzi's death.

The aged fisherman was sitting at the tiller in his fishing launch.
(Continued on Page 8, Column 2.)

Love's Dream Over

MRS. HELENA SOULES RICH-ARDSON, who married Paul Richardson, son of the former governor, when they both were 17, and who now sues for divorce.

RICHARDSON'S SON IS SUED

Paul W. Richardson, son of for-mer Gov. Friend W. Richardson, was sued for divorce in Oakland yester-day.

He has a violent temper, beat her and broke the family furniture, ac-cording to the complaint of his wife, Helena Soules Richardson, who asks a divorce, a cash settlement and her maiden name.

Richardson is understood to be in the East, awaiting the return of his father, who is on a world tour. Mrs. Richardson is at the Errol Arms, 2526 Ashby avenue, Berkeley.

Yesterday's divorce terminates the romance which started at a Sacra-mento high school. Both aged 17, they graduated together, gained the approval of their families in a mar-riage at San Rafael in 1920, before they started their college careers in Berkeley.

Mrs. Richardson, who is the daugh-ter of Mr. and Mrs. A. P. Soules, prominent in Sacramento's social life, asks $150 a month alimony and all of the community property, val-ued at $15,000. Her husband earns between $3,000 and $4,500 a year, the complaint said.

There are no children.

THERE was a time when prospective auto-mobile owners were stopped by one thing—pur-chase price. But how different this is today! The Used Car Want Ads of the San Francisco Exam-iner have fulfilled a long felt need, and it is now pos-sible to buy the car you want at the price you want to pay.

AUTO BLESSING SHRINE PLANNED

CINCINNATI, Aug. 15—(A. P.)—Plans are being formulated here to-day for the establishment of what probably will be the first "automo-bile shrine" or blessing station in the country. The Rev. William P. O'Connor has been granted permis-sion to establish the shrine at his church, St. Vincent de Paul's, by the archbishop of Cincinnati, John T. McNicholas.

St. Vincent de Paul's is located on the Atlantic-Pacific highway, where hundreds of tourists pass daily.

$8,000,000 IS ASKED FOR 5 CITY STREETS

Measure Calling for Vote at November Election Referred by Board to Sub-Committee

A declaratory ordinance calling for a vote next November on an $8,000,000 bond issue for five city boulevard projects was referred to the streets committee for a report by the supervisors yesterday.

This action was taken on the mo-tion of Supervisor Milton Marks, who introduced the proposed ordi-nance. The ordinance asks for a total of $8,030,000. For Bay Shore highway $2,245,000 is asked; for Alemany boulevard, $2,334,000 for widening and improving Junipero Serra boulevard, $500,000; for Sun-set boulevard, $1,900,000, and for an esplanade at the ocean beach, $1,-000,000.

TWO RESOLUTIONS

The board passed finally two res-olutions calling for the start of the year's street reconstruction pro-gram. One authorizes from the good roads fund $114,840 for the reconstruction of eight main streets. The other calls for $100,320 for the reconstruction of seventeen streets. Another measure was passed call-ing for the appropriation of $17,000 for the improvement of Grand View avenue.

Appropriation of $20,000 from the county road fund for the construc-tion of a unit of the Bay Shore highway was given final passage.

ONE-WAY STREETS

Action on the McClintock traffic report and two amendments to the traffic ordinance was delayed when Charles F. Todd moved that the matter be referred to the traffic committee for a report.

An amendment to the traffic ordi-nance was adopted, making one-way streets of the two sections of Bay Street in that portion of the street divided by the street car tracks.

After considerable discussion the board unanimously voted an appro-priation of $100,000 to be spent in improving the upper road at Ocean Beach, between Kirkham and Lincoln way. It was stated that Superintendent of Parks John Mc-Laren has already prepared plans for carrying on this work.

NEW PLANE COULD HOLD SMALL ONE

HULL (England), Aug. 15—(P)—England's newest military airplane is a veritable battleship of the air. It is the largest flying ship in the world, one of the wings alone being almost large enough to provide a landing place for a moth light air-plane. The hull is of duraluminum and stainless steel.

Christened the Iris II, the huge flying boat takes off from the water at a speed of fifty knots. In her hull are ample living quarters and sleeping accommodations for a crew of five. Bunks can be folded up when not in use.

U.S. MOURNS PASSING OF JUDGE GARY

Executive Succumbs at 3:40 in Morning, but News Is Kept From Wall St. Until Eleven

NEW YORK, Aug. 15—(AP)—Elbert H. Gary, chairman of the board of directors of the United States Steel Corporation—and as such the virtual head of the Amer-ican steel industry and a figure of the greatest importance in the American economic world—died in his Fifth avenue home at 3:40 o'clock this morning. He was approaching his eighty-first birth-day.

He had been in ill health for six weeks, but the seriousness of his condition had reached the public's ears only in vague rumors and so his death caught the country by surprise.

Yet the stock market, of which United States Steel is one of the most influential leaders and has been for many years, reacted to the news only slightly.

RUMOR REACHES "STREET"

The announcement of his death was not made public until a few minutes before 11 o'clock.

When the market had opened with steel at 121⅜. Somehow the word had circulated through the street that Gary had died during the night. There was no confirmation. The price of steel edged downward 1⅝ points. Then this brief an-nouncement was made by the steel corporation:

"Elbert H. Gary died at 3:40 a. m. from chronic myocarditis."

(Chronic myocarditis is an in-flammation of the muscular parts of the wall of the heart.)

MARKET RECOVERS.

The market slumped briefly but steel, long a leader on the board, soon rose slightly above its opening price.

The choice of a successor to Gary as chairman of the steel cor-poration is expected in Wall Street to be confined to a group of four men, with the leading can-didate generally believed to be Myron C. Taylor, lawyer, banker, railroad director and industrialist, who was elected to the corporation
(Continued on Page 2, Column 5.)

Curwood Funeral To Be Held Today

OWOSSO (Mich.), Aug. 15—(INS.)—James Oliver Curwood, nov-elist author and conservation leader who died Saturday night after a week's illness from strepto-coccl infection, will be buried here tomorrow afternoon.

Griffith Says Death Report 'Exaggerated'

HOLLYWOOD, Aug. 15—(AP)—D. W. Griffith, motion picture director, in-formed tonight that he was fatally injured according to a New York rumor, flatly denied the charge but later admitted that there might be something in it, and refused to commit himself further until the coroner had looked him over.

"You never can tell," said Griffith, plainly worried at the report from the East. "Maybe I am dead. How does one know anyway?" Griffith said that a flower had run into his automobile last night in Santa Ana, removing some paint.

DOCTOR DIES SAVING GIRL

MONTEREY, Aug. 15—A young San Francisco physician, Dr. Albert Butterfield, 28, who was just begin-ning his medical career, saved a young woman companion from drowning at Moss Landing Sunday, but lost his own life in the rescue.

Just after Dr. Butterfield had brought Miss Dorcas Worsley to safety, he was caught by the treach-erous undertow and disappeared under a large wave.

It was not until 8 o'clock tonight that his body was recovered. Shortly before dark the patrol which had been guarding the beach while the tragedy was the body about 100 feet from where Dr. Butterfield went down, and a swimmer brought it ashore. An inquest will be held at 10:30 a. m. tomorrow.

Dr. Butterfield, Miss Worsley, Miss Eunice Erickson of Pasadena and Joel Smith of Selma were bathing Sunday in the always dan-gerous surf at Moss Landing, now here, in violation of safety regula-tions.

Dr. Butterfield, recently licensed to practice medicine, was a resident physician at the San Francisco Hos-pital. He was graduated from the University of Southern California in 1922, completing his education with the class of 1927 at the Stanford Medical School.

Kellogg, Mexico to Sign Claims Pact

WASHINGTON, Aug. 15—Sec-retary of State Kellogg and Mexican Ambassador Manuel C. Tellez will sign agreements tomorrow extend-ing the life of the Central Claims Commission for a period of two years from September 1.

The Commission has already made awards in claims of nationals of the two governments in excess of $20,000,000, it was learned.

AIR MOUNTS GIVEN FINAL TESTS FOR HONOLULU CLASSIC

By HARRY LANG

Precisely at noon today, a tall man standing at one side of the Oakland airport's 7,000-foot runway, will flash a black-and-white checkered flag in a downward arc—

And on that instant, down from the head of the runway will go careening a fuel-heavy yellow-winged monoplane, to gather speed as it roars down the course, and at last to go climbing into the sky to start the long-awaited Dole race to Honolulu!

NINE TIMES THAT FLAG'LL DROP

Nine times in all—nine times within some twenty minutes, they hope—that tall man will raise and drop that checkered flag. And each time another plane will follow the first until—barring accident or eleventh-hour withdrawal—nine great airplanes will be winging out in a droning bee toward the west; toward a goal some 2,420 miles away, where fame and a $25,000 prize awaits the first to finish in this "air race of the century." For the second, $10,000. And for the others—only the realiza-tion that they, too, have flown.

For a while, yesterday afternoon, it looked as if there would be but eight starters today—instead of all nine. The "City of Peoria" became the center of a flurry over adequacy of gasoline enough. Her tanks will hold 506 gallons, originally believed enough. But comparative checks of speed and gas-consumption roused a doubt that was not dispelled until a gas-consumption test flight had been made in late afternoon, with Art Starbuck, "disinterested pilot," at the controls.

CREW DECIDES TO FLY

When Starbuck came down and reported that the plane had done 99 miles an hour, using 12 gallons of gas an hour, the crew of the ship—Pilot Charles W. Parkhurst and Navigator Ralph Lowes announced:

"We'll fly in the race."

The "City of Peoria" was trundled to its place beside the other eight planes at the starting line—all nine of them officially inspected, tested, and OK'd to go at noon today.

The last to pass, "Lone Star Bill" Erwin of Texas, qualified only yesterday afternoon, when his navigator, Al Eichwaldt, guided him over a 52-mile test course with only a half-mile error.

SCHOOLMA'AM'S PLANE TAMPERED WITH

The others already had their guarantees of qualification—verbal guarantees from Examiner Ben Wyatt, navy lieutenant. Not until just a few minutes before today's start will they be handed their formal certificates of entry, bearing the names of Wyatt and the official starting committee, and certifying that they have passed all tests of plane and personnel—and are eligible for the Dole prizes, if they get there first.

But the last few hours were not without the rumpus. For yesterday morning, Gehenna popped in the "flying schoolma'am's" camp. The plane that is to carry pretty Mildred Doran, the only woman in the race, had been tampered with! In perfect shape Sunday night, the magnetic compass on the red-white-and-blue biplane was found yesterday morning with two magnets removed. Lieutenant Vilas Knope,

---

BOLD BANNER—This huge headline almost overshadows the nameplate of the *Examiner*.

CC THE SAN FRANCISCO EXAMINER: TUESDAY, AUGUST 16, 1927 3

THE CRACK 'NINE' OF PILOTS THAT WILL TRY TO BAT THE HAWAIIAN HOME RUN

Bennett Griffin. Norman A. Goddard. Livingston Irving. Jack Frost. Auggy Pedlar. Chas. W. Parkhurst. Martin Jensen. Art Goebel. William P. Erw

AVERAGE AGE OF RACERS IS LESS THAN 30

It's a Young Man's Game—This Hop for Honolulu; Youngest Is 24, While Oldest is 37

It's a young man's game—this air-racing to Honolulu. For the average age of both pilots and navigators in the contest is less than 30 years!

The pilots are a bit older than the navigators; pilots' average is 29 4-9 years; navigators' average is 29¼ years. The oldest man in the race is Captain Paul Schluter, navigator of Martin Jensen's plane. He is 37. The youngest man is Auggy Pedlar, pilot for Miss Mildred Doran, the "flying schoolma'am." Pedlar is 24.

Of the eight navigators, four are married, and four are single—those single are—Gordon Scott, Paul Schluter, Alvin Eichwaldt, and Lieut. Wm. Davis. Of the nine pilots, four are married—Goddard, Irving, Jensen and Erwin—and the other five are single—Griffin, Frost, Pedlar, Parkhurst and Goebel.

OLDEST PILOT 32.

Goddard is the oldest pilot, 32; Lieut. William J. Davis is the youngest navigator. Now here are some more statistics:

In all, there are 18 persons in this race—nine pilots, eight navigators and one passenger—Miss Doran. Her plane will carry three persons; all the others will carry two except Major Livingston Irving's. He will fly alone.

Of the nine planes in the race, seven are monoplanes and two are biplanes. Their average gasoline load, when they hop off at noon today, will be about 400 gallons. Their average weight at the take-off will be more than two tons each—4,700 pounds, to be exact.

FOUR LACK RADIO.

Of the nine planes, four will carry no radio equipment whatsoever. One—the "Golden Eagle"—carries only a receiving set, and no transmitting apparatus. The other four carry both sending and receiving equipment.

All nine are single-motored planes, and all are powered with the Wright J5 Whirlwind motor, which Lindbergh made famous on his memorable hop across the Atlantic.

These motors will burn between 9 and 14 gallons of gas per hour, depending on how wide open the throttle is.

20 TO 24 HOUR RACE.

The race is expected to be finished in between 20 and 24 hours, which would make the finish between 8 o'clock tomorrow morning and noon, our time. Since Honolulu is 2½ hours behind us, the first planes will land there between 5:30 and 9:30 a. m., their time.

The distance from Oakland airport to Wheeler Field, Honolulu will be approximately 2,420 statute miles, over the Great Circle route which the planes will follow. The distance from the Golden Gate to Honolulu, over the steamer lane, is 2,408 statute miles. The other 12 miles are the distance from Bay Farm Island to the Golden Gate and Honolulu to Wheeler Field.

All Pilots Have Won Air Fame West, South, Midwest in Contest

Twenty hours and more, without rest—cooped up in a tiny, hot, smelly cabin—eyes, nerves, ears, hands, legs ever alert for instantaneous reactions, with death the penalty for a moment's cessation of vigilance!—and all for the glory of winging across the Pacific to Hawaii, with perhaps—only perhaps, mind you!—a prize of $25,000 or $10,000 at the end.

That's the ordeal ahead for these splendidly courageous nine, who will pilot the Dole birds in the race that begins at noon today. "Regular fellows," all of them, most of them as bashful as a school boy. Yet heroes—and here they are, in the order in which they will start their craft at Oakland airport this noon:

1—**BENNETT H. GRIFFIN,** pilot of the **"OKLAHOMA."** Ben Griffin is thirty-one years old—and unmarried. His home is in Oklahoma City, where his parents, Mr. and Mrs. J. B. Griffin, live. He is a graduate of the University of Oklahoma—in fact, he was a football star of that school. In 1917 he entered the Army flying service, and has been "up in the air" ever since.

2—**NORMAN A. GODDARD,** pilot of **"El ENCANTO."** Goddard is thirty-two years old. His wife, Phyllis, will be at the starting line today to cheer him as he takes off. Their home is in San Diego, where he has been engaged in commercial aviation as operator of the Imperial Airport. Goddard is a lieutenant in the naval reserve. He is a native of Liverpool, England, and he flew with the British air corps during the war. After the armistice he went to Canada and in 1921 went to San Diego. He has had 3,000 hours in the air. Incidentally, he himself designed and supervised construction of his Dole race plane.

3—**LIVINGSTON GILSON IRVING,** pilot of the **"PABCO FLYER."** Irving, son of a former mayor of Berkeley, is one of America's war aces, with the Distinguished Service Cross for a brilliant defeat of a squadron of eleven enemy planes, during which he and one other Yankee flyer downed two of the enemy and routed the remainder. Irving holds the rank of major in the flying reserves. He is thirty-one years old, and lives at 1240 Bates road, Oakland, where his wife, Madeline, and their young daughter will await the outcome of the Dole race. Irving is an official of the Paraffine Companies, Inc., and his fellow employes in the San Francisco office have financed his Dole entry by popular subscription. Major Irving, incidentally, is the only Dole entrant who will fly alone, without a navigator.

4—**JOHN W. FROST,** pilot of "The Examiner's **"GOLDEN EAGLE."** Call him "Jack Frost"—he likes it better. Jack is twenty-nine years old—ex-Army flyer, Wall Street bond salesman, wing-stunt man, New York's first aero cop, one-time assistant to a Postmaster General and college sportsman. He is a native of Chicago, and began his flying in 1917, and has 5,000 hours in the air. He is unmarried, and has recently made his home in Los Angeles.

—**JOHN AUGGY PEDLAR,** pilot of the **"MISS DORAN,"** in which Mildred Doran, the "flying schoolma'am" of Flint, Mich., will ride as passenger in the Dole race. Pedlar, who has earned the nickname of "Straw Hat Auggy" by his habit of wearing a straw hat while piloting, is twenty-four years old—and unmarried. His home is in Long Beach, Cal., while his mother, Mrs. E. C. Pedlar, lives in Miami, Fla. Auggy was born in Butte, Mont. He has been flying since 1919, and has 4,000 hours in the air.

6—**CHARLES WILLIAM PARKHURST,** pilot of the **"CITY OF PEORIA."** Parkhurst is thirty years old, unmarried. He has had nine years of flying experience, and has recently been flying as commercial pilot for the National Airways System of Lomax, Ill., which is financing his entry in the Dole race. His home is in Peoria.

7—**MARTIN JENSEN,** pilot of the **"ALOHA."** They call Jensen the "Aloha Kid." He is Honolulu's sole entry in the Dole race, and only got his entry in and his airplane bought at the eleventh hour. Jensen is twenty-six years old, and married. His wife was one of the hardest workers in financing Jensen's entry through popular subscription among Honolulans. The Jensen's home is at 1335 West Kalia road, Honolulu. Jensen has had seven years of air experience, with nearly 2,500 hours in the sky. He has been engaged in commercial inter-island flying in Hawaii, to which he will return when the Dole race is over.

8—**ARTHUR C. GOEBEL,** pilot of the **"WOOLAROC."** Art Goebel is one of the movie's outstanding stunt flyers. He is thirty-one years old, unmarried. His home is in Hollywood. Goebel started flying in 1910, and has had a total of about 2,000 hours in the air. He was in the Army flying service during the war, "gypsied" in 1920, served with the Peruvian army in 1922 and has been movie stunting since then.

9—**WILLIAM P. ERWIN,** pilot of the **"DALLAS SPIRIT."** "Lone Star Bill" Erwin, like Major Livingston Irving, is an American war ace—in fact, the third ranking A. E. F. ace. He has had 4,000 hours in the air. He wears the Distinguished Service Cross, and has an official record of nine victories over enemy planes. Erwin's home is in Dallas, Texas. He is thirty-one and married. His wife, Connie, was to have accompanied him on the race, but withdrew at the last minute because she was under the minimum age limit in the rules for one of the competitions, which Erwin has entered. Erwin is a minister's son—his parents, Rev. and Mrs. W. A. Erwin, are in Pawhuska, Okla.

"Miss Hollydale" Plane Quits Race

LOS ANGELES, Aug. 15.—(I.N.S.)—E. A. Parkford, Los Angeles, real estate operator, whose biplane, "Miss Hollydale," has been entered in the Dole $35,000 air race to Honolulu, with Frank Clark as pilot, definitely announced today that his entry would not compete in the air classic.

Torrential Rainstorms Delay Koennecke Hop

LONDON, Aug. 15.—(A.P.)—A Reuter's dispatch from Cologne says Lieut. Otto Koennecke, German airman, who expects to fly across the Atlantic, has been forced to postpone his attempt by the waterlogged condition of the airdrome as the result of torrential downpours.

"ON THE MARK, Set, Go!" Major Edward P. Howard, official starter, who at noon today at Oakland, will raise the checkered flag and drop it to earth to start, successively, nine pilots on the race to Honolulu, for the Dole prizes of $35,000.

Guiding Is Up to "Avigat[ors]" Pilots Depend on New Bird[s]

In eight of the Dole planes, when they hop for Hawaii, glory and $25,000, will be sitting men whose task it will be to guide these craft to Wheeler Field, Honolulu. Not the pilots—the pilots will only have to follow these men's directions, for these are the navigators—that new breed of birdmen who, to distinguish them from the pilots, are already beginning to be called "avigators."

In a cubicle crammed with instruments and with a maze of figures and calculations, these men will plot the courses along which they will direct their pilots in today's race. If they're right, they'll get to Honolulu. If they're wrong ——!

Here they are, in the order in which their planes will hop from Bay Farm Island today:

1—**AL HENLEY,** navigator of the **"OKLAHOMA."** Al is 31 years old, a resident of Oklahoma City. He is married and has a year-old baby girl. He has served in the army as pilot and instructor for eight of his ten years' air experience and is now a lieutenant in the army air reserve. Henley's wife and baby are in Waco, Texas, to stay with Mrs. Henley's parents until the Dole flight is over.

2—**LIEUT. KENNETH C. HAWKINS,** United States Navy, navigator of **"EL ENCANTO."** Lieut. Hawkins is 28 years old, attached to the navy air station at North Island, San Diego, where he makes his home. He is married, and father of two children. His wife, Sigrid, is now at Oakland to see the plane start in the Dole race. Hawkins was born September 12, 1898, in Wilkesbarre, Pa., graduated from Annapolis Naval Academy in 1920 and has been flying since 1923. His two children, Kenneth Courtney and Flavia Diane, will remain at the Hawkins home, 2426 Upas street, San Diego, until the flight is over. Lieut. Hawkins' mother, Mrs. Mary Hawkins, lives at Paonia, Colo. He has obtained a special leave of absence from the Navy to navigate "El Encanto" in the Dole race.

3—There will be no navigator on the third plane to start today—Major Livingston Irving's. He will act as both pilot and navigator.

4—**GORDON SCOTT,** navigator of the "Examiner's" **"GOLDEN EAGLE."** Gordon is an aeronautical engineer by profession, but has been to sea as professional navigator before engaging in the air business. In 1926 he navigated the 48-foot schooner Jubilo in the Hawaii yacht races—to Honolulu and back to the mainland, earning high commendation for h[is] ... Scott is 26 years old, so[n] ... and Mrs. J. L. Scott of ... street, Santa Monica. H[e] ... married.

5—**LIEUT. VILAS R.** ... United States Navy, ... of the **"MISS DORAN."** L... Hawkins, Lieut. Knope ... tained a special leave o[f] ... from his duties at the N... Diego air station to a... Auggy Pedlar and Mildre[d] ... the "flying schoolma'am," ... lulu in the Dole race. Lie[ut.] ... is 30 years old and mar[ried] ... has a record of four year[s] ... and navigator in the ... service. Lieut. Knope ... tained as navigator of t[he] ... Doran at the eleventh ho[ur] ... place another who had ... qualified in the official te[st].

6—**RALPH C. LOWES,** ... of the **"CITY OF P[EORIA]"** ... Lowes is a graduate of the ... lis Naval Academy, class ... His home is in Peoria, Ill ... is 30 years old and has a ...

7—**PAUL SCHLUTER,** ... of the **"ALOHA."** He ... captain by profession an[d] ... time he was retained b[y] ... Jensen, pilot of the "Alo[ha]" ... serving as master of a ... steamer. Schluter has an ... aerial navigation is the bi[g] ... the future for competent ... gators, and has staked h... gaining a reputation in ... race. He is 37 years old, ... and makes his home in S... cisco.

8—**LIEUT. WILLIAM V**... navigator of the **"WOO[LAROC]"** ... Lieut. Davis obtained ... leave of absence from ... Diego naval air station t... pany Art Goebel in the ... race. He is one of th[e] ... Diego air station men in ... as navigators—the other ... Lieut. Vilas Knope and Li... neth C. Hawkins. The thr[ee] ... graduates of Annapolis ... Academy. Davis is 25 y... native of Georgia. He is ... ried.

9—**ALVIN EICHWALDT** ... gator of the **"DALLAS** ... Eichwaldt's home is at 7... boulevard, Hayward. He is ... old and is unmarried. ... his home with his moth[er] ... Florence Delaney Eichw... went to sea in the navy a[t] ... of 15, and was in east co[ast] ... duty during the beginnin[g] ... war, later serving eight ... mine service in foreign w... held the rank of quart... when he left the Navy. ... tinued at sea, where he h... mate's papers.

Hawaii Governor Sends Pilot Greeting

HONOLULU, Aug. 15.—(AP)—Governor Wallace M. Ferrington today sent a radiogram of greeting and hope for their success to the flyers who will take off tomorrow from Oakland to win the Dole prizes of $35,000 for first and second planes to reach the island of Oahu.

The Governor's message, addressed to Martin Jensen, Honolulu's entrant, said:

"Hawaii's aloha goes out to all messengers of good will. May favoring winds and all good fortune attend your mission."

Light Rations for Flyer Across th[e] ...

Several more of the Do[le] ... yesterday revealed what f... they will carry along on th[e] ... The day before, a number ... Examiner" what they w... now, here are the others:

Major Livingston Irving ... three bars of chocolate, a ... soup, a quart of coffee, a f[ew] ... wiches and some concentra[ted] ... preparation.

Jack Frost and Gordon S[cott] ... carry in the "Golden Eagle" ... chicken sandwiches, two ... coffee and four gallons of ...

EIGHT NAVIGATORS OF THE FLIGHT, WHO WILL KEEP THE SHIPS ON THE COURSE

Al Henley. Kenneth C. Hawkins. Gordon Scott. Vilas Knope. Ralph Lowes. Paul Schluter. W. V. Davis. Alvin Eichwaldt.

CHECKERED FLAG—This center photo in the *Examiner* on race day was the one that started the high-flying adventurers on the deadly nonstop flight to Honolulu.

ODYSSEY OF PACIFIC WRITTEN IN SKIES — SCENES ATTENDING TAKE-OFF

No. 1—SYMBOLIC!—High in the air over the city is seen the Miss Doran Dole plane carrying the Hawaii flyers in the race, soaring over the heroic figure of Joan of Arc, near the Palace of the Legion of Honor.

No. 2—UPS AND DOWNS!—The Pabco Flyer, Major Livingston Irving's plane, the Berkeley entrant, circling above the Oakland airport and performing perfectly in her test flight and in all previous flights. But this was not yesterday. For yesterday—

No. 3—BLASTED HOPES!—Hauling away the wreckage of the Pabco Flyer, a serious smashup. Major Livingston Irving's plane, the Berkeley ship, fell a distance of fifty feet at the end of the airport as she was taking off. Irving was shocked, but otherwise unhurt.

No. 4—"HELLO, HAWAII!"—Martin Jensen, pilot of the "Aloha," the Hawaiian entry in Dole race, and his navigator, Paul Schluter, picked from an ocean liner for the job. Photo taken just before the take-off yesterday. The "Aloha" got away "slick."

No. 5—WORTH FLYING FOR!—Bennett Griffin getting a proper goodby from his sweetheart, Miss Juanita Herrod. Griffin is the pilot of the Oklahoma plane, and if a kiss like that wouldn't make a man fly, well, what would? That's all—what would?

No. 6—"HOLD THE THOUGHT!"—Postmaster Power (left) passing a letter to Jack Frost, pilot of the Golden Eagle, for delivery to the postmaster of Honolulu. George Hearst (center), sponsor for the Golden Eagle, the Hearst airplane entry, for which the three are "holding the thought."

No. 7—A STUDY IN EXPRESSION—Thousands of bay citizens flocked to the Oakland airport yesterday to witness the take-off of the Eagles, and to see the start of a new page of history. This photo shows only a small portion of the huge crowd near the starting line.

DOLE RACE BEGINS—This page from the San Francisco *Examiner* shows some of the scenes at the Oakland Municipal Airport.

HONOLULU OR BUST!---SCENES ENGRAVED UPON THE PAGES OF AERIAL HISTORY

No. 1.—ALL AROUND THE TOWN.—The Hearst entry, the Golden Eagle, piloted by Jack Frost, is seen here, accompanied by her escort, passing the Telephone Building on her way to the Golden Gate and onward to Honolulu without stops for rest, fuel or refreshments.

No. 2.—FOGGING ALONG!—This is the Woolaroc, with her escort, passing over a fog bank as she plunged out into the great pathless aerial distance. The Woolaroc is being piloted by Art Goebel, and has for her navigator Lieutenant "Bill" Davis. The Woolaroc is a monoplane.

No. 3.—ON THEIR TOES!—Or whatever airplanes get on when they are ready to start. This is a scene at the Oakland Airport a minute before the first take-off, showing the Oklahoma at the line waiting word to leap into the air and away on her course.

No. 4.—THE WOUNDED BIRD!—Here is a close-up view of the wreck of El Encanto, the San Diego ship that crashed from the runway as she was preparing for the take-off. The left wing was smashed, but neither the pilot nor the navigator was injured.

No. 5.—FLAG WAVERS!—This was the sacred spot at the Oakland Airport yesterday. Here were the starters and the timers who had to see to it that the planes were started in order and with the proper frequency, and the crowd was kept away from them.

No. 6.—THE ONLY GIRL!—Miss Mildred Doran is shown in this picture listening-in on the radio. Her plane had a bit of hard luck at the start, but she took the air the second time. She is the only girl in the race.

No. 7.—ABOVE SMASH.—This scene shows the flying over Alameda field at runway, returning for the when the premature first plugs caused the pilot, Pedlar to come back to temporary halt.

LEAVING THE FIELD—Some of the Dole race planes are airborne shortly after leaving the airport.

RYING TO MAKE A.IMALS TALK

...nt discoveries which indicate that it is not lack of ...lligence but lack of mechanism of throat and brain cells.

In Next Sunday's Examiner

San Francisco Examiner

AN AMERICAN PAPER FOR THE AMERICAN PEOPLE — AMERICA FIRST

Monarch of the Dailies — REG. U.S. PAT. OFF.

THE WEATHER
Fair, Fog in Evening, Wednesday in San Francisco Bay Region.
Complete Weather Report on Page 23.

CXXVII. NO. 48. CC — SAN FRANCISCO, WEDNESDAY, AUGUST 17, 1927—THIRTY-TWO PAGES — DAILY 5 CENTS, SUNDAY 10 CENTS: DAILY AND SUNDAY, PER MONTH, $1.15

OEBEL RADIOS 'ALL FINE'; 685 MILES OUT; ALOHA SIGHTED; FROST, PEDLAR UNREPORTED

day

...d Farmers.
...ntelligent Land.
...d Submarines.
...s Man.

...ur Brisbane—

...oolidge feels that our ...ppier than they were, ...mers seem to agree ...n July 4, the Presi... ...s country celebrated ...s together, President ... 55th, the United ...ast. The country is ...e times as old as the ...hich shows what a ...try we are.

...armers will be inter... ...that in Manitoba, Ca... ...rs control wheat ex... ..."pool" handling 200,... ...s. The exporters that ...at but got the profit ...trol, and farmers are ...ger price for their ...aps our farmers will ...ng from Canada.

... the way, more pros... ...er in her history, re... ...ated the Dominion's ... and now welcomes ...nces. Everything is ...a's way, including the ... of energetic valuable ...om Europe, the kind ... needs, and stupidly

...Wilfrid Laurier made ..."The nineteenth cen... ...United States' cen... ...ntieth will be Can...

...Canada gains the bet... ...e pleased.

...eth century should ...gh for ourselves and ... Canada has one ad... ...nows that Great Bri... ...g airplanes, intending ...AIR as she has long ...TER.

... ourselves, the Ca... ...t wonder what would ... their prosperity if ...

...ad of our railroads in ...States. Canada has ...f railroad per capita ...ntry in the world. ...ers produced 15,000,... ...f wheat sixty years ...produced 410,000,000 ...year. We have a ...getic nation north of ...ad of it. They are ...kers.

..."take up the subma...

...ch dominates mental... ... the world, except ... Russia, would like ... to have few subma... ... is no protection for ...tic mercantile fleet ... Battleships and

...on Page 10, Col. 5.)

THE BIRD WITH THE BROKEN PINION

HARD LUCK PERCHED atop the wings of El Encanto and grinned in derision when the giant bird started down the runway at the Oakland Airport yesterday at noon. She was the second Dole plane to start, following the take-off of the Oklahoma. As she hurtled down the "ribbon," the San Diego craft swerved onto the rough ground at the side of the runway, smashing a left wing. Neither the pilot, Norman Goddard, nor the navigator, Kenneth C. Hawkins, was injured. That "The Examiner" cameraman was on the job is shown by the fact that this photo was taken before the speeding ambulance or the police car, both seen hurtling down the field, had reached the side of the stricken bird.

—*Photo taken from airplane, by Fraley.*

Mellon Attends Reception to Fuad

VENICE (Italy), Aug. 16.—(A.P.)—Andrew W. Mellon, Secretary of the United States Treasury, attended a gala reception to King Fuad of Egypt last night, tendered by Count Volpi.

General Pershing Is Coolidge Guest

RAPID CITY (S. D.), Aug. 16.—General John J. Pershing was today the guest of President and Mrs. Coolidge at the summer White House.

Mrs. Wilson Guest Of Baruch at Races

WASHINGTON, Aug. 16.—Mrs. Woodrow Wilson, widow of President Wilson, has gone to Saratoga Springs, N. Y., to see the horse races there as the guest of Bernard Baruch and his daughter.

Gen. Helmick, Hurt In Crash, Recovering

WASHINGTON, Aug. 16.—Maj. Gen. Eli A. Helmick, inspector-general of the Army, showed marked recovery at Walter Reed Hospital today from injuries suffered in an auto accident yesterday.

GODDARD, IRVING CRACK UP; ERWIN AND GRIFFIN FORCED DOWN; 'PEORIA' DISQUALIFIED

Chronology Tells Graphic Story of Race

IN THE RACE—The Hearst plane "Golden Eagle"; Martin Jensen's "Aloha"; Art Goebel's "Woolaroc," and the "Miss Doran."

OUT OF THE RACE—"Oklahoma," forced to return; "El Encanto," wrecked; "Pabco Flyer," wrecked; "City of Peoria," disqualified; "Dallas Spirit," forced to return.

Here, in chronological order, are radio bulletins received via Radio Corporation of America, Federal Wireless and Naval Radio reporting the progress of the planes still in the race, after they had passed out over the Golden Gate:

TUESDAY.

1:05 p. m.—Navy radio reports Aloha passes Farallones, flying fifty feet high.

2:35 p. m.—Motorship Silver Fir reports Aloha overhead. Position: Lat. 37.18; long. 125.04. About 185 miles out. Radio report says "light northwest wind; moderate sea; slight haze."

2:45 p. m.—Navy radio reports unidentified plane, believed "Miss Doran" passed over Farallones at 2:43.

2:50 p. m.—S. S. Wilhelmina reports Aloha passing to north. Lat. 36.57; long. 125.31. This position is south of the Silver Fir. Indicates Jensen has turned south into steamer lane.

4 p. m.—Navy radio reports Aloha was 35 miles north of Great Circle steamer route to Honolulu when she passed Wilhelmina. Wilhelmina reports seeing no other planes. Navy has advised destroyers Hazelwood and Meyers, west of Wilhelmina, to watch.

4:35 p. m.—S. S. Wilhelmina reports radiogram received from the Woolaroc, reporting position lat. 36.2; long. 127.2, at 4 o'clock. This is about 350 land miles out.

The radiogram from the Woolaroc reported that the radio beacon was "coming in fine."

5:09 p. m.—U. S. S. La Vallette, 40 miles out, reports 10-mile northwest wind across course, with sky overcast but visibility good.

5:45 p. m.—U. S. S. Sumner, 400 miles out, reports sky obscured; visibility good, and light northwest wind.

8:30 p. m.—Navy radio receives following weather report from observer at Mt. Haleakala, near Honolulu: Wind southeast, velocity 15 miles an hour. Cumulus

(Continued on Page 6, Column 6)

Hidden somewhere in the mystery, darkness and immensity of the Pacific's sky, four history-making Dolebirds late last night were humming along toward Honolulu, $35,000 in prize-money, and the fame of winning the Dole race.

They were the Hearst plane "Golden Eagle," little Martin Jensen's "Aloha," Art Goebel's "Woolaroc," and the biplane that is carrying pretty young Mildred Doran, the flying schoolma'am from Michigan.

Just exactly where three of them were, no one here knew, for no word had come from them for many hours.

Woolaroc Reports 685 Miles Out

But the other—the Woolaroc, which is the only one of the four equipped with a radio transmitter—kept the world aware of her position as the hours went by. "Seven hours out," Goebel reported his position about 595 miles out. That must have been about 7:30, and showed an average speed of 85 miles an hour to that time.

Then at 11:30 last night, the destroyer Corry, out in mid-Pacific with the destroyer squadron steaming east, reported that it had picked up the Woolaroc's radio messages and estimated, by the radio compass, that Goebel's plane was about 685 miles out from San Francisco at 8:30, out time. This indicates that Goebel's speed was increasing with a lighter load and a favorable wind, for in the hour he had gone some 90 miles.

But of the other three there was only silence. Where they were, how fast they were going, which was in the lead—these were things that, like the planes themselves, were hiding in the night.

The last report from Jensen's ship came at 2:50 in the afternoon—two and a quarter hours after he started—when the steamer Wilhelmina reported him passing, at about 200 miles out.

Averages 88 Miles an Hour

This would put the Aloha's speed up to that time at about 88 to 89 miles an hour—a bit better than Goebel's. If Jensen had maintained that, he should be about 20 to 30 miles ahead of the Woolaroc at 8 o'clock.

From the Golden Eagle and the Miss Doran, not a word had come since they passed over the Farallones. But there was no worry here over that, for the weather reports from the lane of flight told of low clouds. The

Examiner ON MORNING AFTER—This bold headline and the aerial shot of the *El Encanto,* which cracked up after swerving off the runway, show the interest in the Hawaiian hop.

TEXAS AVIATION CHAMP—Art Goebel smiles just before taking off and winning the $25,000 first prize from the pineapple king.

DOLE RACE WINNER—*Woolaroc* moves down the field picking up speed for its flight to Wheeler Field.

Miss Doran IN THE AIR—The Dole race plane with three aboard disappeared in the Pacific.

NEVER FOUND—Pilot Auggie Pedlar (1) with pretty brunette Mildred Doran, the flying school teacher, who went as a passenger, and navigator Vilas Knope pose just prior to their takeoff during the Dole flight.

TIN LIZZIES LINE RUNWAY—The *City of Oakland* leaves the field near the Bay.

FIRST CIVILIAN PLANE NONSTOP TO HAWAII—Natives examine the *City of Oakland,* which crashed out of fuel.

ALIVE, WITH FLOWERS—*City of Oakland* navigator Emory Bronte is decorated with leis and clutches a tropical bird in his hands shortly after his crash landing with Ernie Smith on one of Hawaii's outer islands.

shore line was in sight. It turned out to be a river, however, and presently, a mile or so ahead, we saw the glow of lights against the low-hanging clouds. We made for them and found that they were a series of blast furnaces at the edge of a sizable manufacturing town. I thought this was probably Essen, as I knew that the Krupp works were there, but Levine thought it was Bremerhaven, because he had been in Bremerhaven once.

We flew around through the rain, thinking some enterprising manufacturer might have painted his own name and that of his city on a roof, but our search was still unrewarded when we saw some white flares that were being fired into the air off to one side of the town. We flew toward them and discovered a flying field. The attendants there had heard our motor and taken this means of attracting our attention, having guessed our identity. This was Dortmund, although we saw no name on the airdrome as we circled above the little cheering group there, and did not learn until later that we had come through the clouds fairly well on our course after wandering to and fro all night.

I throttled the motor and swooped low over the knot of airdrome attendants, resorting to a trick I had learned long ago.

"Nach Berlin? Nach Berlin?" I shouted, leaning far out the window so that they would be sure to hear as we swept past ten or fifteen feet above their heads. Then I opened the throttle again and did a banking turn to see if they had heard and understood. They all pointed in approximately the same direction and I set the *Columbia* on the course they indicated would bring us to the capital. There was very little gas left now and I wanted to make as much mileage as possible.

When we came through the fog, we had found a gale blowing from the south, and the *Columbia* was buffeted so by the fierce gusts that at first I was sure a part of the tail really had been torn away by our dizzy drop from the clouds. The wind was of some assistance and we made good time after leaving Dortmund, where I had figured that we had about ten gallons of gas left and could go another hundred miles. We flew through rain for the first fifty miles, then it stopped, the ceiling lifted gradually to 2,000 feet and the weather began to clear. If only we had been able to get across the cloud masses blocking us a few hours earlier! How far we would have been now! What a shame that we

couldn't have crossed over into this fair weather area and been far on our way to Berlin or Warsaw!

We were flying about 1,500 feet high now. The Harz Mountains loomed ahead, and because we had no map to indicate how far it would be straight across them we turned to the right to skirt along their edge. There was no use running out of fuel in the middle of a mountain range and cracking up our plane, if we could help it. We had missed disaster at Dortmund merely because we happened to drop out of the clouds over a valley. Twenty-five miles away there were mountains whose tops projected well up into the fog; it was only a matter of luck that we did not come out there instead of where we did. No use riding that luck too hard now.

We had left Dortmund shortly after 4:30 A.M., local time, and it was now nearing six. The gasoline dropped lower and lower in the fuel gauge; the pump from the main tank had run dry before Land's End, England, so we had known for a long time that only one gravity tank in the wing was left. Finally the gauge stood at zero and I knew there was only gas for a few minutes more. There was ample opportunity for a landing—the country here was flat and fertile, small fields, it is true, but large enough for the purpose of a forced landing with the wide choice afforded us by the comfortable height at which we were flying. Unlike America, the farmers in Saxony do not live on their land, but in little villages which we could see here and there at strategic points. The countryside was not yet awake—it was too early for even these rural folk to be up and about their tasks—so we were flying unnoticed toward Berlin.

I wanted to land now, to sit down near one of the larger villages while I still had a few pints of gasoline left and could use the motor in landing. It would be easier to get more fuel if we landed where gasoline was likely to be available. But Levine wanted to go on, to fly literally "to the last drop of gas," and take our chances on getting down without damage to the *Columbia* when the motor finally quit.

"You're the doctor," I told him when he urged me not to stop until we had to. "It's your airplane, but it's brought us a long way and I'd hate to bend it up trying to make four or five extra miles."

I had him climb over the tank and stand in the rear part of the

cabin to keep the plane from nosing over when we came down, in case the field proved to be soft. With her fuel tanks empty, she was decidedly nose-heavy and I needed all the ballast possible in the tail, particularly if the motor was going to be useless when we landed. Ten or fifteen minutes after the fuel gauge quit working and I had recommended landing, the motor faltered for the first time since we had left Roosevelt Field, coughed once or twice and stopped. At the first warning my mind was made up on two likely looking wheat fields below, adjoining each other but separated by a road.

Down came the Bellanca, maneuvering for a "dead stick" landing into the wind. I slipped her into the first field and leveled out, the *Columbia's* wheels swishing along through the wheat before they and the tail skid struck the ground together. She rolled roughly to the road and bounced over it pretty savagely, continuing so far in the short field that I had to "ground loop" to keep her away from a fence. It was a severe test for the landing gear, but everything held. The Bellanca stopped dead still, a little wet from brushing through the standing grain, but unscathed. Our New York–Germany flight was over.

It was a few minutes before six o'clock on the morning of June 6th, and we had been in the air 43 hours. In that time it is probable we had flown well over 4,000 miles, but our air line distance from New York was 3,905 miles and we had broken the long-distance flying record of the world—Lindbergh's mark of two weeks before—by 295 miles.

The water off the West Coast wasn't being ignored either. Almost while Chamberlin was in the air, another aeronautical adventure was being planned—promoted, actually—in California. James D. Dole, the pineapple king of Hawaii, put up $25,000 as a first prize for the first pilot to make a San Francisco to Hawaii nonstop flight. He set up a $10,000 award for the second plane to make the hop over 2,400 miles of the Pacific Ocean.

The multimillionaire pineapple packer started the most astounding and deadly air saga of early aviation. On June 26, 1927, Dole came to Frisco to plan the conquest of the country's other ocean. He had to lock himself in his suite on the top floor of the Clift Hotel to insure his

privacy. Pilots, reporters, and civic officials wanted to assist in the arrangements. Several flyers were in various stages of preparation to try to leave before the prize flight set for August 12. Dole said he was not disturbed by those who wanted to leave before the official time. He did say they would not be eligible for the prize money.

Although the pineapple colossus turned over the regulation of the contest to the National Aeronautical Association, he still was the instrumental man. Some critics said he was sponsoring the flight only to sell more pineapples off the shelves of stores in America. Unlike the unofficial race earlier in the East to see who would be able to take off first, the Dole flight became more and more of an official race. Since several planes would leave at the same time, it was becoming a matter of the fastest pilot and plane or vice versa.

"I am interested in paving the way for regular air service between the islands and the mainland," Dole said when asked what had prompted him to post the prizes. "Second, I want to see inter-island communication by air established. Our islands are separated by channels from 10 to 90 miles in width. I want us to be the first to have such inter-island service, just as we were first in the world to have regular radio telephone service between our various islands."

On June 29, two Army lieutenants, Lester Maitland and Albert Hegenberger, took off in an Army Fokker. The boxy, tri-motored plane left Oakland Airport at 7:08 that Tuesday morning. It landed the next day in Honolulu at 8:59 Pacific time. The 2,406-mile jaunt took 25 hours and 51 minutes. The "Lucky Lindies" of the Pacific had good weather and as easy a ride. Unlike the Bellanca of Chamberlin and Levine, which used its last drop of fuel and went down to a motorless landing, the big Fokker had 250 gallons of gas left when it set down.

The Army had been interested in making the flight for some time. It was spurred by Lindbergh and Chamberlin. Some farsighted brass recognized the potential of Hawaii as a military base.

"In the event of war with an Asiatic power," Major Henry Clagett said, "Hawaii would be our chief base in the Pacific, and it would be the first place the enemy would try to take away from us." Although he certainly wasn't aware of the future course of events, history proved his prophecy accurate. "That will mean," he said of the flight and the

Dole contest, "the Army, in case of war, will have facilities in addition to its own planes to transport to and from the islands anything that a plane can carry."

With the second ocean overcome, Dole evidently decided to make his offer more for the purposes of advertising. "I want it to work out as a sporting proposition," he said, "a race to see who can get off first after the gun and who can reach the islands first." Dole sailed for Hawaii during the middle of July. He had never been in a plane. The press inquired why he wouldn't wait a couple of weeks and fly with one of the racers. He said the thought had never occurred to him!

On July 14, two more men left Oakland hoping to get the hula-girl welcome for their nonstop trip to Honolulu's Wheeler Field. A Pacific Air Transport pilot, Ernest L. Smith, and another civilian, navigator Emory Bronte, had a new single-engine plane, *City of Oakland*, which had been bought by local businessmen backing this venture of the first civilians to fly straight to Hawaii. They noted the flight had been planned for several months, long before Lindbergh took off in May. This trip was the first test of the Pacific with only one motor.

The Travelair monoplane left Oakland at 10:25. It crashed into a thorny kiawe tree on the Hawaiian island of Molokai, some 50 miles from Honolulu. Smith's forehead was slightly cut in the crash landing when they ran out of fuel. Wind, thick fog, a dead radio, and storms had drained their tanks. They almost ditched in the sea a couple of times before making land. Once they had to resort to using an SOS over the shark-infested sea. The fuel gauge malfunctioned, but they beat on the gas tanks to keep a check on the fuel and kept flying. Adding to the suspense, their radio quit right after the distress signals; ships steamed to the area where they were supposedly down. They couldn't relay they had been able to stay up. The plane was smashed, but some thought perhaps it could be reconditioned in time for the contest. Smith and Bronte decided not to enter though.

Dole had set August 12 because it would give Lindbergh, who was very busy with his new international acclaim, a chance to fly another ocean if he wanted. Lindy declined. The pineapple king was greatly concerned when a pilot en route to the Coast for the contest was killed. His parachute did not open when he was forced to leave his disabled plane. Dole wanted to cancel the contest. Then three more were in-

jured when they went down in the Bay while heading to the race. Another plane crashed and burned while flying to the starting point. Dole found the misadventures upsetting, but pilots pressured him to let them fly for the cash prizes.

The perpetual San Francisco Bay breeze wafted heat around the eight planes on the starting line at noon on August 16 at Oakland Municipal Airport. Twice as many planes had been entered. But the crashes had taken some. Others were inspected and ruled unsafe for the flight. Each lifted up from the runway until they all hovered overhead before swinging out to the ocean.

The first airborne was the *Aloha* flown by Martin Jensen and Paul Schluter. They copped second prize. The *Oklahoma*, carrying Al Henley and Bennett Griffin, had to return to Oakland because of engine trouble. Norman Goddard and Lieutenant Kenneth Hawkins died in a crash during the attempted takeoff of the *El Enchanto*. Major Livingston Irving crashed in his *Pacific Flyer* at the airport also. The motors of the heavily loaded planes evidently stalled.

Another plane was lost probably only a short distance from the field. The *Golden Eagle*, piloted by Jack Frost and Gordon Scott, was never heard from again after it passed the Golden Gate Bridge. The *Miss Doran*, the only plane carrying three, was lost at sea. It was christened for Miss Mildred Doran, a pretty Michigan school teacher, the only woman in the contest. Her companions were Lieutenant Vilas R. Knope and John Pedlar.

The seventh plane off the field was the winner, the *Woolaroc*, piloted by Art Goebel, a Texas rancher, and a serviceman, Lieutenant William V. Davis. It landed in Honolulu 26 hours, 27 minutes, and 33 seconds later. The last plane up was the *Dallas Spirit*. Captain William P. Erwin and Alvin Eichwaldt were forced to turn back because of engine trouble. Two days later they went out in the repaired plane to search for the downed *Miss Doran*.

A World War I ace, Captain Erwin kept in radio contact with the mainland. Twice he reported the *Spirit* going into spins.

"It was scary," he said each time, "but all's okay." The third distress signal was never completed.

"Another spin . . . SO . . ." They died before adding the final S to their message for help. The *Spirit* was never found either.

The pineapple contest killed 12 people. Five died during the race, two in crackups at the scene, two in the futile attempt at rescue, and three were killed en route to the starting line. Dole expressed hopes the missing would be found and thanked all those who had participated in any way in the great air derby. Some record fans say the Dole race is one of the top ten sporting events of this century.

The Twenties literally flew into this century. They winged in with high adventure, sporting that unique individualism which was the beauty and daring of the decade. They opened the air around the world. In 1927, man flew and proved he could stay airborne as no other creature.

The following story by Earl Shaub is taken from his book *All in a Day's Work.* It is an intriguing story of a great reporter's assignment.

The early days of aviation produced many good stories. After Charles Lindbergh made his epochal flight to Paris numerous others tried to duplicate it. Some succeeded but many, including Phil Payne, editor of *The Daily Mirror,* failed.

Two of these flights took me and several other New York reporters and cameramen to Canada. The first trip was to Ottawa, destination of two men and a woman who took off from London. Unhappily, they haven't reached Canada yet.

We arrived in Ottawa one morning and, since I was the only one with a reservation at the Chateau Laurier, they all piled their bags and cameras in my room until other quarters became available.

After breakfast we went to the government aviation headquarters to get a forecast on the arrival of the plane. Cordial and courteous officials told us they had received no word that morning and suggested we wait at the hotel where we would be notified in plenty of time to reach the airport.

We stopped in a liquor store and the whiskey was also taken to my room. After a round or two, a crap game started on the floor and a black jack game on the bed. This continued all day and through the night and, happily, someone had the wit to order up sandwiches from time to time.

As the word got around that a party was in progress, other hotel guests came up from the lobby and townspeople came in

from the streets. Even the night watchman who came to caution quiet got interested and forgot to finish his rounds. This went on another day or so until we were informed the Canadian government had abandoned hope for the plane.

The New York *Times* man and I took a sleeping car compartment back to New York. We invited two Canadian nurses to sit in our compartment while their berths were being made down. When my companion introduced me as Mr. Shaub, one of the girls exclaimed, "Are you the Mr. Shaub who gave that big party in Ottawa?"

"Were you there?" I asked.

"No," she replied. "I'm sorry I wasn't, but everybody else in town was there."

So, I guess, it was a pretty good party.

An interesting sidelight concerned my hotel bill. When I settled up at the cashier's window I was charged $12 for the room and $128 for long-distance telephone calls the other boys had made to their wives and sweethearts in New York.

Another less humorous sidelight of that trip is the fact that prohibition officers of that Volstead era stopped our train at the U.S. border and confiscated the bottle I was trying to smuggle home.

The other Canadian trip was to Montreal to meet an English dirigible. The flight was without incident and we filed uneventful stories and interviews.

I must report that I was impressed on that occasion by the manner in which The Canadian National Railroad assumed the responsibility of acting as host to us visiting newspapermen. A vice-president of the road set up a press room for us in the Windsor Hotel with typewriters and telegraph loops and also furnished a special car (equipped with typewriters) to take us to and from the airport. And there were plenty of sandwiches and drinks available at both places.

This thoughtfulness on the part of that railroad and the courtesy of the Canadian officials at Ottawa generated in me a friendly attitude toward Canada that has persisted from that day to this.

I smile as I recall how we prevented a jealous German woman from killing Lady Grace Drummond Hay whom we employed

to circumnavigate the world on the Graf Zeppelin, big German dirigible. This irate woman was apparently motivated by a crush on Karl H. Von Weigand, chief of our Berlin bureau, who also took that 'round the world air voyage for us.

When the big craft sailed east over Europe, Asia and the Pacific with Lady Grace and Weigand aboard, the German woman took a fast liner in the opposite direction to New York with the avowed intention of shooting Lady Grace on her arrival at Lakehurst, N.J.

I was at the airport to report the landing and had with me two husky men Chester Hope had hired to stay close to the jealous woman without her knowledge and prevent a tragedy. There was a tremendous crowd on the field, including our woman and the men at her side, and everybody surged forward against the ropes when the Graf landed.

Then, when the excitement reached its maximum, one of our hired men hauled off with a terrific uppercut and knocked that woman cold. With that, both men yelled, "A woman has fainted," and they carried her off the field to a waiting taxi which took her back to her hotel in New York.

A reporter from a rival paper who had remained close to the woman after her arrival on the field evidently knew her intentions because he gave me a dirty look as though blaming me for crabbing a good murder story.

The next day the titled Lady picked up a fat fee for endorsing a brand of cigarets.

I still regret I may have been instrumental in the retirement from the Hearst organization and the subsequent death of Bradford Merrill, editor of all Hearst morning papers. This happened when Lindbergh flew a crate from St. Louis and announced he was going to fly to Paris. The papers dubbed him "The Flying Fool."

At that time, Hope was allowing me fifty dollars a day to pay for by-line stories by people in the news. I interviewed Lindbergh and gave him fifty dollars. That looked big to him then. Next day, I recommended we sign up the aviator for "$25,000 for his story if he reached Paris." Hope said this involved so much money he would have to consult Merrill, who rejected the idea because, he said, Lindbergh would never make it.

But Lindbergh did make it and The New York *Times* gave him $40,000 for his exclusive story which *Times* men ghosted into a series of articles.

Then Mr. Hearst asked why we didn't sign Lindbergh first. When he was told, Mr. Hearst had a conference with Merrill and the latter retired after being with Hearst for years at a reputed salary of $100,000 a year. Although Merrill was rated as a millionaire with a beautiful home on Long Island, he soon died, presumably of a broken heart.

1 9 2 7

The Golden Age of Jazz

IN 1927, man and music united in a new intimacy. For the first time in history, each individual could dial the mood he wanted. The music could be as mellow as the booze was biting. The notes were syrupy, melted brass and virgin reeds, played on the valves of the heart and a trumpet and a cornet. Gin-mill inspirations could touch genius or be for royalties only. There were the quiet backroom sessions with Willie P., the Beetle, the Lion, and a million other nicknames with the depth of life to them, playing. Playing for the sound, the liberation of a new music, a new time. Those times when the average musicians were elevated to super heights because they suddenly happened to be in that elite league that has all the notes right, the sound.

The world's most-renowned musical thoroughfares—Beale, Bourbon, Basin, and Broadway—were christened during the decade. They were more than just market places. They were music, the microcosm and the macrocosm of this unique time between the wars. Three of the streets are deep in Dixie.

Memphis and the Mississippi mean music. The blues were born on Beale Street. The wailing boulevard was a haven for the tens of thou-

sands of Negro men and women who streamed into the cotton capital during the Civil War. Oppression, emancipation, and song amalgamated into the first—perhaps only authentic—soul street.

The black artery of sin and syncopation lured W. C. Handy from Alabama. He lived Beale for years. One night in 1909, when he was 36 years old, he stood at the mahogany cigar stand in Pee Wee's saloon and wrote "Memphis Blues." But it wouldn't sell. Five years later, he wrote "St. Louis Blues," but he couldn't market it either. Finally, as the decade picked up momentum, so did his songs. Both blues became classics. A new musical medium, the blues, the first expression of the soul *weeping, crying* in melancholy.

Handy's sorrowful sounds made life more amenable. "A Good Man Is Hard to Find," "Yellow Dog Blues," "Harlem Blues," "Joe Turner Blues," and "Hesitation Blues" are among his numbers that were solace for the brown-baritoned and honey guttural laments of living. "The Father of the Blues" also wrote some of the greatest spirituals during the decade, including "Those Who Sow in Tears, Shall Reap in Joy."

The notes wafted into the North. They rode the cigarette smoke in the speakeasies and lowered the temperature of the ice in a highball, as it echoed and melted its way through Prohibition. But the blues are still where they were reared. They are in the toothless reminiscences, and in the knowing eyes of old Memphis Negroes who remember when the blues were transferred from the street to a music sheet.

A few notes and a few hundred miles down the river, New Orleans was playing, too. This time French and Spanish influence was mixed with the Negro heritage. That and other things, and a different environment, made jazz. New Orleans was a riverboat town, too, but it was different from the bluff city of the blues. It was more sophisticated, bigger, and had its own special personality, born from its location. In the Storyville section of the city was a youngster named Louis Armstrong. He was born on the Fourth of July, 1900. When he was 21, he went to Chicago and joined Joe "King" Oliver's band.

Even in the late 20s a bucket of beer was still just a dime in the city of wrought-iron grilles. One could buy directories of brothels that listed their specialties. Bourbon and Basin were just saloon streets then. The tourist clubs came later. Razors and women were backdrops

to fights. Singing and slashing followed the crazy metronome of the times. "Beale had more living and more dying than any other street in the world," the motto said.

Jazz was probably coined in Chicago in 1914, years after the sound had migrated up from the banks of the Mississippi. The derivation of the term is debatable. Some music authorities claim it is a corruption of a bawdy Elizabethan word, *jass*. Other lore maintains it is a bastardization of the name *Charles*, which contracted to *Chas* or *Jas*. The third theory of its origin says it came from *jasbo*, a term describing a minstrel show. In 1915, an ensemble called The Original Dixieland Band was playing at the Boosters Club in Chicago. The patrons were particularly receptive, and the word *jazz* kept coming from the audience. The band decided to incorporate the word in its name. Other local bands followed suit to stay with the sound. *Jazz* probably first appeared on a record label in March 1917 when the Victor Company produced "Livery Stable Blues" and "Tiger Rag." The 20s etched the word into the soul of man and music.

As Memphis fostered the blues, New Orleans gave impetus and opportunity to jazz. The port city was sporting. It was the only town in the country that had legal prostitution. There was jazz, from the bawdy houses to the riverboats.

The individualism of personal expression found extensions on the notes of jazz. They were driving, mysterious, impulses, and emotional thrusts of song and tune. The music was kinesthetic. It was another classification of the blues. And there was the distinct offshoot of ragtime.

Ragtime probably came from the Negro slang word, *ragging*, to describe clog-dancing. It was a chaser with the big dose of wail. It was more stable in composition, leaving the improvisation to the main theme.

By 1927 Armstrong was the jazz king. Oliver's popularity had crested. Louis Armstrong and His Hot Five consisted of Kid Ory, trombone; Johnny St. Cyr, banjo; Lil Hardin, piano; and Johnny Dodds, clarinet. They had hits that year with "Muskrat Ramble" and "Heebie Jeebies." Satchmo's clowning was commercial. His singing and gestures were comical pantomimes to the real purity of the jazz he and his men were blowing. But the goofing helped make money.

"Jelly Roll" Morton was a purist who played only formal jazz on his piano. He added heterophony, solo written music, and inserted improvisations into the total form and development to get his special hybrid of formality. The "Frog-i-more Rag" is one of his most famous works.

Duke Ellington emerged in '27, one of the first formally educated musicians of the era. He didn't blast into the Prohibition concert instantaneously. He eased up to the top stands with finesse. He made it on the jazz tunes that were there. He perfected the old jazz into a new style, updating in his own way. His orchestras were assembled with great care. They had to have more than great horns. The sounds had to complement each other, but he didn't smother the solos. He encouraged the small spotlights, too. "East St. Louis" and "Black Beauty" were among the most popular pieces of his hits of the time.

"Swing King" Benny Goodman was one of the first aware that jazz was moving from the small groups to the big bands. Goodman was not an arranger when he started his orchestra. He liked to extract trios and quartets from his big-band stand. One of the first was a trio composed of Goodman, Teddy Wilson, and Gene Krupa. Goodman never reached the stature of Satchmo during the decade, but his clarinet reached a broader audience.

"Ain't She Sweet" is the jaunty type of tune that gave a headiness to the repertoire of that melodic year. Annette Hanshaw had the hit on the song. "Sweet Lorraine" was one of the more wistful songs with a lady in the title. It was written by Cliff Burwell, the pianist in Rudy Vallee's original band at the Heigh-Ho Club in New York. Paul Whiteman brought "Among My Souvenirs" to lasting popularity, which was one of the few English tunes to make it in America. It was written by Edgar Leslie, and the American lyrics were added by Horatio Nicholls.

"My Heart Stood Still" had a story to it, like almost everything else of the era. In 1927, Richard Rodgers and Lorenz Hart took two girls in Paris on a wild taxi ride. When they almost banged into another car, one of the girls said, "My heart stood still." Hart, who was unruffled, said, "That would make a nice title." Rodgers systematically logged the incident. A few weeks later in London, Rodgers wrote the melody for it.

Some royal showmanship helped initiate the popularity of the song. The Prince of Wales asked an orchestra in a Paris bistro to play it. The band didn't know it, and the Prince sang it until the boys could pick up on it. Naturally, the newspapers made some good copy of it. At the time, the writing team was working on an English musical, *One Dam Thing After Another*. They bought "My Heart" back from the producer and used it as part of the score for another of their hits, *A Connecticut Yankee*.

"My Blue Heaven" was one of the immortal ballads written that year. Three or four singers recorded it, but Gene Austin, then an unknown, was the one who sang it to success. Eddie Cantor used the tune that year in his routine in the Ziegfeld Follies. Tommy Lyman used it as his radio theme.

"The most important element in the success of a record," Austin used to say, "is the song, not the singer. Hit songs don't care who sings 'em."

And the sharply clean and sweet tenor of Austin went on over 12 million records of "My Blue Heaven." The song rocketed him to quick stardom. The flip isn't exactly any lesser known in the annals of hits. It was "My Melancholy Baby." They were recorded on September 14. Austin had more than nostalgia value. He was his own type of jazz. He sang the title song for one of the great silent pictures that year. "Ramona" in film and song was not released until '28, though.

"I'm Looking Over a Four-Leaf Clover" was one of the plinking, jaunty songs written in the year of Lindbergh. Mort Dixon and Harry Woods have helped sell a lot of banjos with the tune.

Of all the musicians who were immersed in the unbelievable decade, Fats Waller was the personification of the hedonism of the times. One of the unbilled musicians on some of Austin's records had been Fats. The 300-pound Harlem-born pianist was quite complex. He loved luxury, and his capacity for pleasure was even larger than his size suggested. He could be caustically satirical, tender, and very funny. Fats had the ability to analyze everything and everyone with an unusual detachment. He laughed at the world and himself. He may have been the most musical cynic of all time.

Fats was generous, spiritually and tangibly. He was always an easy

mark for a handout or a loan, even when he was almost broke. And he usually needed money despite his good income. His standards of fun and living were bountiful and expensive.

Although he liked some of the songs that made him great, he did the others because they were commercial. He realized that he had to make money to permit him to do things he wanted to do. He was not a frustrated artist though, because he did get enjoyment out of all he did. The big satirist and romantic wanted to explore other fields of music, particularly classical. Although he probably had a strong compulsion to compose and work with other types of music, he still was buoyant with the daily joy of living. Life was joy to him. Like the decade, he seemed to be wringing more out of the times than any one individual or the total populace could absorb.

Although he grew up in the colorful squalor of the black ghetto, he had a good background in musical theory and practice. The son of a minister, Fats started studying music when he was 5 years old. By the age of 10 he was doing some public performances. At 16, he became a professional and made $250 for his first records. And he started composing in his teens. His mind was super-fast even if he could not move his bulk quickly. During his 39 years—he died of pneumonia on December 15, 1943—he excelled in several arts.

He wrote over 400 songs, including "Honeysuckle Rose" and "Ain't Misbehavin'." He made some 500 recordings. His enormous rhythm was also on a great number of player-piano rolls. And, all of his tunes were ingrained with his easygoing manner. His pace was incessant. Concerts, gin, partying, writing, and recording. Then European tours, movies.

It was common for him to arrive for a recording session without a song. With his instant creativity, he would write a tune at the studio. He and his group would play it with the inspiration of freshness as part of the essence, for one practice run. Then they would record it. That way, he said, the musicians weren't worn out from rehearsing. Fats always considered melody first. He said a pianist who didn't have a left hand was not worthy of the instrument. The jovial prodigy didn't like big bands, and preferred to lead only six or eight men.

In '27 Fats wrote *Keep Shufflin'*, his first Broadway show. *Hot*

Chocolates, one of his biggest stage successes, came the next year. The serene and smiling titan spent his financial gains on specially built cars and wardrobes of clothes. His hosting was as herculean as everything else he did. Yet he was a deeply religious man in his own way of observance. Some of his close friends said he would have liked to have a traveling religious show with lots of spiritual music.

When a recording arranger tried to be dictatorial, Fats would sabotage him with a parody. And he could be so brilliant, so subtle with his resilient, biting lyrics that his revenge was always genius instead of mere satisfaction. His memory is still in song, not just in sentimentality. In London there's The Thomas "Fats" Waller Appreciation Society.

"Right now, every time someone mentions Fats Waller's name," Louis Armstrong has said several times, "why you can see the grins on all the faces, as if to say, 'Yes, yea, yea, yea!'"

One of Fats' albums is titled with one of his favorite expressions, "One never knows, do one?"

Guy Lombardo was playing "Auld Lang Syne" the year Fats was entertaining the world with his wit and artistry. His Royal Canadians had been ushering in the New Year since '24. Jazz and swing resounded, but he persisted in his velvety smooth style. There has never been any over-orchestration in this family band. Once Guy adulterated his sound a little, and the listeners didn't like it. He pondered. His regular haircut solved his decision.

"It's good," his barber told him, "but it ain't Lombardo."

"We play music people like to hum," Lombardo has said since that day in the early 20s.

Canadian-born of Italian descent, Guy concentrated on the violin as a youngster. Brother Carmen started with the flute and changed to the saxophone. Their father would hide their instruments when he caught them playing jazz. Lebert, another brother, started on drums and switched to the trumpet. Guy's brother-in-law, Kenny Gardner, is a vocalist.

Guy's orchestra has introduced over 300 song hits, including "Little White Lies," "You're Driving Me Crazy," "Seems Like Old Times," and "Easter Parade." "Our drums are practically never heard," Guy

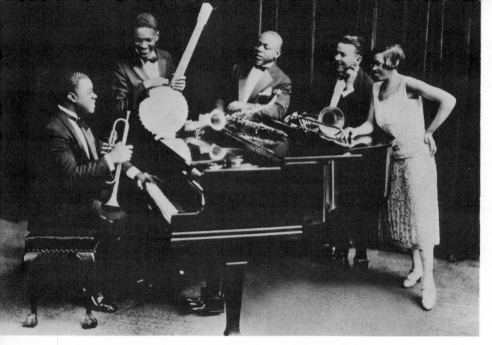

HOT FIVE—Left to right: Louis Satchmo Armstrong, Johnny St. Cyr, Johnny Dodds, Kid Ory, Lil Hardin Armstrong.

SOLEMN OLD JUDGE—George Hay was the first announcer of the Grand Ole Opry and coined the name of the hillbilly program.

EARLY OPRY—Uncle Dave Macon renders a number along with his son Dorris.

GULLY JUMPERS—This group, composed of Roy Hardison, Charlie Arrington, Bert Hutcherson, Paul Warmack, and Fred Shriver, was one of the proliferating hillbilly bands in '27.

FEET BY THE FIRE—Opry announcer George Hay and Uncle Dave talk in the Macon family home.

CROSBY WAS WITH HIM IN '27—Paul Whiteman had one of the top orchestras of the time. *RCA Records*

ELEGANCE OF ELLINGTON—Duke was among the prominent pianists during the 20s. He is still one of the great men of music. *RCA Records*

KING OF SWING—Benny Goodman poses on one of his foreign tours, some 40 years after the 18-year-old "boy wonder" played with Ben Pollack and His Californians. *RCA Records*

LOPEZ THE LEADER—Vincent Lopez had one of the name bands during late Prohibition.

HEIGH-HO EVERYBODY—Rudy Vallee and his megaphone were making millions of women swoon in '27.

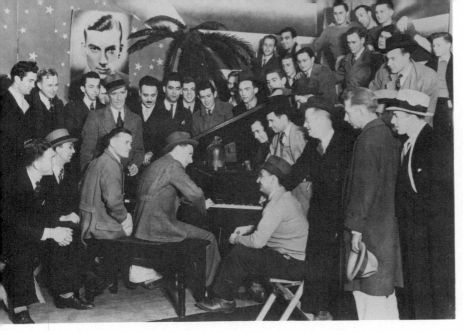

BACK IN THE BOOK NOOK—Hoagy Carmichael sits at the piano where he wrote "Stardust" in '27.

MUSICAL MONTAGE—Most of these stars of the jazz age were already well established by '27.

STILL PLAYING—The New Orleans Preservation Hall Jazz Band, still giving concerts, were all playing with various groups in the jazz age.

PRINCESS OF THE BLUES—Bessie Smith was wailing the sounds of '27 with the best accompanists. She bled to death after an auto accident when no white Mississippi hospital would accept her.

POOL PARTIES IN 20s—Meyer Davis's Le Paradis Band with "Miss Washington" plays this gig in her honor at the Wardman Park Hotel Swimming Pool on August 23, 1924.

1927 BAND—Meyer Davis poses with his boys during the golden days of the society orchestras.

WHEN GIN AND JAZZ WERE GENIUS—Fats is the tinkling piano of the jazz age. *RCA Records*

says. "The lead instrument is the saxophone or trumpet, and the drums follow them instead of the other way around." The Royal Canadians are well into their second thousand records.

Paul Whiteman and Meyer Davis were among those with leading dance bands. They played for the debutantes, fluttering brides, the ballroom circuit of the name clubs, and the strata of the population that considered the white-tie scene a break from the speakeasies.

Female warblers and wigglers added explosive sex appeal to the engagements. Sophie Tucker was one of the "Queens of Jazz." The blonde amazon with the proper blend of *umph* and soul singing changed her image as the fabulous year ended, and she became known as "the last of the Red Hot Mamas."

As '27 was portraying itself as an experimental year for any and all centuries, a slightly built Hoosier college student sat on the "Spooning Wall" at the University of Indiana in Bloomington, staring at the fall night. The twinkling pattern of the heavens inspired him. He whistled a few phrases, then more. As he began blowing them together, he left the wall and hurried over to the Book Nook, a campus restaurant, where there was a piano. That night Hoagy Carmichael wrote "Stardust." It's a classic and therapy. The opening high notes are as shrill and lofty as outer space. Humming or whistling it on those certain nights when one is alone with the stars is inner and outer communication with *the self*.

"Old Buttermilk Sky," "Lazy Bones," and "Georgia on My Mind" were among the tunes that followed his first composition success. His nasal baritone had that distinctiveness even in an era of creativity running amuck, and he had great sales of his own renditions on record. One of his friends and collaborators was Johnny Mercer. The honey-resonant Georgian worked closely with Hoagy during the latter part of Prohibition. Like Hoagy, Johnny had trademark tonsils that allowed him great returns on records of his own tunes. "Chattanooga Shoe Shine Boy" is one of his novelty classics.

But '27 was the jazz year of the era, the climax and the epitaph. For Bix Beiderbecke exited that year, although his shallow body lasted until '31. The young man from Davenport, Iowa, was the top brass of all the clear-bell horns being blown until '28. Then the 25-year-old

cornet player was too far gone to sit with a working band. The brass rails had poured too many bottles into him. He was a rumpot.

His stubby cornet was controlled genius. Everyone knew the purity of his jazz personality, the imprint of his own signature on the song. He probably did more for the exploration of the set rhythm of the medium than anyone. Jazz abides by four-four time with the pace racing through twelve or fifteen basic tempos. Bix blew the range with more acceleration and emotion than any other player. Bix was as drunk on music as he was on the hooch. The boy who wanted to be another Douglas Fairbanks as a youngster blew his life away playing his own dirge in the way he composed. His penetrating solos were inscribed on the music sheets of soul. They were put down with the arcing of his horn as he played.

Bix was young, and the years were wayward. Maybe he had all the music and the times had him. Some say he wanted to bridge the years past with his time. But the jazz years wouldn't blend. They don't adhere. Time has to adhere to them. Bix was on the highest pedestal with the elite, and he knew something was bothering him but couldn't define or diagnose it. Music was the only thing that sobered him.

The dents in his cornet were undoubtedly also on his heart. But he was jazz, maybe Chicago vintage, but jazz such as the Lord allows only in very special instances. Somehow the Almighty meant him as some sort of antidote for the jazz years.

Black hands and white cotton with that long, long sack dragging up and down the rows of the Delta, white hands trying to plow an existence out of the worn-out furrows of poor farms, and the laments of each helped foster country music. The hillbilly sound had been fermenting for two centuries. Maybe the germ came from the minstrels who strummed through Europe for many years before the migration to America. But the 20s made the rural rhythm fans a legitimate musical minority group. The cult has never been really small in number. Hillbillies have always been more isolated from each other than has the urban set.

Some music historians say country music didn't really start to crystallize until the early 20s. By '27 it was tying its strings around the very fiber of working, rural America. The English ballads, folk songs, white

and Negro gospel, and black soul were bonding into a hybrid sound. But it was the domestic mixture of the New South, progressive, cultural, and artistic with an antebellum blend of lyrics from the levees, from the poverty-chinked shacks with guitars and banjos on rickety porches facing dirt roads, and from the joy, violence, and heartbreak of the Southern-born that made it a new medium, and somehow almost all 100 percent American despite its European ancestry. There is the premise that it is more than the South. Individualism is an ingredient, and that is not Dixie's exclusive possession. Students of the sound say it is soul music, gut music, truth with a tempo.

Fiddles and shrill nasal sounds were therapy for the bleakness of that section of the nation that was far removed from the slick hardness of the big-city speakeasy. The guttural slap of the pistons of the Model Ts, which were not very common in sharecropper country, was not in the same league with the muffled, polite coughs of the hearse-long Lincolns and the luxury barge cars of the gangsters and others who could afford them.

In the Appalachians the coal miners and the mountaineers had their own special strains of guitar music. They contributed the depths of their souls to their hillbilly tunes. The music was part of the mountains and hills of Virginia, West Virginia, Kentucky, and Tennessee. The strong miners dug at the coal veins from before sunup until after sunset. They died in the dark bowels of the mountains from foul air, rock and slate slides, and all the other grisly accidents that happened before the advent of better safety equipment. They drank. They fought when provoked. And they fought life. The music supplied ammunition for the siege.

The radio was instrumental in increasing the awareness of the hillbilly world. It connected the farms and villages and mining camps. The initial broadcast of country music occurred on November 28, 1925. The station was WSM in Nashville—the capital of Tennessee and country music—and the only performer was 80-year-old fiddler Uncle Jimmy Thompson. The 1,000-watt transmitter reached a radius of 75 miles. For one hour and five minutes "Uncle" Jimmy played some of the more than one thousand tunes that he claimed to command. He had been fiddling all his life, but hadn't turned professional until he was 56.

"Solemn Old Judge" George D. Hay was the announcer. Within a few weeks, the show had 25 performers and was billed as the "WSM Barn Dance." Dr. Humphrey Bate, a local M.D., came over to the little studio with his harmonica. The audience was so impressed with his artistry of the mouth organ he organized a country band, the Possum Hunters, to appear regularly on the broadcasts. These programs were the first of what was named "The Grand Ole Opry" in January 1926. The sessions got longer and longer air time. Today, the Opry is programmed live each Saturday for over six hours, on Friday nights for three, and hundreds of radio and television stations include its shows, often on a delayed basis, for hundreds of hours weekly.

The Opry is the oldest continuous show in the history of radio. It is the only show with such tenure, and it has the incredible distinctions of never having been preempted, never having been replaced by a summer replacement, and never having had an intermission. Only twice in its broadcast history has it relinquished a little of its time. It contributed a few minutes to one of President Franklin D. Roosevelt's fireside chats and gave time to a special memorial program for Will Rogers.

The origin of the Opry's name is as homespun as its fare. "Judge" Hay was waiting for the show to reach air time one evening. The NBC network program going off was "The Music Appreciation Hour" from New York City. "From here on out folks," Hay said, "it will be nothing but realism, of the realistic kind. You've been up in the clouds with Grand Opera. Now get down to earth with us in a four-hour shindig of Grand Ole Opry."

Paradoxically, as the crowds grew, the Opry had to keep finding new quarters. One of its first moves was to a tabernacle, and it has been in another tabernacle for over 30 years. Officially, the building is the Ryman Auditorium; unofficially, the property has its own unusual, emotion-provoking history.

In 1891 Captain Tom Ryman, a tough riverboat skipper, brought his motley crew ashore into the Cumberland River town in search of a little bawdy leisure. A noted revivalist who had a tent meeting in downtown Nashville challenged the rough riverboat man and his men to attend his sermon one evening. Ryman led his crew to the meeting with the intention of heckling the minister. But they were moved by

the sermon to such an extent, they began praying. Ryman wanted the preacher to have something better than a tent for his humble gatherings. He set up a fund to build a great tabernacle. The red-brick monstrosity was completed in 1892.

Today, Opry fans still sit in the hard pews, and the stained-glass windows add a mystical light to the onstage shenanigans of the country musicians who have quit the barnyard and boondock for sequins and flashy clothes. Gaudiness is next to godliness in the wildest, guitar gathering on earth. But the music is still essentially the same.

The names of some of the early Opry groups emphasize the hayseed appeal stressed then. Paul Warmack and his Gully Jumpers, George Wilkerson and his Fruit Jar Drinkers, Arthur Smith and his Dixie Liners, the Binkley Brothers and their Clod-hoppers, Uncle Ed Poplin and his Old Timers, the Bronco Busters, and Jack Jackson and the Dixie Dew-Drops were among the featured performers.

Uncle Dave Macon was one of the main attractions. He started on the Opry in '26. Carrying three banjos tuned in different keys, he enthralled audiences for over fifteen years. The string band dominated the program until the late 20s. Then singers began to achieve some status on the great hillbilly stage.

The Opry was more than a picking and singing success. It became the hoedown headquarters of the nation. But country music still wasn't very commercial. A thin, young railroad brakeman with a consumptive cough from Meridian, Mississippi, proved there was money in the music, though. Jimmie Rodgers, the Blue Yodeler, set his misery to music, wailed chords of despair, and much of America listened. He had known poverty and pain, and moaned the blues. His lonesome lyrics are legend in mountain music, but he died at the age of 35. When tuberculosis killed him, he was wealthy. He sang from a cot in the New York recording studios almost until his last breath of the blues.

But the singing brakeman inspired others during his short career. Bill Monroe came to the Opry with his banjo picking so fast fans saw only a blur of his fingers, and bluegrass music was born. The Carter Family from southwestern Virginia was achieving some acclaim in '27 with its folk tunes and gospel songs. Others, like Roy Acuff, wailed about hard times and the rails—maybe some knew Black Friday was

coming and was going to make things even worse for them—and train songs became a part of country music.

Nashville and the Opry became the Hillbilly Broadway. The music sided with the outcasts of society. It first became associated with the good, manual laboring class of the South. Then it jumped geography and became national. Below the Mason-Dixon Line, hillbilly was the only music of many in '27. It was—still is—mountain good. Religion and country music are closely related. Honky-tonks and beer and hard labor were—are—a type of religion to the Southern mountaineers.

In '27, as now, not all of the hillbilly fans were rubes. Will Rogers was one of the celebrities of the era who praised it as his music. City dwellers found out over the years that country music isn't just about the country. It's about hard times, drinking, gambling, jail, big trucks, two-timing men and women, and all that. All of it earthy. And every bit as true in '27 as today.

And for other opera aficionados, there was another kind.

In February 1927 the Metropolitan Opera House in New York was enjoying its busiest season in the decade. *The King's Henchman* was getting storms of applause. Poetess Edna St. Vincent Millay had based the libretto on an old Saxon legend, a mélange of feudal ideals, the romanticism of Sir Walter Scott, pre-Raphaelistic modes, and pseudo-Gothicism. Critics hailed the premiere as a triumph of the stage. There were 37 curtain calls. One magazine review noted the sincerity of the ovation was quite evident since no one fled for his limousine as the musical drama ended. It was last performed in 1929.

Awesomely prophetic of today's progressive ballet, George Antheil staged a New York showing of his *Ballet Mecanique*. The European-educated American nearly caused a riot when his show premiered in Paris. The young composer tried to portray the texture of the U.S. in sound—a cacophony of gears, assembly lines, and brute power. Instead of relying on jazz, which had become a cliché for modern times, he used a battery of percussion instruments, mechanical pianos, bells, wind machines, xylophones, and airplane propellers. The percussive happening was too much of a time machine for the critics. It was almost a half-century ahead of them.

"This is making a mountain out of an *antheil*," Sam Chotzinoff, the *World*'s aisleman, said, who got a good line out of his play on words.

The New York *Times* elected not to review the concert. It ran a news feature story, calling the ballet a gaudy sideshow of the arts. *Time* magazine gave Antheil's ballet some commendation. The young director had some wind of his own. During his Paris show, he had a plane prop turned the wrong direction, which almost blew away the audience.

In July, Southerners in Fletcher, North Carolina, held a memorial ceremony for Daniel Decatur Emmett, a native of Ohio, who wrote "Dixie." The adopted son of "Dixieland" never thought the song was his best, preferring "Old Dan Tucker," instead. "Dixie" was too hastily composed, he thought. One Saturday night, while touring with a minstrel show, the leader had asked Emmett to crank out a stage march tune, a "walk around." He needed it the next day for a show.

An expression used by Southern circus performers working in the cold North came to him.

"I wish I was in Dixieland," the line went. Emmett worked up a tune from this inspiration, and gave what he considered a poor job to the "interlocutor" the next day. That evening the audience canonized it.

1 9 2 7

CHAPTER 8

Vaudeville to Video

VAUDEVILLE still had its variety in 1927, but the evolution and revolution of life and the entertainment media were making some adaptations. The bumps, grinds, skits, songs, dances, comic monologues, acrobats, and animal acts had competition from other areas of show business. From its infancy in 1885 until its demise in 1929, vaudeville was like a great awakening to the American entertainment scene. It played to the nation, urban and rural.

As an art form that still refuses to surrender its memory, its talents and color left a profound impact on the public. It was more than a medium. It was the vessel that helped make the U.S. a melting-pot nation. The comedy and the routines served as a link between the natives and the influx of immigrants coming into the country during those years. The zipping up and down of the curtains of vaudeville helped the nation to accept and understand the tremendous changes taking place. Vaudeville was communal showbiz.

No one entertainer could emerge too far from the mass of attractions. It was a gregarious troupe, and each showman contributed his part to the whole. Three to four dozen acts were often on one show,

each striving to add its own impact to an incessant extravaganza. Vaudeville catered to the public's needs and was the first modern mass entertainment.

By the 20s the star system was being molded. Salaries soared from $35 to $3,500 a week for many. The average ticket to see a show was a half-dollar, and some theaters often ran from 10:00 A.M. to 11:00 P.M. And the houses made money, too. A 2,000-seat theater at a little better than half capacity with 30 performances a week could gross about $20,000 per week. But the glitter generally came out only on stage. It was packed in trunks between show houses. Entertainers had to keep moving on the circuit in order to survive.

The competition mixed aggression with zaniness. Showbiz matured on the vaudeville route. Spontaneity and improvisation were the real directors of the great acts. It was an apprenticeship that graduated some of the most magnificent names in the entertainment industry.

Ed Wynn was one of those who perfected a role on the vaudeville platform and used it the rest of his long career. The whimsical, lisping, "perfect fool" was his design. Always costumed, always in character, Wynn refused to pose seriously for photographs. He was always on stage. The son of a hat maker, Wynn ran away from home at 15 to join a road show.

"I had a very definite urge for the stage," Wynn once said, "an urge I felt from about 8 years of age." His odd costumes were highlighted by horn-rimmed glasses and high thick-soled shoes. His voice was his outstanding character label. For radio he used a hysterical falsetto. On stage he used a normal pitch with a lisp.

A sandpaper voice and a monstrous nose were among the many trademarks of another comedian. Jimmy Durante's comedy during vaudeville was raucous, cyclonic, but never really naughty. He loved the piano and was harder on that instrument than anyone else has been before or since. By 1910 he was playing piano at Coney Island, Chinatown, and Harlem. He was often billed as "Ragtime Jimmy, the King of Harlem." Before he plunged into vaudeville, most places he worked were tough.

In '27 Durante, Eddie Jackson, and Lou Clayton had a trio that worked at Durante's nightspot, Club Durante. They sang, danced, and joked. They worked at the Palace and did some shows for Ziegfeld.

The strident-voiced Durante wrote and sang songs like "I Can Do Without Broadway (But Can Broadway Do Without Me?)." Durante didn't do any single gigs during 1927, nor any until 1931, when he accepted a movie contract.

"Schnozzola" was Clayton's name for Durante's ponderous proboscis, and it has been an accepted synonym for nose since. His picturesque language and piano destruction were just as much a part of him in the 20s as in the 70s.

George Burns and his wife Gracie Allen became big on the vaudeville marquees. George tried every conceivable type of act until he hit as a comic. Jack Benny was another comic who worked vaudeville. Eddie Cantor was with the "Ziegfeld Follies" in '27. He had been working with Durante since before making the famous troupe.

Florenz Ziegfeld's "Follies" are the 20s as well as '27. Flo's magic formula had been working superbly for over two decades. He found the most beautiful showgirls around and built the most elaborate sets against which they could drape their sex appeal and enticingly beautiful bodies in brief costumes. Engineering combined with pulchritude to swing alluring ladies from hooks and raise them on platforms. Whirling chandeliers glittered with girls riding on them. Spiced and spliced into the brigades of lovelies was an assortment of acts. Big-eyed Eddie Cantor sang and danced and cracked jokes. His dancing started then, he said, because he was so nervous at being in the big time. His moving around set him at ease to work.

Earl Carroll's "Vanities" were Ziegfeld's biggest competition. He used the same sensationalism and gimmicks to display his bevy of shapely bodies. His girls were just as attractive and drew almost as well as Flo's did. It was burlesque at its peak and peek of the decade, a shimmering scene of undulating hips and sculptured legs. The girls of Flo and Earl exhaled with some of the biggest and best bosoms of womanhood.

Will Rogers roped and wisecracked in the "Follies" from 1914 to 1924. He remained very close to Ziegfeld and his gorgeous revue even after he left the show. The Oklahoma cowboy, who became a living legend, was sort of a fatherly adviser to the world's most beautiful girls. His homely counseling included persuading the girls not to smoke cigarettes. Some levels of society did not consider showbiz a

very proper profession. Tobacco use by women wasn't accepted by the upper classes. "The more decent women the stage can get," Will contended, "the better it will be for the stage."

Of all the hoofers who tapped and shuffled on stage, Bill "Bojangles" Robinson was the uncontested master. The handsome dancer started with traveling shows in his teens for $5 a week. He had danced to Broadway stardom by '27. The suave, gold-toothed dancer starred in many Negro musicals as his salary climbed to $2,000 a week. The agile and swift rhythmic feet were among the fastest the world has seen. He could run faster backwards than the average athlete could run forwards. For a while, he held the world's record for running 75 yards backwards. In an era when Negroes were still being lynched with deadly regularity in the South, he was highly respected by both races. Dozens of cities made him an honorary police officer because of his many charitable activities. Much of his income was given to scholarships and to orphanages.

Bing Crosby was not too well known in '27. The Tacoma, Washington, crooner started as a drummer. He, Al Rinkler, and Harry Barris formed a trio called the Rhythm Boys in Los Angeles. The three were achieving some local popularity when they joined Paul Whiteman's band and toured with it for three years, including '27.

Vaudeville songs and humor were bulwarks of the business. Standup comics emerged from the route. And the songs said it all. "Take Your Girlie to the Movies (When You Can't Make Love at Home)" and "When You Know You're Not Forgotten by the Girl You Can't Forget" were catchy and catch-as-catch-can. George Burns knew many hundreds of these tunes. Part of his act was trying to act like a singer. He started the 70s with the same skits.

In '27 the advent of talkie movies caused some changes on the vaudeville billing. Theaters began showing the new motion pictures with added live performances. Radio was also edging into the acts, which were starting to diminish in number. But the world was turning its head to get the sound. Hollywood was speaking.

There was more wiggling in the theater seats in '26. Audience boredom with silent slapstick was more than evident at the ticket booth. Early talkies alone were not the total solution. Writers were delivering new comic scripts that cut down on slapstick and introduced some

straight drama. Comic characters were being given human attributes for the first time. They were given the status of live people.

This new format was in Keaton's *Go West*, where his attachment to a cow brought tears of sympathy instead of laughter for the melancholy-faced actor. He helped the bovine by removing a stone from her hoof. She reciprocated by shielding him from an angry bull a reel later. When the time came for the cow to go to the slaughter house, the comic freed a herd from the railroad boxcars. The sad-panned performer's antics again called for emotional concern rather than belly laughs. As with slapstick, the public soon became weary of the straight silent drama. The movie studios pondered the problems of sagging attendance and advancing technology.

"Quantity and quality are equal," Hollywood decided in its own celluloid and amoebic simplicity. By '27 the universal focus on sex had become somewhat of a disturbing commercial nuisance. It was fashionable among the middle and upper reaches of life to have had an affair before the age of 30. It was a social badge. Adultery was more status than love and lust. The sex merchants were a generation quicker to realize the realism of the medium than were the legitimate studios. Stag movies had been on the market almost since Tom Edison left his motion-picture baby untended for a few minutes. Some of the financially sordid studios weren't above using their lots for moon-lit productions of blue flicks. Several aspiring starlets got into their familiar positions on the casting couches and performed with partners for stag reels. Hollywood has always had rumors about established actresses starring in stags during its early years in clown town. And there was more than a subtle undercurrent of erotica in '27 and its surrounding years. Bootleg party records had been spinning for years with their dirty jokes and obvious euphemisms.

The gin generation didn't get anything near its true representation from Hollywood during the jazz age. Censorship and innuendos kept life as it was off the screen. Some of the best writers called the times the "most expensive orgy" ever. Unfortunately for posterity it couldn't be filmed that way, they noted belatedly. Some of the prophets and analysts of the era said a widespread neurosis started crusting on society in '27. It was not evident in sight and sound in the new films.

Since sex was sex and Hollywood felt it couldn't be overdone, it

was the primary appeal and the secondary one. A background of chorus girls was the prop for almost everything. Flo's "Follies" were transferred to film with some editing in certain cases. Sound accompaniment was the prelude to the first talkies. Warner Brothers premiered *Don Juan* on August 26, 1926, at the Manhattan Opera House in New York. John of the New York Barrymores starred in the "honeyed" version of the movie. An orchestra arrangement of the score was played on the vitaphone, a wax record which synchronized the sound with the film. *The Better Ole* and *When a Man Loves* were among the flicks that followed that used the synchronization records. These were the buildup to October 6, 1927, when *The Jazz Singer* was released by Warner. It was the first feature film with simultaneous speech and music and other sound devices. Although it was fundamentally a musical with a feeble plot, the audience response was quite favorable.

Al Jolson would have smeared burnt cork on his face, dropped to his knees and sung "Mammy" anyway, but his starring in *The Jazz Singer* made it easier for him to become an institution. The Russian-born singer was the sentimentalist who invented the emotional method of combining lyrics and talk. He talked the second verse of many of his songs, turning singing into conversation and back again.

Before his role in the first real talkie, he made a silent picture but was so dissatisfied with it he bought up the film and shelved it. He accepted the lead in *Jazz Singer* only after George Jessel had turned it down. Actually he spoke only one line of pure dialogue in the film.

"Come on, Ma, listen to this" was the extent of his language except for the songs. The plot paralleled his own life fairly closely. It chronicled the son of a Jewish cantor who broke away from his father's wishes that he also become a cantor, in order to seek a stage career. Jolson's father was indeed a cantor and wished Al—real name Asa Yoelson—to become the seventh of a direct line of Yoelson cantors, but the boy desired a more sumptuous pulpit and a different audience.

Jolson was squiring Ruby Keeler in '27 and married her the next year. She was a well-known dancer and actress. The singer said after their wedding that he had the most beautiful wife in the world and two million dollars. Jolson had been singing "Swanee" since 1918. That year, he had been working in a New York show when a young

composer named George Gershwin kept bothering him backstage.

"I tried to brush him off," Jolson said, "but he wouldn't brush off. Finally, I stopped the rehearsal and agreed to listen to the tune. It sounded okay so I sang it in the show. They say it made Gershwin famous. I know it made me $40,000 through sheet-music royalties."

Jolson's characteristic singing position down on one knee with his arms outstretched wasn't showmanly inspiration, the legends contend. The expansive gesture was due to an ingrown toenail, he told the press on occasions. The foot was so painful he got down on one knee while singing "You Made Me Love You, I Didn't Want to Do It" in *Honeymoon Express*. The gestures with the hands were an attempt to make the posture seem more natural, and it did take the pressure off his sore foot.

Toastmaster general George Jessel maintains his friend Jolson started singing on his knees due to another emergency. He said Al had a big green salad just before a singing engagement. He said he began hitting himself with his hands when the radishes hit him. When the onions hit him, he had to drop to his knees.

Fred Murnau, a German, was one of the first producers to contribute something to the new film mode. In *Sunrise*, his first American production, he had action and camera movement. He also employed some good mood devices. His scenes offered holiday excitement, traveling, and some notable frames of sensual seduction with some darkness and drowsiness to help create the exotic effects.

The maker of the shiniest stars and the master of the supercolossal cinema epic was Cecil Blount De Mille. Many of his pictures had Biblical themes. Some of his critics said his multi-millon-dollar productions were religious orgies. But the near-nude damsels were as authentically attired as history could support. The ski-nosed, mild-spoken little man was very religious. His father studied theology and had considered becoming an Episcopal minister.

De Mille customarily read two chapters from the Bible each night, one from the Old Testament and one from the New. He attended to every detail of his pictures, including how the extras parted their hair. His props were meticulous replicas. He developed more stars than any other man, but none was better known to the public than he was. His finds included Gloria Swanson, Wallace Reid, Thomas Meighan, Agnes

Ayres, House Peters, Jack Holt, Phyllis Haver, Rod La Rocque, Richard Dix, Leatrice Joy, H. B. Warner, Florence Vidor, and Theodore Roberts. He went to Broadway to get some of his personalities and brought Geraldine Farrar from the operatic stage.

"The people in the Bible weren't characters in a book," De Mille said in his later years. "They were real individual entities to me. Mighty warriors like Joshua were my heroes. They were like the cowboys and supermen who are heroes of the children today."

The King of Kings was playing the major theaters in '27. The lavish film was beyond anything movieland had done before, and very few since have attained such impact and magnitude. The story of the life of Jesus was still being shown somewhere in the world for thirty years, and it still gets some limited showings today. The energetic little man who liked to wear riding boots on location didn't realize any personal profit from the release. All the earnings he would have realized, millions of dollars, went to charity. Leading evangelists of the 20s and a generation later called him a prophet in celluloid who brought the Word of God to more people than any other man.

Among the many unknowns who were coming into prominence on the studio lots was Gary Cooper. He was working as a stunt man primarily in westerns, when in '27 he was selected for his first major role, the lead in *The Virginian*, which was released the following year. Joan Crawford was doing very minor parts and got her first film contract on New Year's Day in '26. She was making $75 a week the following year. She and Douglas Fairbanks, Jr., were seeing each other on and off the lot. They married the year of the crash. Gloria Swanson was 28 years old in '27. The veteran with the well-defined features, light eyes, retroussé nose, and flashing teeth made the transition easily from the silent to the talkies. One of her '27 films was *The Loves of Sonya*. Her hip-waving charm entertained many men when she filmed *Sadie Thompson*.

Edward G. Robinson was 34 years old when Chamberlin was looking for a field to set down the *Columbia* when it ran out of gas. The 5'8" Romanian-born actor had a swarthy complexion and expressive lips that almost vised a cigar, pipe, or cigarette. He was described by one reviewer during those days as "this fascinatingly ugly little man."

Born Emanuel Goldenberg, he became "Little Caesar," the tough

mobster with a tommy gun, and became stereotyped as the leading gangster actor. But he was successful on stage in a variety of roles before coming to California. In '27 he did some play writing and was married. He wed the former Gladys Cassell of New York City, an actress known professionally as Gladys Lloyd. On screen his normal manner was forcefully friendly and quiet, but as in real life he could turn explosive in an instant when provoked.

"Live beyond your means," Robinson said as a rule of success. "Then you have to succeed."

Twenty-seven-year-old Helen Hayes was living in a 22-room mansion in Nyack, New York, during the *great year*. The attractive actress was married to playwright Charles MacArthur. She was working in *Coquette* that year. It was a long-running hit—366 performances.

Diminutive Mary Pickford was "America's sweetheart." The well-built little lady with long golden curls and a dimpled smile reigned supreme for many years in Hollywood. The yellow hair was her trademark, her symbol of virtue and innocence. She would not permit any of her silent films or her talkies to be re-released. She said she did not want to compete with modern starlets who had the advantages of better techniques and technology than were available in her era. Her social reign in Hollywood was almost omnipotent during the 20s.

She married Douglas Fairbanks in '20, divorced him in '30. They had the biggest mansion in filmdom. Pickfair—a combination of their names—was a social mecca. It was called the "White House of Hollywood." It was said film premieres didn't begin until Mary and Doug arrived in style. Society column cynics said the script marriage was too ideal to be permanent. She was the biggest money-maker of the screen ladies of the time.

Charlie Chaplin was still very much on the '27 screen scene. Born on April 16, 1889, in London of theatrical parents, Chaplin made his stage debut as a baby. As a forlorn but lovable tramp wearing baggy pants, flapping shoes, battered derby, twirling a rickety cane, and with a scrub-brush mustache, Chaplin was in the heart of mirthful America. His wistful screen personality gave him universal acceptance. His comedy overshadowed his other exploits. He was not only an accomplished actor but also an adept writer, director, and producer. Jackie "the Kid" Coogan was one of his discoveries.

Chaplin resisted the talkies. The mighty comic actor stood in the midst of the old and the new rather adamantly. He insisted he didn't like or need sound and didn't want one audible word to do with talkies. And he continued to make silents although he did use some synchronized music for his pantomimic comedy.

There was some spectrum sex appeal on and off the screen, but the film could only show the black and white. Somehow the color got through with the glamour girls, though. There were many beautiful girls who were the spirit of the 20s, with great legs and bodies and faces that were as sensual as the times were wild.

Gilda Gray was a Polish girl. She interpreted African dances in American troupes. The superbly endowed amazon with rhythm was a sculptured blonde. She glittered in a chemise which had enough air and texture to show a lot of her. She initiated a new dance on the Continent.

The "Shimmy" came about from her own variation of the dance. When she was asked what she was doing to make her anatomy move so appealingly, she said, "I'm shaking my chemise." With mispronunciation over a period, "chemise" became "Shimmy."

The "It" girl was Clara Bow. In 1927 she appeared in *Rough House Rosie*. Between 1923 and 1933 she made 35 movies. She was the bubbling buoyancy of all the flappers, the bob-haired vixen, the All-American reincarnation of what the well-built and razz-mah-tazz queen of jazz was all about. She was the vibrant beauty of all that was deliciously and delectably wicked in the jazz age. Her wink was the flirtation of '27 and of all other years. Her electric eyes had all the luminosity of the honesty and the excellence of the days.

Prohibition night life had other regal ladies, too. Mary Louise Cecelia Guinan, better known as Texas, came to New York in '22. The Waco girl made some fame as an actress and singer, but she became the mistress of ceremonies of the plush clubs. She also operated several clubs of her own. Gangster and rumrunner Larry Fay was the first to sponsor her. Fay liked the showgirl clubs. He had an interest during late Prohibition in such spots as the Silver Slipper, the Rendezvous, Les Ambassadeurs, the Cotton Club, and the Casablanca.

Texas' clubs included the 300 Club, the Argonaut, the Century, the Salon Royal, the Club Intime, and two or three Texas Guinan Clubs.

SHOWBIZ COMICS—Joe E. Brown, Will Rogers, and Eddie Cantor clown for the lens in a theater lobby.

MOST REPRODUCED PHOTO—This print was widely used in many billings for Will Rogers, who could get a rope to do amazing things in his lariat demonstrations.

CLUB SCENE—Jolson sings with face and body in this scene from *The Jazz Singer*. *Released through United Artists Television*

"THE JAZZ SINGER"

DECLARATION—Father makes a point while mother is more shaken than son. *Released through United Artists Television*

"THE JAZZ SINGER"

CLASPS OF LOVE—The singer has a song of affection for his mother. *Released through United Artists Television*

"THE JAZZ SINGER"

MOTHER-SON CLUTCH—Jolson hugs his mother. *Released through United Artists Television.*

COSMETIC MAKEUP—Pretty May cajoles the jazz singer. *Released through United Artists Television*

"THE JAZZ SINGER"

IN THE WINGS—Mother, father, and May watch the singer. *Released through United Artists Television*

"THE JAZZ SINGER"

HAPPY DRESSING ROOM—This is a light scene in the first talkie. *Released through United Artists Television*

"THE JAZZ SINGER"

TWO LOVES—May and mother express concern in one of the several emotional scenes. *Released through United Artists Television*

"THE JAZZ SINGER"

WHITE PALMS, BLACK FACE—Jolson sings another in the movie. *Released through United Artists Television*

She was suspected of having syndicate connections, and all her clubs were raided frequently. The shapely dancer with a flair for club management was often arrested but never went to jail. She was brash and vivacious, with excitement always with her. She was the queen of the night clubs. The flapper entrepreneur was the most renowned noise in New York and was rivaled as the top night club attraction only by Helen Morgan from the middle 20s to 1931 or 1932. Few entertainers have had a peak of popularity which climbed so high over Manhattan.

"I have spent many wakeful hours trying to bring into camp such persons as Texas Guinan," a leading Prohibition officer wrote in '27. One year she reputedly banked almost a million dollars from her club profits.

"Hello, sucker" was Texas' greeting to her hundreds of thousands of customers. It is a part of Broadway history. Some of her other phrases have also become a part of night club and underworld argot. "Give this little girl a great big hand," Texas would shout when one of her singers was getting only token applause. She made millions but left an estate of less than $30,000 when she died in '33 in Vancouver, B.C., where she had been appearing with some dancing girls. The little, long-jawed Fay, who liked to be called the "Beau Brummel of Broadway," died the same year. The flashy hood who gave Texas her start forgot to wear his bulletproof vest under his gaudy raiment and was shot down in front of one of his clubs.

Belle Livingston, the Kansas Sunshine Baby, was another lady club operator who gave the Prohibition agents a lot of trouble and her patrons a lot of pleasurable drinking and dining. In '27 she was running one of her three clubs. It was her best known, the Fifty-eighth Street Country Club. Five floors of bars, grills, private rooms, and recreational dens were in the speakeasy. Belle was six feet tall and weighed a well-distributed 175 pounds. She had been a Broadway showgirl in the 1890s and usually served as her own bouncer.

Documentary realism was finally getting on the screen. Producer Rex Ingram's *The Magician* contained a sequence of a surgical operation. *Seventh Heaven* starred Janet Gaynor and Charles Farrell. It offended British tastes, which made it even more popular in America. Vilma Banky starred in *The Winning of Barbara Worth*, with Janet Ford doubling for her in the dangerous scenes. (Gary Cooper ap-

peared in a role that led to his stardom.) And there was some sociological comment in *The Wind,* which was directed by a Swede, Victor
Seastrom. It was a study of the effects of environmental conditions and
generally rough living on a sensitive girl who was unable to cope with
the circumstances.

The Barrymores graduated to talkies with finesse, naturally. They
were not among the thespians who thought speech conflicted with
freedom of movement. Voices had to have personalities, too. Elocution
institutes began to capitalize on teaching all the aspiring actors and
actresses who wanted to do talkies how to speak. Every silent dropout
had to be replaced. The farsighted saw that silents were not going to
persist in doing any percentage of the film business. Talkies merged
the stage and screen. Tom Mix horse operas and Madge Bellamy posh
romance specials were running around the merry-go-round of entertainment. The big bands were still doing encores, Sophie Tucker and
the swing girls were still anatomical and adenoidal, John Philip Sousa
marches still made the old World War I bullet wounds ache a little,
and every swimmer was Gertrude Ederle fighting the Channel current
and coldness.

Leave 'em Laughing was a Stan Laurel and Oliver Hardy feature
with some sound in '27 before their status had technically reached
stardom. It was a pantomime pandemonium in a dentist's office with
the complications of a toothache and laughing gas. Their Hal Roach
productions elevated them to the top of the comics. Movies were made
sometimes in less than a week. Some were made in three days. *Sugar
Daddies* had Stan cast as a harassed lawyer and Ollie as an ex-
asperating butler who team their talents to expose a blackmail ring.
Their attempts to solve the caper results in one of the most hilarious
chase scenes of the era when they romp jerkily through the amusement
parks of Southern California.

The ranking juveniles on the lots included the "Our Gang" kids.
Farina, Joe, Wheezer, and all the Gang did *Spook Spoofing,* among
other flicks, in '27. "The Little Rascals" kept doing silents for three
years after talkies. Their misadventures often had pathos and comedy.
They could flit from one emotion to another with incredible speed.
Roscoe "Fatty" Arbuckle was combining his humorous bulk with
beauty background plots. The ponderous screen buffoon did not object

to being in *femme* camps for the sake of comedy or serious pursuits. Offscreen he pursued the party life until it spelled finis to his career.

What Price Glory was making big money in '27. Its director, Raoul Walsh, suggested that Marion Michael Morrison change his name. Morrison, a former prop man, had pinch-hit as a stunt man when no one else wanted to plunge into the sharky waters off Catalina Island during a scene. He became an actor in '27. Walsh told the young giant that he "looked more like a John Wayne than a Marion." Wayne got into the industry when a studio executive needed some extras and turned to the local football team. Wayne, a big lineman for UCLA, said he could get some of his teammates. His friend Ward Bond was among the beef he got for the parts. The muscular pair were among the roughest during their early years when they made the drinking clubs.

Maybe the advent of sound made the medium more challenging, but for some reason more actors and actresses turned to directing and producing in '27 or soon after. Fairbanks, Chaplin, and Pickford were among the producers, as were Harold Lloyd and Norma Talmadge. Several of the veteran silent and neophyte talkie movie people formed their own production companies, but few of them were successful. Even cowboy star William S. Hart failed to make it. Fox Studio launched its Movietone system of putting sound on film in '27. Warner and Fox were the only producers of talkies until May 15, 1928.

Theater patronage went from 60 million to 110 million almost entirely because of sound. The increase would have been even more phenomenal if more theaters had been capable of using sound films the year they were introduced. The addition of the sense of sound to movies lifted film from a restricted channel to the mass media.

The year 1927 was probably Broadway's best ever. There were 268 shows produced—a record never equaled since.

The aisleman from *Time* magazine was among the critics who gave *Burlesque* credit for being the first hit of the play season on Broadway in '27. Barbara Stanwyck was cast as a burlesque queen in love with a no-good husband who was a comic dancer, played by Hal Skelly. He runs off with a chorus girl, but Barbara can't overcome her loss enough to marry a cattle baron who offers her half of Texas. In the last scene,

Stanwyck and Skelly are doing a dance routine. His sodden limbs quake. She gives him the old morale-building speech.

"Can you make it?" she asks.

"I can—if you'll stick, kid," he replies.

She says, "I'll stick—always." The curtain falls.

Burlesque played for 372 Broadway nights.

Two years earlier, Barbara had been singing jazz tunes in night clubs.

Oh, Please opened the Broadway calendar year in '27. The musical comedy concerned an actress who raided the home of a civic reformer while his spouse was away. Beatrice Lillie sang her brand of novelty songs. In the cast of the short-lived (75 performances) musical were Helen Broderick and Charles Winninger. The music was by Vincent Youmans.

The Letter got short but pleasant reviews in October. The Somerset Maugham play starred Katharine Cornell as an attractive murderess whom most men in the audience would not have wanted around the house despite her beauty and build. She shot a guy as the curtain rose and remained evil throughout.

Coquette opened in November. Helen Hayes, in a magnificent performance, played a frivolous lady who falls in love with a rough villager, ably played by Elliot Cabot. Her father shoots him and passion becomes death.

Fred Astaire and his pretty sister Adele sang and danced their hearts out in *Funny Face*, a Gershwin triumph. Numbers included "High Hat" and "He Loves and She Loves." In the cast: Victor Moore and Betty Compton.

Although much less widely popular than movie and vaudeville, the radio was becoming a necessary item in the standard of living by '27. In October a Radio Fair was held in Madison Square Garden. Some 300 exhibits were a maze of earphones, galena crystals, cat's whiskers, binding posts, wires, coils, and huge refillable batteries. Radio was now a sophisticated, simplified apparatus. There were sets shown that did away with batteries. This would reduce the cost of radios and make them sell quickly during the next three years. There were receiving sets in only 7 million of the nation's 27 million homes in '27.

The radio was also bonding the family together. "They all used to scatter in the evening," mothers were saying. "Now, the children sit around and listen to the radio."

Between July 1926 and February 1927 some 200 new stations went on the air because of new radio legislation. The radio was an insane maze of waves. Dial twisting was a necessity, because stations changed frequencies at will. They would be on one side of the dial one day, on the other the next. Interference turned into a power game. Stations would increase their power at will. All the stations literally fused. Everyone was on the air, and no one could be heard. President Coolidge had appealed to Congress in his message of December 7, 1926, to enact a comprehensive radio law.

The Radio Act of 1927 resulted. The plight of the airwaves was basically evident. It was obvious that everyone in the nation could not set up his own radio station. The act proclaimed that the airwaves belonged to the people of the United States and were to be used by individuals only with the authority of short-term licenses granted by the government when the "public interest, convenience, or necessity" would be served. The law revoked the license of all stations then operating and allowed them 60 days to apply for a new permit which had to be filed with the Federal Radio Commission. The FRC regulated the power, frequency, and time limitations of broadcasting.

"Radio regulation is as necessary to its development as traffic control was to the development of the automobile," the Supreme Court said.

The Columbia Broadcasting System started on January 27, 1927, under the name of United Independent Broadcasters, Inc. Its first purpose was to contract time for a network of 16 stations, to sell advertising time, and to broadcast programs.

Rudy Vallee was radio's earliest crooner. He had a band in '27 that was playing the New York clubs, and the engagements were broadcast by a local station. The radio was an audio tabloid revival of vaudeville in many ways. Variety programs were coming into popularity. A constellation of comedians was getting ready to come on the air. Many of them were still doing stage acts as vaudeville started to decline. Eddie Cantor, Jack Benny, Bob Hope, Fibber McGee and Molly, and Jimmy Durante were among those who would soon have regular programs.

Fred Allen and Edgar Bergen were foremost in broadcasting. Allen was the reigning pungent wit of the day. The former librarian flunked with his vaudeville juggling act but scored with his humorous monologues. He married Portland Hoffa in '27. She became one of the most renowned names in history through his acidulous and winning talent. Lum and Abner—real names Lauck and Goff—were also on the vaudeville circuit in '27. Their radio did not come until '31.

Music was the main ingredient in programming, as it still is. The Hotsey Totsey Boys were playing "I Got the Gimme's, So Gimme Another One Too" over station WKD in Albany, New York, while "Dixie" radiated from the transmitters in the South during the late evening. The airwaves were starting to function as a news source, but most of the electronic journalists did little more than read newspaper headlines from late editions.

H. V. Kaltenborn, an associate editor of the Brooklyn *Eagle*, went on the air in April of '22 to discuss a coal strike. Soon he started giving 30-minute news analyses over station WEAF in New York. In '27 he covered a revolution in China, among other significant stories. His "Kaltenborn Edits the News" broadcasts were delivered in sharply clipped tones, and with a robust but dignified diction. He was so adept at backgrounding the news that he needed only partial scripts. Generations after '27 also heard his emphatic "Good Night" that ended each program.

Early sound-effects men provided the real grunts and smacking of leather as radio brought the major boxing matches to millions of homes. The microphones were not so sensitive or so near the rings as they were later. But the drama was real. During the suspenseful interlude while the Dempsey-Tunney decision was being figured, some men died of heart attacks while waiting for the announcement.

1 9 2 7

The Writers

THE picture of F. Scott Fitzgerald crawling on all fours to a Samuel Goldwyn party is one of the literary legends of the 20s. Campus libraries now bulge with biographies on Scott and his wife Zelda. They repetitiously—and with rare exception superficially—recount the antics of the pair. They were jealous of each other, but some sort of weird love did connect a runner chain between them. Their handsomeness as a couple is a poignant accent to their story. He had a high forehead with very fair wavy hair. His mouth was delicate, almost effeminate. Hemingway said Scott's mouth bothered him when he first met him. It was worse as a focus fetish after one knew Scott for awhile, Hemingway said. They were in Paris together with Gertrude Stein's colony. Scott was already well known, but Hemingway still hadn't sold a book.

Scott met Zelda in 1918 in Montgomery, Alabama. She was a society belle who possibly had a leaning toward schizophrenia then. The memoirs say she was chased around the dining table by her father the first Scott was invited to her house. She liked men and a good time. They married, and the parties, marathon drunks, squabbles, and traveling began. He was the wealthy, precocious author, she a Southern

belle with a great figure and a haunting look beneath the facade of her clean and attractive face.

"Let's do something" was her motto. And *do* they did. Europe, the Riviera, the scene of the moment.

Some who were there said she kept him as drunk and occupied as possible to keep him from writing. She was that jealous of his work. They also liked to taunt each other with their brief, torrid romances. On the foreign beaches she was shapely, tanned, lovely. He was not in very good physical condition, rather soft, unlike his unknown friend-acquaintance Hemingway, who was powerful. Scott came into a New York club one night with a shillelagh. He said it was the best stick made, unbreakable. Hemingway was sitting at the table. He took the police club from the slightly built Scott and broke it across his head with a booming laugh.

Zelda's obsession with excitement led to fits of hysteria. Her young daughter also complicated her mental condition. Scott did not do any work of literary impact in '27. He sold little that year, but the royalties from *The Great Gatsby* and other books were sufficient to keep him in the wasteful luxury to which he had long been accustomed. Some critics said Zelda is in each of his best books. She is Daisy Buchanan in *Gatsby* and acidic Gloria Patch in *The Beautiful and Damned.*

The romance of Scott and Zelda climaxed in the crisis year of 1927. She was admitted to the first of many mental hospitals the next year. Her mind swept from love to beratement while she was in institutions. She devoted much of her time to correspondence. Even during their courtship days she had been a prodigious letter writer. The missives certainly did not contribute to the mental peace of Scott. He had other loves while she was away, but he refused to divorce her. The stark terror of their relationship ended only when Scott died in 1940 at the age of 44. She was burned to death in a hospital fire in 1948.

Scott was a word merchant. He prostituted his talent to get money to be able to write books, he said. He was true to himself, he confessed to some friends, in that he wrote magazine stories the way he wanted. To make them salable, he did the rewriting necessary. Maybe it was the whoring of the times instead of the whoring of his talent. Maybe it was both. Some of his works are permanent. Others are not. He could produce short stories rather quickly and get thousands of dollars for

each from the *Saturday Evening Post* and other slicks of the era. He was able to write for money and mankind. And himself. But he short-changed himself too much. He had his sensitive hands on the pulse of the Prohibition years, The jazz-age writer was able to push his prose to genius heights, but he could blow badly when he had deteriorated. There were some fragile intervals. He worked. Zelda was released. She tried to maintain stability. But the relapses were worse each time for both. Scott reflected on the decade in the November 1931 *Scribner's* magazine, in an article "Echoes of the Jazz Age." It was an excellent reverberation by a writer who was still hearing the years, but for him the nights were not so tender.

Ernest Miller Hemingway was an expatriate in Paris during most of the early and middle 20s. He wrote while he was hungry, and he was happy as he prowled the streets of the resurgent city. Drinking, conversing, and writing hard were the elements of discipline to his "lost generation." The forlorn, sometimes funny, sometimes brutal years away from the jazz age of the USA were instrumental therapy to the expatriate writers. Decades later, Hemingway's memoirs revealed how important the Paris tenure had been. His spare style had been distilled then. He worked meticulously, writing and rewriting, on short stories as training for the longer haul of a novel. And in the winter of '26 *The Sun Also Rises* was published.

In '27 he produced a book of short stories. *Men Without Women* included one of his most famous stories, "The Killers." It is about two men who go into a restaurant to shoot Ole Anderson. It is about life. It is about death. It has been reprinted in many anthologies and adapted to stage and screen more than once. The collection also included "Fifty Grand," "Today Is Friday," and "A Pursuit Race."

"Hemingway first showed us through his writing that violence is a human trait," Sinclair Lewis said. "He's been able to write about war without being coy or cute."

The heavily built, square-featured son of a doctor from Oak Park, Illinois, was an author-adventurer. He had shrapnel in his legs from World War I, and he picked up other injuries on his safaris and from fighting in other wars. He said his body was etched with his active life.

In September 1969 an investigation uncovered a trove of unpublished Hemingway stories. The literary find yielded 4 novels, 19 short

stories, and 11 articles, plus several poems, notes, and letters. Most of the manuscripts were found in a backroom of Sloppy Joe's Bar in Key West, one of his favorite saloons all his life. A Cuban bank vault yielded some of the works. *Jimmy Breen,* one of the books found, was written in '27.

Sinclair Lewis's *Main Street* portrayed a drab existence of life in a smug and complacent small town. The 1920 novel stirred furious debate over whether Gopher Prairie and its inhabitants were typical of the nation's small incorporated towns. But the controversy sold books. Within a few months, the novel went through eleven printings, and the tall, lean, and lanky author was famous. *Babbitt* upset small-town businessmen. They arose to denounce the composite image of themselves in the person of George F. Babbitt, the real-estate man in the little city of Zenith.

In '25 Lewis was selected as the winner of the Pulitzer Prize for *Arrowsmith,* a novel about a young Midwestern doctor whose devotion to medical science triumphed over the local ignorance and prejudices of his colleagues and the community. When the 40-year-old red-haired writer turned the Pulitzer down, his fame as an iconoclast became entrenched forever. In '30 he did accept the Nobel Prize primarily for *Babbitt.* He later reflected on why he accepted one award and declined the other:

> The reason is the enormous difference between the two. The Nobel Prize, with no strings attached, is awarded on the basis of excellence of work. The Pulitzer Prize, on the other hand, is cramped by the provision of Mr. Pulitzer's will that it shall be given for the American novel published during the year which shall best represent the wholesome atmosphere of American life and the highest standard of American manhood. This suggests not only literary merit, but an obedience to whatever code of good form may chance to be popular at the moment.

In '27 his literary lightning flashed with more voltage than ever before. Just before *Elmer Gantry* was released that year, Lewis spoke at the Linwood Boulevard Christian Church in Kansas City. He ridiculed Fundamentalism, and, as an experiment, challenged God. "If He is a Fundamentalist God, let Him strike me dead within ten minutes,"

Lewis said. He placed his watch on the pulpit and continued his talk.

When *Elmer Gantry* came out, he became even more a focal point for religious criticisms. Many clergymen condemned him in sermons. Gantry was a hard-drinking, passionate preacher. He dispensed canvas salvation and salved his own conscience with profit. The seamy evangelist is the original con man on the Bible circuit. He set the stereotype for all of them. The frail-looking novelist slashed into the garb of hypocrisy that clothed many of the country's pseudo-sanctified institutions. He exposed what was beneath regardless of whom or what the vestments hid.

Lewis's personal life in '27 was not peaceful. His wife obtained a Reno divorce in '28. As a writer is supposed to do, he worked at various jobs from coast to coast before becoming an established author. Even after his literary successes, he worked for long periods as a newspaperman. The intense writer was also an actor and held an Equity card. He had the ability to put even strangers at immediate ease and to make friends easily. His stories flowed with the same intimacy. His books, or exposés, were not written out of emotion.

Lewis prepared reams of notes and outlines for his books. He researched with such scrutiny that his notebooks frequently ran 300 pages. "My novels are just about people," he said. "Elmer Gantry just happened to be a preacher. I said some nice things about preachers in the book. You might as well say I glorified preachers as to say I exposed them." To a great degree, he looked at his books like news stories. He said he felt he never did get a good news story to write while he was a reporter.

Lewis dedicated *Elmer Gantry* to H. L. Mencken. "The Bad Boy of Baltimore" was still scourging the boobs. Mencken contributed new words to the language and was an authority on language. His scholarly tome *The American Language* is still considered a standard reference. He was the bass drummer of the jazz age. The son of a Baltimore cigar manufacturer, Mencken looked upon the mores and foibles of the 20s with a critical and amused eye. He was the undisputed satirical mischief king of the literary world. The fair-complexioned wit took a ridiculing, vicious assault against any convention that struck him as false or hypocritical.

"H. L. Mencken is the most powerful personal influence on this

whole generation of educated people," Walter Lippmann said in '27. Like Lewis, he had some barbs for hypocrisy in religion. He was widely denounced from many pulpits. In 1926, a prominent New York preacher said that H. L. "had a good heart but a weak head." Mencken referred to many ministers as "the reverend clergy." In 1903, at the age of 23, he became city editor of the Baltimore *Morning Herald*. Three years later, with two books already published, he joined the Baltimore *Sun* and was associated with it for 50 years. In '27 he was publisher of the *American Mercury*, which he had founded three years earlier. His editor was George Jean Nathan.

"The only advice he ever gave me," Nathan said, "was to never make love to a woman in a hammock because it will break your back."

He didn't like the cult in the 20s that criticized the country. "The issue of Americanism is being murdered by idiots," he said. "Day by day its exponents pile up proofs that to be an American, as they conceive it, is to be a poltroon and an ass." He had a Nietzsche and beer philosophy that blistered the land. His toleration for ignorance was low.

"The truth to the overwhelming majority of mankind is indistinguishable from a headache," the irrepressible author once wrote.

During the 20s Mencken liked "to stir up the animals," a term by which he referred to humanity. One of his most amusing stories he used in the *Mercury* was about a prostitute who operated from a cemetery. The Boston Watch and Ward Society banned the edition. To the glee of the flapper era, he hurried to Boston and sold a copy to the chairman of the Society of Brimstone Corner. The courts shortly vindicated the writer and made him even more of a celebrity. He dumped a scathing attack on the South in an essay titled "The Sahara of the Bozart." He said the South was a cultural cesspool. Almost overnight, three literary magazines were founded in Dixie.

The public remembered his antics at the Monkey Trial in Dayton, where Clarence Darrow and William Jennings Bryan tried to put evolution on the witness stand. He said no one gave a damn about that school teacher. The object is to "make a fool out of Bryan." He personally covered the case for the *Sun*. He came up with labels that are still common language. He said the South was the Bible Belt, and

Dayton, Tennessee, was the buckle on it. The presence of the author-editor-critic-philosopher was one of the major features of the world-renowned trial.

"A gorilla, true enough, cannot write poetry," Mencken said. "But if it could only speak English, it could be made into a competent train conductor or a congressman in 30 days."

He did not marry until he was 50 years old, in 1930. Throughout his bachelor days he loved fat women, the more obese the better. He liked beer and big broads. His war against Prohibition and the hypocritical chastity-belt respectables is one of the most monumental battles of all time. He helped to turn the faucet on and drown the Noble Experiment.

"He is the most powerful private citizen in America," the New York *Times* said of him in the 20s and 30s.

While Mencken was creating new words and expressions, Damon Runyon was writing a new language on Broadway. The flashy sports writer for the Hearst newspapers walked the famous street in his $50 shoes, for which he hired a man to break in for him. He could dash off short stories and sell them to slicks with seemingly no labor. Born in Manhattan, Kansas, in 1884, Runyon was raised with newpapers. His father was an itinerant compositor who sometimes established newspapers of his own.

His breezy fiction buzzed and glowed with all the fervor of the gnarled neon scrawled up and down the most revered boulevard in the world. He knew the gamblers, the fighters, their managers, the shills, the pitchmen, the society notables on every level of life. The big shots, the people of the city, and the hangers-on. They knew him, too. Many of them turned into characters in his hundreds of stories, many of which became movies. All "the guys, all the dolls."

The soft-spoken reporter was always with the most alluring show-girls and in company with the most colorful personalities of the times. He inspired a newspaper friend to start freelancing stories during the 20s. Walter Winchell not only started selling fiction himself; he was immortalized as Waldo Winchester in one of Runyon's stories.

Jeweled studs fastened Runyon's shirts. His flashy attire was in keeping with that of his lingo-talking friends. He always wore a for-

tune in jewelry. His stories were almost always in the present tense, and his genius for describing people launched an era in characterization.

Lindy's Restaurant was his favorite spot. He headquartered there. As "Mindy's," it was the locale for many of his tales. He wrote novels, plays, poetry, news, and feature stories with equal success. His picturesque fiction creations—all based on characters he knew—include Harry the Horse, Little Isadore, Spanish John, Dave the Dude, Apple Annie, Light Finger Moe, Broadway Rose, Broadway Sam, Regret, the horse player, and Sorrowful, the bookmaker.

"I took one little section of New York," he once said, "and made half a million writing about it." He was more than lively; he was humorous. But there is depth to his work; his unique realism probes feelingly the people and life on the street of dreams. Runyonese and Broadway-esque are the same language.

In '27 Runyon covered Sacco-Vanzetti, Lindbergh, crime, and many other major stories. Although he favored sports, he enjoyed general reporting also. When an army of reporters broke from a news scene frantically to write or phone in their stories, the natty Runyon would calmly dictate his story spontaneously over the phone to his newspaper. He would then, just as calmly, go to one of his favorite hangouts for coffee. The bespectacled novelist-short story writer-journalist never drank whiskey, but he reputedly drank 40 cups of coffee a day. He undoubtedly had a photographic mind, and tape recorders for ears. He absorbed every detail, every word.

"Damon," Bing Crosby told him in amazement in a club one night, "you must listen to everything you hear." The world is still hearing the jargon and seeing the habitués of the Great White Way because Runyon painted and recorded it all in his prose.

In 1927, Dorothy Parker was one of the wittiest women of that generation. She was nationally acclaimed for her prose and poetry when she was arrested for picketing the Massachusetts State House as a Sacco-Vanzetti sympathizer. She was charged with sauntering and fined $5. As the drama and literary critic for *Vanity Fair*, Dorothy Parker formed a close association with John Dos Passos and the other major writers who lived and frequented New York. Dos Passos was another of the writers who crusaded to save the lives of the Italian

anarchists. He was fined during the same demonstration. Their execution was a moral crisis for the established novelist.

Dorothy and her first husband were having domestic problems in '27, and the sophisticated, yet earthy, authoress and poetess was granted a divorce from Edwin Pond Parker II the next year. She retained his name as her pen name.

One of the bestselling lady writers prior to, during, and after Prohibition was Mary Roberts Rinehart. The famed mystery writer was 51 years old in '27. Her sometimes brutally stark tales are excursions into quiet terror, and paid her enormously in wealth and stature. She felt close to her fictional creations and made it a rule "never to kill nice people" in her plots. Many of her 60 books are still on the paperback racks, including the first one, *The Circular Staircase,* published originally in 1908 and now considered a crime classic.

The attractive Mrs. Rinehart did all her writing in longhand with a fountain pen. Hemingway was another writer of the era who said he could express himself better in longhand. Then, as now, some writers felt a typewriter is too much of a barrier between the mind and the moving hand. She used the same pen for over a quarter of a century and cherished it more than any other possession.

"I might leave a diamond bracelet lying around," she said, "but never that pen." During the 20s she wrote more general novels than mysteries. *The Red Lamp* was being extensively read in '27 and had been out for two years. *Lost Ecstasy* was published that year, an appropriate title for those months. Her work, she said, helped the readers go off into another realm and share adventures they most likely would never have themselves.

Tarzan was swinging as wildly in '27 as today. The superbly muscled white man of the jungle rode his first grapevine 14 years earlier. Edgar Rice Burroughs was 35 years old when he conceived his apeman. The solidly built writer was mild looking. He never visited the Dark Continent where his main character lived. But he extracted many millions of dollars from inner Africa with the exploits of his grapevine swinger.

Into an imaginary jungle, Burroughs sent an Englishman and his wife and then had them die immediately after blessing them with the birth of a son. An ape raised the boy. *Tar* means white and *zan*

means man, Burroughs said in his manufactured ape vocabulary. He was an international author in the jazz age. Tarzan was translated into 56 languages over the years. The Chicago-born writer lived well and in relative seclusion almost all his life. He said he was aware he was not doing the most serious literature, but he was content to make money and provide the public with his white jungle lord to take people to lost cities, hidden valleys, and treasure- and adventure-loaded paradises.

Helen Keller could not see or hear the 20s in the normal sense. Her dark soundless world could not imprison her spirit or restrain her faith, however. She was one of the great personages of the decade. Born at Tuscumbia, Alabama, in 1880, she had a normal babyhood. When she was 19 months old an illness left her blind and deaf. Muteness resulted because she had not yet learned to talk except for a few childish words. During her early childhood she developed into a half-wild creature, able to make her wants known only by crude motions and guttural noises. When she could not communicate, she often went into rages. Her wealthy, influential parents sought the advice of inventor Alexander Graham Bell—a pioneer in the education of the deaf—on what to do for the child. He told them to secure a teacher for her. When she was 7, Miss Anne Sullivan was obtained from the Perkins Institution for the Blind in Boston. The two were inseparable for a half-century, until Miss Sullivan died in her seventies.

Anne taught her through the manual or finger alphabet, but there were severe problems in getting the little girl to respond to any affection or instruction. A water pump was the breakthrough. Anne spelled "water" into Helen's little hand and then held it under the spout. The connection between word and object was made. That day the little handicapped girl learned 30 words. She literally was totally committed to learning from that first instance of communication. With Anne always with her, she went to prep school, graduated with honors from Radcliffe College, and began her tremendous career as an author and educator and humanitarian supreme.

During these trying years, as they applied themselves to so many monumental tasks and achievements, the dramatic story became even

more one of life's most warming friendships. Anne went blind because of the strain in serving as the eyes of Helen. They lived together in darkness and ran a nationally known household on a fantastically normal basis without special aids. By 1927, the world had known her for well over a quarter of a century. She and Anne had performed an unusual vaudeville act. Both gave lectures which enthralled the audiences between acrobats, antics, and animals.

Miss Keller wrote over a dozen books, many articles, essays, and stories. *My Religion* was published in '27. Her favorite literature was the Bible and volumes of poetry and philosophy. She and Anne did much work for the deaf and the blind in that year, as they did in others.

"The two most interesting characters of the 19th Century are Napoleon and Helen Keller," Mark Twain said. She was an eternal light that glowed through '27, and her incandescence was perhaps needed more then than at any other time.

John Steinbeck was one of the writers seeking himself and acceptance in '27. He was getting acquainted with the underprivileged migrants he would write about. In his native Monterey County, California, he lived and worked with Mexican and other foreign laborers. He watched the hapless trek in old autos from the Dust Bowl to the promised land of the fertile orchards and farms. The nomadic young dropout from Stanford University worked in the fields, was a caretaker on an estate in the High Sierras, and took some freighter trips. He was probably still gathering some material for his fourth novel in '27. His first three books were not published.

Cup of Gold was not published until '29. That it coincided with the crash and did not sell well was in keeping with the difficulty the wide-shouldered writer was having in carving his own niche in the writing world.

The Hoosier writer Booth Tarkington had a bestseller with *The Plutocrat* in '27. He was essentially a romantic and sentimentalist. He disliked the blunt impact of the fiction of the roaring period. He was an admitted conservative.

Louis Bromfield had a bestseller with *A Good Woman* in '27. He

PROFILE OF SUCCESS—F. Scott Fitzgerald was wealthy when Hemingway wasn't eating well in '27. *Courtesy of Charles Scribner's Sons*

DURING PARIS DAYS—Hemingway poses for a promotional picture for his publisher, Charles Scribner's Sons. *Courtesy of Charles Scribner's Sons. Photo by Helen Breaker, Paris*

PORTRAIT IN INDIANA HOME—Booth Tarkington was a top novelist by '27.

AUTHORED *Mosquitoes* IN '27—Faulkner was not well known when Liveright Publishers took this photo that year. Liveright Publishing Co., publishers of *Mosquitoes*

POET FOUND—Ezra Pound was one of the burning zealots of verse and political philosophy of the Lost Generation. *Photo: Boris De Rachewiltz. Courtesy New Directions Publishing Corp.*

won the Pulitzer Prize in '26 for *Early Autumn*. His flowing vapor of glamour came across best with female characters, and most of his successes were with heroines.

"Sparkling, bubbling, dauntless, and enthusiastic" were common word choices for the personal life of Richard Halliburton. The playboy liked to be on the move since travel books were most profitable for him. He said his female companions who accompanied him on his escapades "stayed at separate hotels." Some critics duly noted that there might have been traffic between the hostelries. One of his most popular travelogues—*The Glorious Adventure*—was released in '27. It chronicled his tour of Greece. The prim New York *Herald Tribune* noted he was not a great writer or adventurer, but he had sound formulas.

William Faulkner was 30 years old in '27. The short, distinguished writer was born in New Albany, Mississippi. He was raised in Oxford, the site of the University of Mississippi, and spent his 65 years there except for sojourns to New Orleans, Hollywood, New York, Virginia, and abroad. His first book, *The Marble Faun*, a poetry collection, was published in '24. *Soldier's Pay*, his first novel, was released in '26. *Mosquitoes* was published in '27. Two years later he did his first book about Yoknapatawpha County and the fortunes and misfortunes of aristocratic families and the rise of the Snopes clan. The rambling stream of consciousness style of the man who preferred to call himself a farmer rather than a novelist still confuses many readers just discovering his books. An acquaintance with all his novels is almost mandatory before one can grasp his intricate cross-narratives. The devilments of his characters, their violence, sensuousness, and shocking immoralities, and his sociological comments about the South, racism and the place of man combine to give valuable insight into the heart of his fictional county in his native state.

"If a story is in you," Faulkner said, "it has got to come out."

Although the 20s were the most productive period for Willa Cather, she still could not locate the fulfillment through beauty that she wanted. Faulkner was not well known in '27, but even then he possessed that serenity which always made him appear reserved even when he was pulling pranks or demonstrating against something he considered incorrect. Willa never found this mental peace. She became

openly hostile against "modern America" when she discovered she could not find perfection in certain areas of life.

In '27 she experienced a turning point and made a literary and probably a personal change. Starting with *Death Comes for the Archbishop*, published that year, she turned to historical novels and fictionalized reminiscences of her childhood. The book is a vivid reconstruction of the works of the first Roman Catholic bishop of New Mexico. Her ability graphically to portray scenery makes her books seem almost illustrated with color slides. Her mastery of description was a reflection of her meticulous research.

"Poor Thornton," father Wilder said of his son when he was a child, "he'll be a burden all his life." But his father blundered rather badly with his prophecy, for the frail, skinny boy won the Pulitzer Prize three times.

In 1927, the 30-year-old playwright hit his literary stride with his most famous book, *The Bridge of San Luis Rey*. He had been writing since his undergraduate days at Yale. The son of a Maine Congregationalist who became a U.S. consul in Shanghai, Thornton was cosmopolitan and had an excellent education, with a year's sojourn at the American Academy in Rome adding to his background.

His 1927 success was regarded as a delicate contribution to the book world by the critics, too. The book explores the lives of five travelers who died when a bridge in Peru broke in 1714. Each victim is subjected to an ironical, intellectual autopsy, which tells us something about life and fate.

Of all of Wilder's interests in writing, the theater ranked first. He was an author who relished the intimacies and insanities of the jazz age. Even while in college, his room was a literary salon, and some of his professors assayed him then as a literary genius. Wilder saw humor in life and he unleashed it and showed its existence even in the most trying of times.

"Literature is the orchestration of platitudes," Wilder said of book lore. His work catalogued him as more interested in issues than in individuals, in broad ideas rather than in specific situations. *The Bridge* bears this out.

"The gift to the public of laughter without malice is one of the most useful things a man can do," Wilder once observed.

Billy Rose, the mighty midget of Broadway, did everything on the grandest scale. The five-foot three-inch master of many theatrical trades was a dynamo rolling up and down New York. He was born on a kitchen table in a tenement in 1899. In high school he concentrated on stenography because it would get him a quick job and a fast cash return. When he was 19, he became chief steno to Bernard M. Baruch, who was then chairman of the War Industries Board. In the early years of the second decade, Billy decided to become a writer.

The competition didn't bother him, and neither did the rejections of his stories by magazines. He advertised himself and his wares in newspapers.

"This is the first of a series of little pieces I intend to run in this gazette," his first ad read. "I shall publicly deliver myself of miscellaneous notions on Life, Art, Reforestation and Sex Among the Aborigines. The purpose of these pipsqueak paragraphs will be not so much to improve the mind of the populace as to inveigle it into my Diamond Horseshoe." His gem shoe was all in his mind and manner then. During the late 30s his most famous nightspot was named the Diamond Horseshoe.

"Long-stemmed American beauties" were the chorus girls who worked in his sophisticated honky-tonk. A "tony" he called it. I boast the usual 50 lovely girls, he said, but in 49 costumes. His floor shows were as talented as they were gorgeous.

The little night club entrepreneur with electric eyes was credited with some of the greatest song hits of all time. Several of the tunes that were smashes during the late Prohibition days were "It's Only a Paper Moon," "That Old Gang of Mine," "More Than You Know," and "You Gotta See Mama Every Night." His royalties helped make his nightspots among the most lavish layouts. He lived in equal splendor. His five-story town house near exclusive Beekman Place on New York's posh Upper East Side was a study in plushness. Old paintings by masters were on the walls, and the mansion was filled with gadgets, which Billy called "the latest antiques."

"I sell ballyhoo, not genius," Billy said of his great ventures. He was squiring some of the most beautiful showgirls in the business in '27. Celebrated comedienne Fanny Brice was one of them. He married her the year of the crash. He produced musical revues on and off Broad-

way. Even though some of his shows were always running to capacity
audiences, he still lost money because they were so resplendent. He
paid Flo Ziegfeld $630,000 cash for his theater.

The short showman with the expensive suits was one of the happy
masters of ceremonies of the speakeasy era, a toastmaster to the times
who lived and profited by them in experience, revelry, and other re-
wards. That was the man who wrote the tune "Barney Google."

The young poets in '27 were the ones who are now required reading
in high school and college literature courses. Among those who had
volumes of verse published that year was Ezra Pound. He was a wild
man who was American only by birth. His sympathies were in other
climes—fascist Italy, for one. His language was as violent as his philosophy and his gestures. With a satanic beard and a ribbon around
his head, he was piercingly erratic. However, Ford Madox Ford, the
underrated English novelist, who spent some time with Stein and
Hemingway in the Paris colony, said Pound was the "greatest living
poet." In February, *Personae: The Collected Poems of Ezra Pound*
was published.

In May 1927 Edwin Arlington Robinson had his just released *Tris-
tram* read by Mrs. August Belmont in a Manhattan theater. The 4,000-
line blank-verse dramatic narrative—a study of characters ruled by
passion—was awarded the Pulitzer Prize in 1928.

The bustling vitality and the rasping and bowing of life in the jazz
age were captured with more stark realism in verse by Carl Sandburg
than by anyone else. His word choices were not flowery. The world
found it could not only tolerate but enjoy poetry that was visceral.
The porcelain-slick poets of academe found faults in his free-verse
style and were appalled at his use of slang and subject matter like
slaughter houses and slums. But his verse communicated with the
masses. He was writing out of experience and acute observation. He
hopped freights westward out of his native Illinois and worked as a
dishwasher in Kansas City, Denver, and Omaha. He swung a heavy
hammer as a railroad section hand in Missouri, harvested the infinite
wheat fields in Kansas, painted houses in his hometown of Galesburg
where he was born in 1878. He was 36 years old before achieving any
recognition for his poetry.

Folk music was always with him in his ramblings. He was so

interested in it that by '27 he became a troubadour. In his resonant baritone, Sandburg gave poetry-reading and folk-singing concerts, strumming on the guitar. *Chicago Poems,* published in 1916, had a phenomenal domestic and foreign sale.

In '27 his two-volume *The Prairie Years,* published the year before, was selling well, and it still does. His eyes had that gay, sad light that X-rays all. His grin and voice had that same husky pity for the follies of men. In 1927 he was living in Harbert, Michigan, in a house high upon a Lake Michigan dune. The mystery and paradox of the water impressed him. The sea replenished him as he marveled at its calmness, suddenly sunny and benign, then washingly melancholy, then thrashing and wild in its primitive fury. His house, where he lived with his wife and three daughters, was a citadel of hospitality flavored with warm old wine and many friends coming and going. The man, like his verse, was open and real. Nothing vain, or nonfunctional. The beauty of simplicity, the love or understanding of all things natural. He perhaps was one of the foremost authorities on the study of the conflicting traits of man. The ability of man to change in a second from a clown to a killer, from a baby to a primeval beast was one of the traits of man he found very odd in human behavior.

But he was also a playful, ironic spirit who could find all the richness in the young. His children's stories are now standards. "Slang is language that rolls up its sleeves, spits on its hands and goes to work," Sandburg said of his picturesque phraseology. Of his own medium he said, "Poetry is an art practiced with the terribly plastic material of human language."

The generation of exiles was liberated by its own pens by '27. Paris still had its American literary tourists. In April one of the most notable of the little magazines was published there. *Transition* gave a streak of the spectrum of new writing, including one of Faulkner's stories in that initial issue.

1 9 2 7

CHAPTER 10

Jazzy Journalism

JAZZ journalism was as zany as the people and events it covered in
'27. The labels "Lawless Decade" and "Torrid Twenties" seem much
more appropriate than any others when one considers the press of the
period. Not only were newspapers covering the endless significant
stories, but they were inundated with more sensational news features
than they had seen before or have seen since.

Prohibition booze and the potent era itself intoxicated editors, reporters, and publishers as they did everyone else. But being journalists,
most of them were able to retain enough sobriety to keep the presses
running while Billy Sunday was screaming for the execution of Sacco
and Vanzetti, while Prohibition was pickling graft and corruption,
while gang wars were killing children in their cross fires, and while
everything and everyone seemed to be running amuck. The press can't
be penalized for its conduct during those years. The men and women
who comprised it were not from an alien planet. They were people of
their time. No miraculous inoculations were available to make them
unhuman, totally objective creatures.

Reporters were a callous, cynical lot during the 20s when circulation

wars were ruthless. In the major cities they often toted police badges, phony search warrants, and an array of snooping devices. They were not above sneaking through windows to steal the diaries of murdered mistresses. On a few occasions suspects were kidnaped for exclusive interviews, and planting a few clues helped plug the holes on page one. On at least one slow news day, a New York paper hired some hoods to come in and shoot up the city room a little.

Police and reporters were great friends then. They worked together. Reporters accompanied them on raids, carrying their own pistols. The trenchcoated reporter-detective was a hybrid of the day. Crime news was priority because it had more interest for the masses who were watching the robbers and killers, with concern ranging from admiration to frustration.

Tabloids appeared in the 20s, small format newspapers which were primarily pictorial and could be easily read on the subways and commuter trains. Their sex and crime stories were sometimes wholly fictitious. Bernarr "Body Love" Macfadden published the most notorious of these degenerate sheets. His New York *Evening Graphic,* generally called the *Porno-Graphic,* exploited the scandalous during its existence from 1924 to 1932 as did no other newspaper in the nation. "My paper's purpose is to fight for all forms of abolition of government censorship and for the elimination of graft and favoritism in politics and business," the 56-year-old physical culturist-journalist piously said.

The *Graphic* came into national prominence in '25 when it used the first composograph, a faked news picture, in its coverage of the Kip Rhinelander divorce case. The wealthy Long Islander was suing his attractive bride, Alice Jones, on the grounds that she had concealed her Negro blood. When Alice dropped her dress to her waist to show the judge and jury that Rhinelander was well aware of her skin tone, photographers were barred from the court. Macfadden had the scene re-created with a gang of reporters and a model. After the picture was shot, photos of the heads of the jury members were superimposed on the resulting photo. A shapely showgirl posed with her bare back to the camera. The tab's circulation jumped 100,000 overnight.

In February 1927, the *Graphic* embraced the divorce proceedings of Edward "Daddy" Browning, a 51-year-old real-estate millionaire, and his teenaged wife "Peaches." Orgies and intimacies filled the records,

and the newspaper reported them as graphically as it dared. Its composograph included a pillow fight with Peaches on the bed on her knees, a love-nest shot with the teen seductress stretched out on a love seat showing a lot of leg, and her "Daddy" husband putting a shoe on her while she perched on a stool in her lingerie. It was Macfadden's "chemise policy" in the photos to pose his models only in panties or peekaboo negligees. The tab's artistic concoctions sold papers and opened up the boudoir whenever it had the opportunity. As always, the real heads of the men and women in the cases were pasted on the faked art work. New York's two other big tabloids, the *Mirror* and the *Daily News,* used closeup portraits of the Brownings with as much emotion and sex interest as these real pictures could inspire.

In Paris, the hijinks of Daddy and Peaches caught the fancy of James Joyce, and that magpie of the Western world set the pair among the coupling constellations in his *Finnegans Wake,* thus guaranteeing them immortality.

"Flaming Youth" was one headline in the *Mirror.* "His Mania Causes Peculiar Love for Young Girls," read the subhead on the story. The *Daily News* used heads like "Peaches's Bridal Secrets" and "Hunt Peaches's 50 Sheiks."

Harry K. Thaw had just been released when the *Graphic* started focusing on his antics. He had spent 20 years in an insane asylum for the murder of famed architect Stanford White, whom he had shot to death in the old Madison Square Garden on 26th Street—a building designed by White. The tab did a feature on Thaw to warn young girls not to go out with him. The paper used a composite shot representing Thaw trying to strangle a damsel in his apartment. The misleading heads and stories were used with the same splash of sex. One of the many heads read, "Thaw Attacks Pretty Girl in His Luxurious Rooms." The luxury was modest even though Thaw was an eccentric millionaire. The *femme* was a dance-hall girl, and her beating was some playing-around blows with a hairbrush. That week in February, Macfadden was given a court summons charging him with violation of that clause of the penal code prohibiting literature "principally made up of criminal news, police reports, or pictures or stories of deeds of bloodshed, lust or crime." He hadn't been arrested since 1905, when he sponsored a beauty show in Madison Square Garden

that attracted huge mobs. Four years earlier one of his beauty-pageant posters depicting a girl in tights had prompted his first problem with censorship. The bathing suit was quite modest, but a little brief for the first year of the century.

The extent of the Macfadden empire encompassed far more than the lurid tabloid. He was an eminently successful magazine publisher. His periodicals in '27 included *Physical Culture*, with 400,000 readers; *True Story*, weekly, with 2,000,000; *Movie Weekly*, 440,000; *True Romances*, with 650,000; *Dream World*, with 200,000; *True Detective Mysteries*, with 150,000; and *Muscle Builder*, with 80,000.

In March 1927, the *Graphic* decided to capitalize on the memory of Rudolph Valentino, who died the year before. Millions of women were still mourning the great lover of the silent cinema. The tab employed the late star's acquaintances to assist in making a series of fake photos and spirit messages. Some editor had decided it would be great copy and art for the dead man to describe the hereafter, the torment of his soul leaving his body, and his memories. The spiritual con story also had Valentino meet with Enrico Caruso. The husky singer draped in a sheet posed beside a massive pillar, and the deceased was clad likewise in the faked portion of the picture.

In one Saturday special edition, "Rudy's spirit" was captured in sepia. The photo was a still from one of his movies showing him tanned and stripped to the waist, posed against a shield.

"Tabloids are just as inevitable as jazz," a *Graphic* editor said. "They are as truly expressive of modern America as World's Series baseball, skyscrapers, radio, the movies, Billy Sunday, and beauty contests."

The tabloids loved murders, and they went to town when Judd Gray, a corset salesman, murdered a middle-aged art editor with the help of the victim's wife, Ruth Snyder. The murder had all the ingredients: sex, insurance, and a particularly morbid killing. Poisoned whiskey, picture-wire binding, and a skull-pounding window-sash weight were among the specifics of the case.

From his cell the corset peddler pleaded insanity and said he had been debauched by the love affair with Mrs. Snyder. From her cell, she called her former paramour a "jackal." The *Graphic* spotted the importance of the trial before the rest of the newspapers, and put its master picture composers to work. It used several composographs and

wrote tens of thousands of words about the case after first trying in vain to get the Gotham newspapers to agree to limit their daily court reports of the case to 500 words. Reams of hot copy spurted into the tab's columns.

But the January 14, 1928, edition of the *Daily News* scooped every other paper in town when it ran a full-page photo—page one—of Ruth Snyder being electrocuted in the chair at Sing Sing. The ghastly picture was made by a *News* reporter who secretly had a small camera taped to his leg while he was among those who witnessed the death. It ranks as the first of the most sensational news pictures. The *Graphic* had no peers pictorially in most stories, though. Still, the paper wasn't very profitable.

"That damned *Graphic* lost $5,000 a day the first year or two," Macfadden said in later years, "but I was making $10,000 a day uptown so it didn't make any difference." *True Story* alone made him a profit of over $2 million a year.

The *Graphic* helped to inaugurate the personal column type of journalism. Bernarr Macfadden had Walter Winchell, Louis Sobel, and Ed Sullivan on his newspaper staff. Of all the *Graphic* stories, the newspapermen of the 1920s applauded the headline Macfadden used when a maniac escaped from an institution and then raped a woman.

"Nut Bolts and Screws," the head boldly announced in type two inches high.

William Randolph Hearst was the proprietor of a diluted version of the *Graphic*—the *Daily Mirror*. "The Chief" also owned the New York *American* and published a tab insert in it for a while. The multimillionaire son of a U.S. senator was perhaps the most powerful private citizen in the nation in 1927. He controlled at least twenty-five newspapers, eight magazines, two press syndicates, and other holdings.

Hearst lived like a Croesus. For many years his personal expenses ran over one million dollars a month, sometimes millions more. Art by the Old Masters he bought by the warehouse. His San Simeon estate cost over $40 million. Today the castle is run by the state of California and is open to the public. The fantastic main house was his hobby, and work never stopped.

The palpitating tabloids almost licked him, but the man who had been battling Joseph Pulitzer since 1895 was too canny a veteran to

lose. His favorite newspaper was the San Francisco *Examiner,* which he obtained while in his early 20s. He had the ability to find brilliant editors to run his mass-media empire. Some of his men became extremely wealthy. One of his New York editors, Arthur Brisbane, was one of the highest-salaried editors of the jazz age—a multimillionaire, in fact. He helped Hearst accumulate some $40 million worth of property in New York.

Hearst needed an astronomical income. Even when his newspapers alone were making over a million a month, and his magazines, ranches, and other interests added untold millions each month to his monies, he was spending wildly. He kept up five other castles in addition to San Simeon, and owned the 220-foot yacht *Oneida.* The luxurious ship was as ornate as his houses. It was kept docked in the Hudson while he was in New York, and sailed via the Panama Canal back to California when he was there. He used it very little, and let Flo Ziegfeld and other friends enjoy it when he was not using it.

All his income was spending money, as far as he personally was concerned.

His extravaganzas are gilded and legion. When he got interested in movie production, he once had a river frozen for a scene so skaters could use it. He loved to take guests on camping trips at San Simeon where they would have caviar picnics and eat off the most kingly silver.

When Lindbergh landed, Hearst offered him a half-million-dollar contract to make an MGM movie for him. Modest Lindy rejected the offer, and the flamboyant king of the media let the young airman have the honor of tearing up the contract before a crowd.

During the years Hearst was separated from his wife, he kept a very jealous eye on Hollywood glamour star Marion Davies. The pretty blonde actress was very close to him until his death. He built her a mansion just as a dressing house and for entertaining on the studio lot. She had a 90-room beach house herself.

He bought things on impulse. Gadgets impressed him, too. From the Prince of Monaco he bought a yacht that had a floor that would disappear at the push of a button to reveal a glass bottom. The superbly appointed ship was put in a Brooklyn yacht basin and never moved during his life by him. Window displays lured him. If he

passed a store with a shirt he liked, he bought a hundred of them. One day he went shopping for boats for two of his sons. He bought big sport crafts. He saw a boat he liked for $50,000 and took it also. An Oriental rug in a window got his attention. He bought it for $40,000 and dumped it in one of his storage warehouses where it stayed for many years. Hundreds of items were purchased and never used. Whole rooms from castles in Europe were in the basement of San Simeon.

In May 1927, "The Chief" was given an honorary degree by Oglethorpe University in Atlanta. He had been expelled from Harvard during his youth after having commodes delivered to each of his professors just prior to some final examinations. During his college days, he had an alligator that drank wine.

Hollywood society was divided into two castes by '27, those who had been invited to San Simeon and those who had not. The grandeur of the 40-bedroom main house was staggering even to the very wealthy. There were miles of ornamental gardens; two huge guest mansions flanked the great house called Casa Grande. Mosaic swimming pools, private theaters, and game rooms were the utmost in artistic elegance. They dined on duck, roast guinea fowl, and other gourmet dishes. Drinking was kept to a minimum. The media king did not approve of immoderate consumption of alcoholic beverages. Dinner cocktails were permissible, but the great host frowned on anyone who might wish more than one.

Film writer Irvin S. Cobb, who often contributed stories to the Hearst magazines, especially *Cosmopolitan,* was astonished during one of Hearst's 1927 parties at San Simeon. He entertained 70 guests one weekend and had them brought the 200 miles to the estate from Los Angeles by a private train furnished by the host. Naturally, it had the finest dining and musicians for entertainment. When a few dozen of the guests decided to stay on a few more days, Hearst ordered two special trains to take them back to Los Angeles. Some of his movie mogul friends were astounded at the expense. Private cars they could grasp as a fine gesture, but to charter two entire trains was very expensive. The big man with the pipsqueak voice said he did not want his guests to be disturbed by any trains banging around on sidings or having to stop en route to Los Angeles.

Despite his constant entertaining and his closeness to many of his editors and his many close acquaintances, no one ever seemed to understand this powerful man of mystery.

One of the biggest and best-read newspapers in the daffy decade was the Denver *Post*, the yellowest, most irresponsible and sensational journal in the nation. It was the most conniving, conning, and degenerate sheet for a generation. Harry Tammen and Frederick G. Bonfils were the most notorious publishers who ever owned a printing press. Hoaxes and blackmail were their beats.

The tall, suave Bonfils claimed kinship to Napoleon on the Corsican side of his family. Born in Missouri in 1861, he attended West Point for a short time. The slim, coal-eyed character became a criminal. After several arrests and serving time, he became a Mississippi riverboat gambler and later a Kansas City land shark. Tammen was a bunco artist and a bartender. He worked in the Palmer House in Chicago and then moved on to the bars in Denver, but he was fired. Back in Chicago, the five-seven, 240-pound native of Baltimore met Bonfils, who was four years his senior.

Naturally, they first tried to con each other. It was a standoff. Then Tammen told Bonfils the Denver *Post* could be purchased for just $12,500. The little penny paper could be used to exploit the richness of the Rockies, the chubby little con man noted. On October 28, 1895, the pair took over the newspaper. The three other newspapers in town considered the paper nothing more than a journalistic joke, until Bonfils and Tammen coerced by questionable means advertisers to leave the competition. By 1920 the paper was a national phenomenon.

Red ink and bold heads were mixed throughout the makeup of the paper. Pictures and art were never sedate. Fake news stories and distortions were used almost every day. The publication was a carnival, so the publishers bought a big circus. They also bought a burlesque house and had the strippers wear bikini editions of the *Post*. Arthur Brisbane once went to Denver just to see if the tales circulating were true. Lions snarled from cages flanking the *Post* building. That same day he saw the hefty Tammen throw bags of silver into the street as a promotion gimmick. Hearst said the paper looked like a red omelet.

In 1922 they somehow found out about the Teapot Dome oil scandal. They blackmailed Harry Ford Sinclair, the oil magnate, for a

quarter of a million dollars cash and a million dollars' worth of oil leases. The two had documented evidence that U.S. Secretary of the Interior Albert Fall had accepted a $200,000 bribe to let Sinclair have illegal drilling leases in Wyoming. It was two years before Congress uncovered the graft. Sinclair and Fall went to jail, another major figure in the case committed suicide, and Bonfils and Tammen came off with nothing but profit. In July 1924 Tammen died. Like his partner, he had lived in luxury. He left a 22-room mansion that had marble bathtubs, gold-plated fixtures, and a revolving dance floor.

In 1926 the Scripps-Howard chain bought the *Times* and the *News* in Denver and formed the powerful *Evening News*. Roy Howard took charge of the new paper himself. At first, the dynamic Howard slowed the pace of the *Post*. Bonfils was 64 years old in 1927, and engaged in one of the most vicious circulation wars in newspaper history. The thin ex-gambler was offered $15 million for the *Post*. He declined, preferring to fight.

The much younger Howard was a veteran of great newspaper battles. He used the same type of promotion stunts and premiums his competition had used. The *Evening News* started giving away three gallons of gas with the purchase of every 25-cent classified ad. Bonfils increased his offer to four. Howard made it five. When the gas-war promotion ended, the papers had lost some $50,000 each. They held outdoor banquets and festivities for the entire city. Planes flew above the buildings broadcasting news headlines. Bonfils had a table built one-third of a mile long inside the Moffat Tunnel being bored through the Great Divide and fed 1,500 people at it. Howard got him with some news scoops, including the Lindbergh flight. But the gaunt Bonfils, even with health deteriorating, let 100 dogs loose in City Hall during a council meeting. He had a dozen monkeys smuggled into the state capitol. The monkeys climbed to the lights and unscrewed the bulbs and threw them at the politicians. Howard capitulated. The 25-newspaper chain pulled out of the Rockies after losing over two million dollars. Bonfils possibly lost more, but it didn't affect his holdings to any degree. He could have held out for tens of millions.

When Bonfils died in '33 he still had his silver-headed cane with the built-in gun, his 51-room mansion, and several million dollars. Although he and Tammen gave widely to charities before their deaths,

they also made some unusual dispositions of their wealth. Bonfils, for instance, left $50,000 to be awarded to the first person to communicate with Mars. Today the *Post* is one of the most respected and most prestigious newspapers in the country, but its past is one of the most checkered in American journalism.

Scores of other famous, or soon to be outstanding, journalists were working ethically in '27. Drew Pearson was a 30-year-old foreign and diplomatic correspondent for overseas newspapers. Westbrook Pegler was 33 years old and working as a general assignment and sports reporter for the Chicago *Tribune* that year. The most famous correspondent of World War II left Indiana on Saturday, Christmas Eve in '27. Ernie Pyle went to Washington, D.C., and started to work as a telegraph editor on Monday morning for the Washington *News*.

The changes made by the Associated Press in '27 were indicative of the journalism revolution of progress wrought during the most hectic decade of major news events. Manager Ted Boyle, who was a very young reporter then, reflected recently:

> It was a big year at AP. We converted state wires from Morse to Teletype. I'm told also that we shed the old "fuddy-duddy" image and went in for livelier treatment of news. We sent our first specialists into Hollywood. We entered the newsphoto business—something we had deliberately shunned in the past. We established a large-scale feature service and began hiring artists to illustrate the productions. We began centralizing in New York many operations that previously had been left to local handling by headquarters of various geographical divisions. We gave heavy treatment to sports news.

One of the most amusing and enlightening looks into the Chicago school of journalism during the period Pegler dubbed "The wonderful age of nonsense" is the following incident by Mr. Earl Shaub, taken from his book *All in a Day's Work*:

> One phase of the good old days, also my rambling days, was brought back vividly when I attended a swank cocktail party in Chicago recently.
> While mixing my drink the bartender asked, "What ever became of Walter Howey?"

"Where did you know Howey?" I asked in amazement.

"I knew you, too," he replied, "when I was bartender in various clubs in New York during the prohibition era but I can't recall your name at the moment."

I identified myself, and he said, "Sure, I remember now. I knew a lot of you fellows then—Jack Lait, Gene Fowler—"

I interrupted, "Two of my very best friends."

"Lait was the only man I ever saw who could drink a pint of whiskey and then carry on a coherent conversation in five-syllable words," he continued. I knew he was telling the truth because I had seen Jack do that very thing on a bet.

"A great bunch, a great bunch," the bartender repeated, after I told him Howey, Lait and Fowler had passed on.

That conversation recalled my first meeting with Walter Howey when I blew into Chicago during my wandering days and headed for the *Tribune* office. Howey was city editor and I told him I was looking for a job. He peered at me with his one eye and said, "We haven't had a vacancy in more than a year and I don't anticipate one in the next five years."

I went over to the *Examiner* and asked the head of the copy desk, a Mr. McLean (everybody called him "Mac") for a job. During our brief conversation I mentioned that I had worked for J. W. McCammon.

Then he said, "The best damned man in the business. I knew him in St. Louis, Omaha and Denver. If you were good enough for McCammon you are good enough for McLean. Sit down." He pointed to a chair on the rim.

Within five minutes another fellow breezed in and gave me a cold stare when he saw me sitting in his place. McLean reached in his drawer, pulled out a pad, wrote a voucher, handed it to the man and calmly told him that he wasn't with the *Examiner* any more. That's the way we got on and off in those days.

The other man went straight to the *Trib* and went to work for Howey who had told me just an hour before they wouldn't need anybody for five years. Two weeks later, Mr. Hearst hired Howey away from the *Tribune* and he served as one of the top Hearst editors and trouble shooters the rest of his life. He and I became good friends after I went to New York.

Speaking of my first meeting with Howey recalls other experiences I had during my early attempt to break into Chicago. One

HISTORIC HOOK-UP—While a battery of AT & T officials listen, President W. S. Clifford conducts the first conversation at the opening of the New York–London telephone line on January 7, 1927.

ERNIE WENT TO WORK IN '27—The most famed war correspondent in history, Ernie Pyle left the University of Indiana in 1927. Here Ernie, right, talks to a former classmate, Prof. John Stempel of the journalism department, on a visit to the campus in 1944, only a few months before he was killed by a Jap bullet on Iwo Jima.

ATTRACTIVE ENGINEER—Miss Dixie Tighe, a wire service reporter, rode in the cab of this record-breaking train to get the flavor of the epic ride. The train, carrying motion pictures of Charles Lindbergh's Washington, D.C., reception, set a world's speed record for a train by covering the 226 miles from D.C. to New York in 191 minutes. A photo lab had been built in one of the cars so the film could be processed en route.

ONE OF WORLD'S GREAT RESIDENCES—The 250-room French Renaissance palace of George Washington Vanderbilt was built in 1895 in Asheville, North Carolina. Like San Simeon, it is a palatial structure, crammed with the finest furniture and conve-

GRANDE CASA—The entrance to the main house at San Simeon is lined with flowers and statuary.

AERIAL VIEW OF HEARST MANOR—San Simeon's complex reigns over this California mountain top some 200 miles from Los Angeles.

FLOOD STORIES—On April 24 the *Times-Picayune* had more copy on the rampaging waters than on all the other subjects on the front page totaled together.

PROTECTION
The break in the Caernarvon levee will give valuable protection to New Orleans during the height of the flood, engineers predict.

The Times-Picayune

THE WEATHER

VOLUME XCI — NO. 96   Issued Every Morning at 601-631 North St. BY THE TIMES-PICAYUNE PUBLISHING CO. Founded January 25, 1837   NEW ORLEANS, SATURDAY, APRIL 30, 1927   Entered N.O. Postoffice as Second Class Matter Under Act of March 3, 1879   SINGLE COPY 5 C

CITY TO FEEL RELIEF FROM LEVEE BREACH IN 48 HOURS

HOUSES FALLING AS NEW FLOOD HITS CROWDED ARKANSAS TOWN

Rush of Water from South Bend Break Sweeps Over McGehee and All Southeastern Part of State

THOUSANDS PERILED IN TORRENT'S PATH

Inundation Bears Down Upon Northeast Louisiana Parishes as Population Flees from Lowlands

NAVAL CONFERENCE SCENE TO GENEVA

Coolidge's Choice Reported Acceptable to Britain and Japan

Caernarvon Levee Blasted to Release Floodwaters

GIST of THE NEWS

GAP TO SPREAD 1600-2000 FEET IN FOUR DAYS SAY ENGINEERS

Opening 50 Yards Wide Expected This Morning River Finishes Work Begun by Dynamite

LEVEES' STRENGTH REVEALED BY BLAST

Repeated Blasts and Digging Are Required to Break Bulwark; Solidity of River Defense Klorer Points Out

Four Fliers Die as Lightning Hits Naval Airplane

Craft Hurled to Earth During Severe Storm on Chesapeake Bay

THREE INDICTED IN COUNTERFEIT CURRENCY RING

Ex-Secret Service Man Accused of Passing Bogus Money

Times-Picayune Telephones News of Mississippi Flood to London Evening News

'Take a Chance' Spirit Is Blamed for Flood Danger

River Commission Chairman Says Menace Must Be Eliminated

Reporter Talks 1500-Word Story on Latest River Situation

COOLIDGE REFUSES SPECIAL SESSION FOR FLOOD AID

President Opposes Diversion of Treasury Funds to Relief

Dr. Cline Urges All Precautions for Upper River

Points to Special Flood Warning and Rapid Rise at Vicksburg

Crosby Is Named Flood Dictator for Mississippi

Appointment of Lumberman Follows Conference With Hoover

Hoover Promises Government Help to Louisiana to Battle Menace of Mississippi Flood

Medical Statute of State Held Valid by Court

Supreme Tribunal Renders Decision in Fife Brothers Case

TANKER INSPECTOR STILL FAST IN MUD

Efforts Continued to Free Big Ship from Crevasse

LEVEES ABOVE CITY IN GOOD CONDITION

No Weak Spots Discovered, Captain Stamps Reports

SLIGHT DECREASE IN RIVER HERE

The Times-Picayune Free for Two Weeks

SIX DAYS LATER—The New Orleans newspaper—one of the country's most attractively made up—was the publication of record in covering the flood.

was the shortest interview in history with "Uncle" Joe Cannon, elderly Speaker of the House of Representatives, when I asked him for a message to the people on the occasion of his birthday. I was sent by the city editor of the *Examiner* to interview the Speaker who was registered at the Congress Hotel.

When I told Cannon what I wanted, he said gruffly, "No. Goddamnit. No!" Then he slammed the door. I learned later that was not only a short interview but a very unusual one for a politician.

After reporting my encounter with Cannon to the city editor, I asked if he had another assignment and he said, "No, Goddamnit. No!"

I thought that was it, but he gave me another chance next day and I redeemed myself by stealing a huge prize-winning painting out of the Art Museum and taking it to the office to be photographed. This blue ribbon picture had been painted by a museum guard who was working his way through art school, and that is why it was a good story.

The guard-artist was delighted to be interviewed but the management would not permit an *Examiner* photographer to take a picture of the painting on account of the smoke that old time flash guns made before smokeless bulbs were invented.

But there is always a way. The guard naturally wanted all the publicity he could get so he concealed our photographer and me until the museum closed at 5 P.M. Then he assisted us to smuggle the picture through a basement half window. It was difficult to carry this huge canvas against the stiff wind as we crossed Michigan Boulevard but we made it to the office on Madison Avenue where we photographed the painting. We got an express company to return it to the Museum next morning and get a receipt.

Another brief but memorable interview I got during that period was with Alice Roosevelt on the subject of short skirts. We were tipped off that the former President's daughter was wearing one of the first short skirts that had been seen in Chicago in the lobby of the Blackstone Hotel.

I hurried to interview her, and she said, "Short skirts are another sign of freedom for women. They are here to stay."

As she gracefully raised her skirt another inch, she added facetiously, "Legs! See! Legs! You men will get used to that."

The only time I was reprimanded by a prelate in church occurred during those first days in Chicago. It was Christmas Eve and I was sitting next to Bob Casey reading copy on the old *Inter-Ocean*. Tiny Maxwell was in the slot. The bottle passed around the desk freely that night and Casey suggested all of us should go to midnight mass. Some of us did.

The cathedral was crowded and we took seats on the front row. Before the priest started the service, he looked directly at us, and said, "Aren't you a fine bunch of drunks?" Then he switched to Latin and went on with the service.

When the *Inter-Ocean* collapsed shortly after that, Casey went to the *Daily News* where he became one of the country's outstanding reporters and feature writers.

The following news chronology from the Philadelphia *Bulletin* is typical of the local coverage by one of the big metropolitan dailies in '27.

LOCAL CHRONOLOGY, 1927

January

1—Jack Hines' Old Timers win mummers' fancy crown; Frank A. Collins Assn. tops comic division, and Ferko Band gets string band award.

4—Pinchot delivers scorching farewell address at Harrisburg. Public Service Commission engages Chas. C. McChord to make survey of Phila. transit.

5—Morris L. Clothier gives $100,000 to Swarthmore.

7—Fire in automobile row, 215–17 N. Broad, destroys 50 cars.

10—Hadley subpoenas Mayor to furnish Sesqui accounts.
Pinchot forwards "certificate of doubt" on Vare's election.
60 pupils rescued in fire at Mother of Sorrows school.

13—Wm. Slook, policeman, fatally shot by Wm. Myers.
Director Austin sends Sesqui furniture and clerks to Hadley's office.

14—Mayor signs drastic central parking bill.

18—Penna. Supreme Court refuses to halt removal of Vare ballots to Washington.
John S. Fisher inaugurated as Governor.

Oaklyn, N.J., votes to change from Commission to Council-manic government.

21—Sam'l O. Wynne appointed Prohibition administrator for Eastern Penna.

24—McCown & Co., brokers, fail.

26—Mercury down to 4; zero in suburbs.

Media garage fire threatens central block.

Camden riverfront warehouse burned, $100,000 loss.

29—First Phila.-London phone call; Provost Penniman to Lord Dawson.

Home of J. W. Mercur, Media, destroyed by fire; $175,000 loss.

February

1—Warburton House, women's hotel, opens.

Dr. Wm. C. Hunsicker chosen State Senator.

4—Wm. Myers convicted of murder of policeman Slook.

Anthony M. Ruffo, Jr., becomes Mayor of Atlantic City.

5—Phila. and Edinburgh linked by radiophone.

Temple Univ. opens $5,250,000 drive.

6—Rev. Dr. Clarence E. Macartney resigns Arch St. Presb'n pulpit to go to Pittsburgh.

9—Dr. Chevalier Jackson wins Phila. Award for 1926.

10—Quaker City Cab goes into receivership.

12—S. S. *Evangeline* launched at Cramps; last to be built there.

13—Churches throughout nation observe Conwell Sunday.

14—Market St. merchants protest central parking ban.

18—Transport Henderson sails for Nicaragua.

County building at Media afire; $25,000 damage.

19—Coastal storm sweeps city, doing much damage; seashore resorts flooded; schooner ashore at Brigantine. 8 lost.

22—Dr. John H. Finley is orator at University Day exercises.

P. O. S. of A. dedicates new home, 1317–19 N. Broad.

25—Gunmen kill one and wound 2 at Club Cadix.

March

1—Magistrate Rowland arrested in liquor case scandals.

7—North Phila. grain elevator razed by fire.

Four Olney Bank bandits electrocuted at Rockview.

Governor signs bill for observance of March 4 as Pennsylvania Day.

South Phila. homes of Di Silvestro brothers wrecked by bombs.

10—Public Service Com. orders 5 grade crossings at Fernwood abolished.

11—Family of 6 burned to death, at Brown's Mills, N.J.

Mayor signs bill for Filbert St. track removal in Pennsy terminal plans.

16—Lower Merion Township adopts zoning ordinance.

17—Central High dedicates tablet to soldier alumni.

20—Fox-Locust Theatre dedicated.

22—McChord transit reporter advocates city purchase of underliers.

24—N.J. Legislature passes two-cent gas tax and bond issue to finance new highways.

25—Business bodies petition for 40-foot channel to sea.

Germantown Hospital opens campaign for $600,000.

27—Ferry companies reduce auto toll to 25 cents to compete with bridge.

28—German textile mfrs. and merchants visit city.

29—Police Lt. Elwood Gaynor, Lancaster, found slain near Sharon Hill.

One-hour parking permitted on Broad, Market and Arch Sts.

30—Public Service Com. rejects proposed revision of Frankford L lease, but approves Chestnut St. subway pact; Erdenheim loop to be retained.

Two battalions of Marines leave for China.

Gov. Fisher defends compromise on ballot reform bills.

April

1—Coal prices reduced $1 to $2 a ton.

Council has long debate on Grand Jury's presentment on condition of city streets.

Policeman Martin Tallett gets first Valor Medal from city.

4—Mayor revokes dance license of Club Cadix.

6—North Second St. markets observe 125th year of city ownership.

11—House at Harrisburg defeats Old Age Pension proposal.

Fire wrecks Sturtevant plant in Camden.

14—Legislature adjourns; praised by Governor.

15—P. R. T. asks Public Service Commission to O.K. bridge trolley cars.

Cramps Shipyard announces it will build no more ships.

21—City Council extends Frankford L lease for 30 years.

22—Gov. Fisher vetoes bill for division of Phila. wards of more than 70,000 pop.; approves bill fixing City Council membership at 22.

23—J. Ramsay MacDonald, former British Premier, taken from train to hospital with infected throat.

27—Mrs. Mary McConnel, 53, found murdered by strangler in West Phila. home.

29—Magistrate Rowland pleads guilty of graft and extortion; later sentenced to 6 years in prison.

30—National Federation of Men's Adult Bible Class parades up Broad St., despite driving rain.

May

2—Forest fires damage large area in Atlantic County, N.J.

11—Commander Francesco de Pinedo, Italian flier, lands in Phila. on four-continent flight.

12—Gov. Fisher vetoes bill requiring all teachers to be native or naturalized citizens.

14—One killed, 50 hurt, when grandstand collapses at Phillies' ball park.

18—Bandits hold up West Conshohocken bank and escape with $1,046.

25—Steamship *Malolo*, built at Cramps, collides with freighter off Nantucket on trial run; no casualties.

30—Jos. Zanghi and Vincent Cocozza shot to death in gang warfare at 8th and Christian Sts.

June

1—Bandits get city payroll of $13,000 at entrance of Municipal Hospital.

Ferdinand G. Zweig appointed to succeed Magistrate Rowland.

2—New Public Library on the Parkway opened.

8—Chester Hand, 51, Bridgeton, N.J., farmer, kills step-daughter and ends own life.

10—Councilman Crossan criticises P. R. T. for failure to make service improvements.

Harry J. Haas, Phila., elected president of Penna. Bankers Assn. at Pittsburgh session.

13—Col. Lindbergh flies over city on way to New York from Washington.

18—Delaware County Grand Jury scores graft in Chester police force.

25—State Supreme Court bars Sunday baseball in Phila. in test case against the Athletics.

30—Katherine Miller, convicted slayer of student, escapes from insane hospital at Norristown.

July

1—Allen M. Stearn appointed to additional seat in Orphans' Court.

4—Seven holiday bathers drowned, 11 motor fatalities, in city and vicinity.

5—Fire sweeps Boardwalk block in Atlantic City; loss $250,000.

6—B. Y. P. U. begins annual national convention at Baptist Temple.

"Rusty" Callow signs up to coach Penn oarsmen.

8—Restaurant owner shot and killed by negro bandit at Burlington, N.J.

Workman killed in 5-alarm fire that razed factory at Front and Clearfield.

12—U.S. District Court dismisses suit of Reed committee to seize Delaware County ballot boxes.

Frank G. Zimmerman, 45, theatrical man, a suicide.

14—Joseph L. Kun appointed to bench of Common Pleas No. 1.

19—Rain breaks hot wave; 27 heat deaths in Phila. district in 6 days.

Ernest E. Rieker, who killed wife and Sheriff Kulp, hangs himself in Bucks County jail.

22—Lottery headquarters in West Phila. raided; 13 arrested.

28—Penna. Railroad breaks ground for great terminal project that will wipe out the "Chinese Wall."

August

3—Mayor Kendrick awarded gold medal by Sesqui Assn.

4—The *Bulletin* offers $25,000 prize for first non-stop flight from Europe to Philadelphia.

5—Bomb, planted by Sacco-Vanzetti cranks, damages Emmanuel Presbyterian Church, 42nd and Girard Ave.

6—Major E. E. Hollenback, Villanova, elected State Commander of American Legion at York.

8—Seven radicals arrested for distributing circulars calling for strike in behalf of Sacco and Vanzetti.

10—Republican Organization picks Mackey for Mayor.

Albert H. Ladner, Jr., resigns as minority member of Registration Board under Democratic pressure.

12—Heyman & Goodman get S. Broad St. subway contract for $7,269,000.

14—Secretary of Labor Davis delivers address at initiation of big Moose class.

15—J. Hampton Moore announces independent candidacy for Mayor and attacks Vare and the Organization.

17—Two men held in $15,000 bail, charged with smuggling narcotics into Eastern Penitentiary.

Sven D. Berg, young Dane, held in $50,000 bail for theft of U. S. scout cruiser plans.

24—Secretary of Labor Davis attends Moose convention here.

26—Marion Shoemaker, 17, attacked and thrown from motor; Chas. Snyder, 38, arrested later as assailant.

Figures show August the coldest in Phila. in 90 years.

September

1—War Dept. approves plans for Tacony-Palmyra bridge.

2—Frank C. McCown, bankrupt broker, arrested on charge of fraudulent conversion.

4—Two long-termers beat tower guard and escape from Eastern Penitentiary.

7—Removal of central trolley tracks and establishment of bus
terminals recommended by Chief Engineer of Public Service
Commission.

"Revelry" withdrawn from Garrick Theatre; had aroused crit-
icism for its treatment of Harding Administration.

9—Motor crash at Lawnside, N.J., kills 2; 5 hurt.

The *Bulletin* withdraws $25,000 prize for flight from Europe,
declaring season too advanced for successful venture.

9–11—Sesqui-Centennial of Battle of Brandywine observed.

12—Sixteen men, released in bail after seizure of rum-runner
Bulko, fail to appear at hearing.

Radio Rodeo opens week's exhibits.

15—Dr. A. Wm. Lilliendahl, 70, murdered while motoring with
wife near Hammonton, N.J.; she says two colored men attacked them.

21—Moore makes surprising run in Republican Mayoralty pri-
maries, carrying 12 big residential wards, but Mackey wins
by 74,000.

23—Merger of Phila. Electric and U. G. I. urged by joint committee.

26—Big mass meeting urges Moore to head independent ticket.

Navy officials in Washington aroused by criticisms in magazine article by Admiral Thomas P. Magruder, Commandant
at League Island.

27—Warrant issued for Willis Beach, 57, as accessory in murder
of Dr. Lilliendahl.

29—J. Hampton Moore announces independent candidacy for
Mayor.

30—Sesqui-Centennial of Battle of Germantown (observance continued on Oct. 1).

October

1—Rose Sarlo, 16, Woodbury, N.J., beaten and murdered near
Mantua; Geo. Yarrow, bus driver, arrested for crime.

5—Independents choose "Citizens Party" as campaign title.

7—Mrs. Margaret Lilliendahl and Willis Beach indicted by Atlantic County Grand Jury for murder.

Criminal trials without jury declared illegal by Pennsylvania
Superior Court.

8—Dempsey-Tunney fight films seized by Federal officers at 3 theatres.

11—Fire destroys section of Boardwalk district at Ocean City; loss $1,500,000.

12—Scottish Rite Temple, Broad and Race, dedicated.

14—Fairmount Park Commission stripped of Parkway control by court decision on land exchange with the Philadelphia Club.

15—Bank guards slain by bandits attempting to rob Belmont Trust branch near 49th and Woodland Av.

22—Sesqui-Centennial of Battle of Red Bank, N.J.

Col. Lindbergh feted in Phila.; 40,000 cheer him at the Stadium.

26—James M. Beck named as Republican candidate for Congress from First District.

Admiral Magruder relieved of command at the Navy Yard; Secretary Wilbur names Rear Adm. Julian L. Latimer as successor.

27—President Coolidge refuses to intervene in case of Admiral Magruder.

U. S. S. *Scorpion* mustered out of commission in Navy Day ceremony.

Presbyterian Synod, at Chester, reverses conviction of Rev. Harry H. Crawford, of Frankford, and exonerates him of all charges.

28—Mayor Kendrick, defending his administration, calls Mackey and Moore "four-flushers."

Fred Masciulli, South Phila. High, dies of football injuries.

November

1—Court upholds right of Wallace Bromley, State legislator, to appointment as Personal Property Assessor.

3—U. S. Senator Smoot, "razzed" at Republican Organization rally, rebukes interrupters and cuts address short.

5—Rear Adm. Latimer takes command of Phila. Navy Yard.

8—Harry Mackey elected Mayor; Organization sweeps Council and rest of ticket.

9—Gratz Senior High School dedicated.

10—Mayor submits Binns report on operation of Broad St. subway to Council.

13—New St. Joseph's College at Overbrook dedicated.

15—Transit survey of Chief Engineer of Public Service Commission suggests changes at estimated cost of $78,000,000.

17—President Coolidge delivers Founders' Day address at Union League; receives League's gold medal and is made honorary member.

Tornado sweeps across Eastern Penna., causing heavy damage in Berks County and loss of two lives.

18—Miss Maria J. Gilpin, 65, killed in fall from 18th floor at Broad and Locust Sts.

21—Wm. W. Thompson, mfr., killed in 5-story fall in Stephen Girard Bldg.

Two Camden motorists killed at rail crossing at Westmont, N.J.

City Council votes to transfer $5,000,000 from Sinking Fund to make good budget deficiency.

23—Airplane carrier *Saratoga* moved from Camden shipyard to League Island.

Thos. A. Logue, defeated Democratic candidate for Mayor, appointed to the Registration Board by Gov. Fisher.

30—Federal Grand Jury indicts 19 members of crew of the rumrunner *Bulko*.

December

3—John (Racetrack Johnny) Paone, 38, killed by gunman in front of his cigar store on E. Passyunk Av.

5—James M. Beck seated as Congressman, pending investigation of charge of non-residence in Phila.

7—New buildings of the Phila. General Hospital dedicated; cost $5,000,000.

Ground broken on Parkway for the Rodin Museum.

George D. Yarrow sentenced to death at Woodbury for murder of Rose Sarlo.

8—Mrs. Margaret Lilliendahl and Willis Beach found guilty of voluntary manslaughter at Mays Landing; later sentenced to 10 years at hard labor.

Jos. Cucinotta, 13, shoots and kills his father in Camden home while defending his mother.

9—U. S. Senate denies seat to Vare, 56 to 30, pending Reed committee's final report.

12—John M. Stinnette, shell-shocked veteran, kills his French war bride and escapes.

13—City Council passes 20-cent tax rise.

Thieves halt Reading fast freight near Langhorne, throw out $100,000 of raw silk, but flee after pistol fight with crew.

14—President Dice announces the Reading's $31,000,000 electrification and improvement program.

15—Proposed agreement between City and B. & O. for Schuylkill Embankment improvements sent to City Council.

16—District Attorney Fox opens inquiry into straw bail evil.

17—Engineers Club observes 50th anniversary.

Charles M. Schwab, John Hays Hammond and Howard Elliott get honorary degrees from U. of P.

Drexel Institute given new engineering building by C. H. K. Curtis.

Two bank guards murdered in Real Estate Trust vaults.

19—Valley Forge sesqui-centennial program opened with address by Geo. Nox McCain.

Fortieth Ward protests proposed West Phila. abattoir.

Magistrate Perri arrested in straw bail probe.

Mrs. Isabelle J. Shedaker, Burlington, N.J., slain by admirer.

23—Fire damages Union League.

Judge Taulane opens probe into divorce frauds.

Three girls killed at Monroeville, N.J., grade crossing.

24—St. Luke's and Children's Hospitals announce merger.

26—State Supreme Court adopts severe code for admission to the bar.

Bristol opens new municipal building.

27—Judge Audenried, retiring from bench, honored by colleagues. New buildings at House of Correction, Holmesburg, dedicated.

1 9 2 7

CHAPTER 11

Silent Cal Speaks Out

SILENT Cal, the solemn-faced President of the United States from 1923 to 1929, was born in Vermont, the descendant of a long line of New England farmers. When he was 24 years old, he moved to Massachusetts to study and practice law. After an apprenticeship in local politics, he was elected governor for two terms. During the Boston police strike in 1919, he gained national attention for his role in restoring order. The next year he was elected vice president and succeeded to the presidency in '23 when Harding died. He was popular and won reelection the following year on his own. His period in office was in sharp contrast to the times, being characterized by a reduction of taxes, a favorable business climate, and a devotion to economy and thrift in government that owed much to the careful habits of his native state.

Christmas in '26 was somewhat more festive than the holidays the First Family had enjoyed in the last two years. The White House had a Christmas tree for the first time since '24, the year his teenage son, Calvin Coolidge, Jr., had died after an accident.

One of Cal's first public duties of the new year was an address on

the 150th anniversary of the Battle of Trenton. His speech writer always did an excellent job of preserving his somber image. He confined himself to revolutionary history and morality.

"We are placing a great deal of emphasis on prosperity," President Coolidge said. "Our people ought to desire to be prosperous, but it ought not to be their main desire. There are other things that they ought to want more. Prosperity is not a cause; it is a result. It is all summed up in a single word. It is character.

"Under our institutions the only way to perfect our government is to perfect the individual citizen. It is necessary to reach the mind and the soul of the individual. I know of no way that this can be done save through the influences of religion and education."

In late January the President's physicians prescribed a diet of ham and eggs for breakfast instead of New England sausages. They said they were too fattening. A month later, Silent Cal began taking two-mile daily walks around the White House grounds to combat the calories.

Vermont chose four mountains and christened them "Coolidge Range." In March the First Family moved to No. 15 Dupont Circle while the White House was being modernized. A construction worker was arrested for selling tourists rusty nails from the White House roof for a dollar each. In April the President revoked the Executive Order of President Harding under which Secretary of the Interior Fall had illegally leased oil reserves owned by the Navy Department.

One of the White House visitors in April was Clarence W. Barron, the powerful financial publisher. He reported to the President that hard times were becoming a thing of the past.

Silent Cal bought new shoes on the strength of that promise. He was as choosy about his dress as he was his word choices. Although he was no womanizing dandy like Harding, in his neat way he was one of the best-dressed men in the country. His suits usually cost $125–$150, and he liked hard collars. He preferred no cuffs on his trousers, and wore no jewelry. Formality didn't bother him because he could not have cared less about pomp and circumstance.

Mrs. Coolidge, one of the most attractive First Ladies ever to live in the White House, charmed the country with her warmth.

"Isn't it nice that Calvin is President?" she once said. "You know we really never had room before for a dog."

On August 2 Coolidge made one of the most important surprise announcements of all time. At noon he asked the reporters in the press room to come to his office. His stenographer had just typed a 10-word sentence on several slips of paper. Everett Sanders, his secretary, stood at the door after the newspapermen assembled. Cal unsmilingly knocked some ash off the cigar he held in an ivory holder.

"Is everyone here now?" he asked. He directed each of the newsmen to file past his desk. As they did, he handed each a slip of paper.

"I do not choose to run for President in 1928," the slip said. Silent Cal would not say more to the startled press corps as questions started.

While the political analysts were trying to determine why Silent Cal was not going to run, the nation talked about it. The White House doorman said it was the biggest shock of his six administrations there. Although he would not add another word to his statement to the press, the President did confess a little more to some of his callers. "There are plenty of other men in the country for the job," he said. "This is not a one-man country. Ten years is a long time to be President." In the meantime, he was President and would continue so for another 15 months.

Someone recalled that Mrs. Coolidge had knitted a bedspread nearly a year ago. The spread, which was to be left in the White House, bore a prophecy. The First Lady had knitted "Lincoln 1861–1865" on one side. On the other she had put "Calvin Coolidge 1923–1929." A friend was amazed. "I know what I'm doing," Mrs. Coolidge said.

Later that month, while the Sacco-Vanzetti case was the most important news story in the nation, Coolidge went to South Dakota. Before he left he gave a speech calling for the establishment of municipal airports in major cities. He had long been an aviation enthusiast, and the relatively inexpensive efficiency of airmail impressed him.

In 1927, Secretary of the Treasury Andrew Mellon found a way to save money. The Treasury printing bill amounted to millions annually. In order to conserve on paper and printing expense, he announced the size of paperback money was going to be reduced. The new bills measured 6⅛ inches by 2⅝ inches, an inch and a half shorter and

half an inch narrower than the old ones. He pointed out that the new size would last longer because it would not have to be folded so much.

One of the most important pieces of legislation before Congress in '27 was a bill authorizing federal funds for the construction of a huge dam—known as the Boulder Canyon Project—on the Colorado River, to provide for flood control, irrigation, and power. Sponsored by California Senator Hiram Johnson, the bill was strenuously opposed by Arizona, which felt it owned the water that came through its state. California would benefit at the expense of Arizona, some legislators claimed. The debate started a filibuster, one of the most heated in decades. The New York *Times* said it was the biggest display of "sectional feeling since the Civil War."

The filibusterers held the floor hour after hour. Some of the senators began leaving. Then more. By early morning, only 29 senators were left in the chamber. Some were sleeping on lounges. The talkers on the floor became perturbed. They had the sergeant-at-arms authorized to arrest the absentees. Aides telephoned their senator bosses to get down to the floor. One senator said he had to go to a funeral, another's phone had been disconnected, eight said they were sick, and a dozen could not be located. But the word was out.

Slowly, the senators began to return—grumpily. Finally, a quorum was present, but the determined filibusterers kept the floor and allowed no one to offer a motion on the Boulder Dam bill. The marathon won after almost 29 hours. Nevertheless, the bill passed the following year.

Silent Cal seemed to sense that perhaps something was not right with the economy. Most of the men invited to the White House were business executives. He kept tuned to the world of high finance. Reporters had noticed this heavy leaning toward the cash register for some months.

"Why don't you have artists, musicians, actors, poets around the White House as Wilson and Roosevelt did, and sometimes Taft and Harding?" a reporter asked.

"I knew a poet once," Silent Cal said in his parched way, "when I was in Amherst; class poet, name of Smith." He paused in his famous assessment of culture. "Never have heard of him since!"

William Allen White, the famous small-town journalist, editor, and

MOUNT RUSHMORE BEFORE BORGLUM—The granite mountain looms blankly in 1927 just before the sculptor went to work on the likenesses of the four Presidents. *National Park Service*

PRIME MINISTER OF GREAT BRITAIN—While President Calvin Coolidge was getting inducted into the American tribes in South Dakota, Stanley Baldwin, accompanied by his wife here, was made a chief in Banff, Canada. He did not enjoy the political prosperity of Silent Cal, and his government was in trouble in late '27. *Canadian Pacific*

SILENT CAL AT RUSHMORE—President Coolidge hands Gutzon Borglum his hammer and chisel during the conservation ceremony on August 10, 1927. *National Park Service*

DICTATORIAL KINGFISH—Huey Long was just starting to rise to unprecedented heights in Louisiana politics in '27.

RUSHMORE NOW—The 60-foot heads of Washington, Jefferson, Theodore Roosevelt, and Lincoln have lured millions of tourists from all over the world. *National Park Service*

publisher of the little Emporia (Kansas) *Gazette,* was an admirer of the President. But the widely quoted editorial writer was critical of Cal for being unable to slow down the speeding economy. He said the public should be shocked out of its greedy materialism. In the wild bull market of 1927, the President could send stocks to great heights with a short speech.

In Rapid City, South Dakota, in late August, the police impounded an abandoned wrecked car. Painted on the windshield was "I do not choose to run in 1928." But Silent Cal liked the Dakotas. That summer he vacationed in Custer Park, South Dakota.

Flashing Mexican spurs and cowboy garb, the grim-faced President rode a horse three miles up the side of Mount Rushmore in the Black Hills. Following a 21-tree salute—the timber was toppled with individual explosions—President Coolidge dedicated the national memorial, which Gutzon Borglum began to carve on the granite face of the mountain. "We have come home to dedicate a cornerstone that was laid by the hand of the Almighty," he said. Republican newspapers editorially noted that the unusual salute—wood instead of gunpowder—was functional, another example of Coolidge thrift.

One of the most important foreign developments concerning the Coolidge administration in '27 was the power struggle within Russia's Communist hierarchy. Even before the death of Lenin in '24, General Secretary Joseph Stalin and War Commissar Leon Trotsky had been fighting for control of the party. Trotsky lost. In March he spoke in Moscow's Trade Union Hall, his first public appearance in four months. The crowd cheered and applauded him for a quarter of an hour. Nevertheless, he avoided internal politics but shook a fist at the free world.

"The lands bordering the Pacific will be the scene of the world's most important events," the prophetic politician said. "Europe does not relish this any more than it relishes the fact that the United States has become the most dominant power in the world ..."

Soon afterwards, his successful rival spoke in the courtyard of Moscow's Railway Shop. Workers had left their forges and lathes to hear Comrade Stalin hold forth on the election to the local Moscow Councils. A slow rain trickled down the slicker of the dictator, and rivulets ran from his soggy hat.

"Will there be war this year?" a worker called to him, in a "spontaneous" dialogue.

"No, comrade," Stalin said. "There will be no war this year. A war danger does exist, but our enemies are as yet unprepared and the workers of the world do not wish to fight Russia. Because our policy is directed to peace, it is difficult to pick a quarrel with us."

In America the Reds were trying to gain members for the party among the factory workers and employees from other areas of labor. The fervor being generated by the Reds was evident in March when 5,000 Russians living in New York City paid $6,000 to hear a former Russian premier speak. Aleksandr Kerensky was in power briefly after the fall of the tsar, but he was replaced by Lenin after the Bolsheviks seized power during the revolution in 1917. Kerensky later moved to the U.S.

The former prime minister spoke at the Century Theatre in Manhattan. A 1,000-pound candelabra was toppled by the crowd. Bolsheviks and Tsarists fought the revolution again. Neither side cared for Kerensky. Finally, amid furious excitement, order was attained. A Tsarist girl approached the ex-premier on stage with a bunch of roses. As he bent to accept the flowers, she slapped him in the face.

"You ordered my fiancé to be shot in Russia," she yelled. "I now avenge him!"

When the police charged up to arrest her, Kerensky said, "Let her go." He then said to the audience in Russian, "Oh, you poor little monarchists. You have lost your manhood. Not one of your army officers dares to come upon this stage! Instead you send a girl." This inflamed the crowd again. Two dozen Russians were ousted. One of those forced to leave was Andrew Tolstoi.

"He says," a patrolman said, "he is related to some wop count that's dead, and used to write books." The cop's ignorance, not knowing the young man was a descendant of Leo Tolstoi, who wrote *War and Peace,* was too much for some of the reporters, who shook their heads at the irony of the incident.

While Kerensky was berating Tsarist and Bolshevik as enemies of Russia, Trotsky was telling an American labor group in Russia, "We are the same old revolutionaries, and if our enemies think we have grown sleepy and lazy through administration, they will get a rude

shock. All humanity is divided into two camps, the proletariat and the imperialistic bourgeoisie, and those who attempt to turn us back to capitalism will be received with hard knocks."

A month later capitalism's foe was kicked out of the Communist party. The august Central Committee, which ceremoniously cut him from the ranks, did not get away without some eloquent defiance from the rather meek-looking little revolutionary. He called them Bonapartist dictators and usurpers. To no avail. The brush-mustachioed orator with the burning-ray eyes spent the rest of his life in exile.

Although there was turmoil in much of the world, America was making technological advances so quickly they were difficult to keep in perspective as to how they were changing life. The nation was drinking from a flask even if there were some teetotalers clamoring about all the sin from the stills, and it was literally dancing in the dark in some of the speakeasies. Even the federal government had opened a swanky honky-tonk in an effort to curb some of the illicit-liquor running.

The Prohibition Bureau leased the premises at 14 East 44th Street in New York, just a few doors from Delmonico's. It set up the plush Bridge Whist Club, which sold booze and even had a free lunch and tidbit counter for those who liked to wallow in the Western tradition when the saloons also gave grub to thirsty cowboys.

Silent Cal accepted this and everything else that went on in his administration without much comment or emotion. The fads and foibles of the times might have been abrasive to the Vermont Republican, but no one knows. Cal couldn't be read, and he wasn't inclined to speak. He didn't have to be audible. His most special year said it all.

1 9 2 7

CHAPTER 12

The Best of Prosperity
and the Biggest Budget

THE automobile industry has always been a good barometer of the American economy. Most of the population was riding with money in its pockets in '27. According to *Motor* magazine, there were 22,342,457 motor vehicles registered, some 10 percent more than in '25. The six heaviest populated states—New York, California, Ohio, Pennsylvania, Illinois, and Michigan—had more than a million cars each.

Silent Cal's business and financial advisers noted that the competition between the car manufacturers was becoming much more intense. General Motors passed U. S. Steel in gross revenue in '27 to become the nation's largest corporation. Early in the year Secretary of the Treasury Mellon said, "All signs and indications at the moment point to the country's enjoying a successful business year." Contrary to predictions, the auto and steel industries dropped in production. Installment buying was slumping but did not appear to be drastic. The labor market was not as steady as it had been the last two years. Iron and steel makers had cut production and increased unemployment.

Although people were saving less money, consumer sales were still

high. While the larger corporations were not complacent, they were not overly concerned over a slight dip in revenues. High finance accepted it as a little valley in the cycle of profits.

Lindbergh's flight injected a surge in international business for the nation and caused an awakening in commercial aviation in the U.S. and other countries. Department of Commerce officials believed the transatlantic flights of Lindbergh and Chamberlin had stirred up a big foreign demand for American aircraft and materials allied to flying. The federal government began to take a more mercenary interest in the development of the overall aeronautics potential. Wall Street declared a special holiday on the day Lindbergh returned from Paris and closed the New York Stock Exchange. One of the first effects of the flight was the increase in value of the Wright Aeronautical Corporation listing on the market.

Big business did exercise some restraint after the ex-airmail pilot made his historic trip. It wanted to be sure that "Lucky Lindy" had more going for him on the flight than spiritual blessings. When only a few days later Chamberlin repeated the performance under even more trying conditions and with a passenger, high finance was convinced. Within hours after Chamberlin landed, the U.S. Department of Commerce received cables from Germany and Argentina desiring to buy exact duplicates of the *Columbia* and the *Spirit of St. Louis*. The sales were made, and the Commerce commissioner said, "The sale of American equipment abroad should be largely stimulated as a result of these record-breaking exploits." And more orders came.

New airlines began operation before Chamberlin and Lindbergh could get back to the U. S. There were eight airlines in service by August, all advertising well-appointed cabins with meals aboard. The two hops to Europe weren't enough to sway most of those who wanted to stay with surface travel, though. The masses were skeptical of flying. Since the jazz age was the era of plush trains, some of the airlines began to call their planes "flying trains." Planes took one-third of the time of rail travel. Their fare was triple that of trains.

The approximate time and rates of the new airlines are contrasted with the speed and expense of rail travel on the following chart:

	TRAIN		PLANE	
San Diego to L.A.	3½ hours	$ 4.00	1 hour	$ 15.00
Detroit to Grand Rapids	4 hours	5.00	2 hours	20.00
New York to Boston	5½ hours	8.00	3 hours	30.00
Cheyenne, Wyo., to Pueblo, Colo.	8 hours	8.00	3 hours	25.00
Chicago to Minneapolis	12 hours	15.00	6 hours	40.00
Salt Lake City to L.A.	30 hours	28.00	7¼ hours	60.00
Portland, Ore., to L.A.	39½ hours	40.00	11¼ hours	115.00
Chicago to San Francisco	68 hours	80.00	22½ hours	200.00

Auto magnate Ford closed down his big shops in the spring of '27. He scrapped the Model T and put the country in suspense with the announcement that he was building a new car. His secrecy generated talk as interest mounted across the country. Speculation stories increased in the newspapers. By fall the stories were competing for space along with the coverage of Sacco and Vanzetti, Lindbergh, and the lurid murder cases in the tabloids.

On December 2, Henry Ford introduced the Model "A" Ford. Just before Convention Hall doors in Detroit were opened, the acknowledged prophet of the mass-production society, along with his son Edsel and his grandsons Benson and Henry II, looked over the new car again before letting 100,000 people inside. In Manhattan the crowds were even bigger than in the auto city. Police had to work to keep congestion from becoming chaotic. Flivvers seemed from another age as the "A's" sat on the floor, the sedans more solidly boxy, the coupes more sculptured and sporty than the spidery Model "T's" that had sputtered around the highways of the nation by the millions. Half the cars on the roads were Fords, some 10 million of them.

A five-day series of full-page advertisements in 2,000 daily newspapers at a cost of $1,300,000 heralded the unveiling. The New York *Herald Tribune* estimated that a million people tried to see the new Fords on the first day of their showing in Manhattan. The exhibits of the "A's" in Cleveland, Kansas City, and Miami brought huge crowds eager to look and to order. But the star of *The Jazz Singer* continued to drive his 21-foot custom-built Mercedes, which he had purchased for $8,200 the year before.

Sore arms, wrenched shoulder sockets, and broken bones were common to those who had to crank their "T's" in order to start them. One also had to hold the "T" to keep it from idling off after it fired. Just how many men had a foot run over trying to stop their runaway flivver will never be known and neither will the number of cuss words they uttered. The "A" carried a self-starter as standard equipment. The gas tank was in front of the windshield. It had steel instead of wood-spoked wheels. Its dash featured a speedometer, a gas gauge, and an ammeter. And there was a gear shift. One could control the rate of his ratio instead of alternating between the three pedals in the floor of the "T." Except for the semi-elliptic transverse springs, the new car was completely different from the old.

The Model "A" motor was more powerful and faster than the "T." It had a guttural noise and could be revved down to where one could count the pistons slapping. Today antique-car connoisseurs praise the incredible durability of the "A." It is a miracle of automotive Americana. As with many antiques, the cars sell for several times their original purchase price. The Classic Car Club of America considers any car made between 1925 and 1942 a classic. The "A" is the most common vintage car of the collectors. There are more of them today than all of the other autos from the era combined. Due to the good economy and relatively cheap price, several families had two cars during the Coolidge terms.

"If the past is any indication of the future," suave General Motors president Alfred Pritchard Sloan, Jr., said after the introduction of the Model "A," "the new Ford car will be a car that will appeal to a great mass of people. General Motors is in quite a different position. General Motors' idea is to make a car of greater luxury than the Ford, a car that properly belongs to the next higher-price class." He declared there was no war contemplated between the two auto makers.

Prosperity had forced Ford to come out with a better car. Flivver sales had declined because people wanted more elegance in their automobile. The motor car was already entrenched as a status symbol. Outside of the engineering innovations, paint was the biggest automotive change. The public had become color conscious. Almost all the cars until '27 were black or brown. Green, red, yellow, blue, and almost every other hue came out that year. Many of the colors popular

today made their appearance the year the Model "A" rolled into the automotive heart of the nation.

In January the National Auto Show opened at the Grand Central Palace in Manhattan. Ford was absent, but most other manufacturers were there. People pushed until they could get close enough to peer at and fondle the many models on the floor. They stroked the new richness and artistry in the upholstery, kicked the tires, which not too many years back had often been solid rubber, no air. Some of the designs and the quality of the coachwork were superb. The prices ranged from the economy models costing only a few hundred dollars to the huge luxury barges that were more like plush tanks or trains. These makes were exhibited; the dates beside some of them indicate the year they ceased making the model:

Auburn (1936)	Franklin (1934)	Paige (1928)
Buick	Gardner (1931)	Peerless (1932)
Cadillac	Hudson (1957)	Pierce-Arrow (1938)
Chandler (1928)	Hupmobile (1941)	Pontiac
Chevrolet	Jordan (1932)	Reo (1936)
Chrysler	Kissel (1931)	Rickenbacker (1927)
Davis (1928)	Lincoln	Star (1931)
Diana (1928)	Locomobile (1930)	Stearns-Knight (1930)
Dodge	Marmon (1933)	Studebaker (1965)
Duesenberg (1937)	McFarland (1928)	Stutz (1934)
Du Pont (1932)	Moon (1931)	Velie (1929)
Elcar (1931)	Nash (1957)	Whippet (1931)
Erskine (1930)	Oakland (1931)	Wills–Ste. Claire (1927)
Essex (1932)	Oldsmobile	Willys-Knight (1933)
Flint (1927)	Packard (1958)	

Touring cars offered the upper classes a wide choice. To increase their appeal for the status of anonymity, isinglass side curtains were easy to see through from within but difficult to look through from the outside.

The big, boxy cars were favorites for gangsters. They armor-plated them and substituted bulletproof glass for the curtains. Although few had more than 100-horsepower mills, they were very fast once they got their three- and four-ton loads moving. Getaway cars were one of

the major expenses—provided they weren't stolen—of the hoodlums.
Dillinger stole only Fords after '31, when the V-8 replaced the "A", and
he once wrote a note to Henry Ford saying, "Your slogan should be:
Drive a Ford and watch the other car take a Ford's dust." Bonnie and
Clyde liked Fords. Ma Barker and her brood preferred Cadillacs and
the more expensive lines. Ironically, they usually bought them.

Whiskey runners actually began introducing the hotrod during the
last years of Prohibition. They put helper springs in the cars to handle
the heavy liquor loads, used special speed carburetors, and started bor-
ing for more power. Acceleration was important to the runners and
the robbers. The Checker and Model A were among the wild, wild getaway cars of the less-prosperous criminals.

In sharp contrast to today, many of the big-city police departments
drove the most expensive cars. One reason no one paid much attention
to the 1925 Cadillac parked outside the garage on Clark Street on
Valentine's Day in 1929 was that the Chicago police used the same
car. The massacrers who decimated the Bugs Moran gang used a
Caddy that duplicated those driven by the local law.

The automobile was already a mass murderer. A major insurance
firm counted 21,716 deaths attributed to cars in '27. In proportion to
the number of vehicles today and the number of miles they are driven,
the percentage today is not as high as it was then. The high death rate
was attributed to the poor roads, a lack of enough road signs, and a
higher factor of mechanical failures than today.

The Eskimo Pie Corporation went public in March '27. The firm,
which had been delighting people with its ice cream on a stick for six
years, had become a $25 million property. People were eating two
million of the chocolate-covered ice cream treats daily. Christian K.
Nelson and Russell Stover were the two men who founded the firm.
Nelson said that year he was going to buy the biggest and best-looking
car that money would buy and drive it down the main street of his
little hometown, Onawa, Iowa.

The top professors of business and economy were usually at the
White House with Silent Cal, but Professor Irving Fisher of Yale came
out with some of his statistics on the money situation in December. He
said eight out of ten people were earning little more than the minimum
living expenses. He estimated total U. S. income at $90 billion. His

RICHEST AND FUNNIEST—John D. Rockefeller attended a Will Rogers lecture on February 3, 1927, in Daytona Beach while the comic was on tour and the business tycoon was on a Florida vacation.

MODEL "A" MAKER MEETS COMIC—Henry Ford visits with the most noted wit in '27, Will Rogers.

La Salle

1927

FAMOUS 1927 LA SALLE—This was the first car in the auto industry to be completely designed from front to back bumpers by a professional stylist. Harley J. Earl, who had been in the custom car field in Los Angeles, designed this car as a consultant to Cadillac. Its success led General Motors to hire him and start its own styling staff.

VIEWING IMPERIAL—New York Governor Al Smith, far left, talks about the appointments of the luxurious auto with W. P. Chrysler.

ALMOST DOUBLE FORD PRICE—Even Chrysler's cheaper models were still some $300 higher than the cars of Henry Ford.

SLEEK "60" ROADSTER—This Chrysler model sold well to the upper-middle-income and high-income groups.

Presenting the New
Standard Five-Passenger
SEDAN
$2675
F.O.B. DETROIT

CHRYSLER
IMPERIAL
"80"

*Eight body styles, priced from $2495 to $3595,
f. o. b. Detroit, subject to current Federal excise tax.*

Chrysler now announces a new Imperial "80" body style—the Standard five-passenger Sedan at $2675.

All the superlative performance, which has won the unbounded enthusiasm of thousands of Imperial "80" owners during the past year, with distinctive luxury of upholstery and appointment detail, is thus offered at this price, which instantly makes this car the *one incomparable* value in the finer car field.

The same chassis in every detail of engineering; the same smart design and appearance; the same brilliant mastery of speed and distance assured by its *92 horsepower* and capacity of *80 miles and more an hour*; the same smooth and inspiring operation; the same relaxed, luxurious riding; the same easeful driving; the same live rubber shock insulation which does away with squeaks and rattles and the annoying need of chassis lubrication.

By one master stroke of manufacturing genius, made possible by the Chrysler plan of Standardized Quality, this new Standard five-passenger Sedan makes available the unique and refreshing qualities of the Chrysler Imperial "80" to that wider group which has desired these virtues. Now, for the first time, in this great closed car value, this wider group is able to satisfy its fullest ideals of the ultimate in motoring enjoyment.

CHRYSLER SALES CORPORATION, DETROIT, MICHIGAN
CHRYSLER CORPORATION OF CANADA, LIMITED, WINDSOR, ONT.

CHRYSLER MODEL NUMBERS MEAN MILES PER HOU

MORE LUXURIOUS THAN FORD CARS—Chrysler concentrated on a higher-price line for its share of the automotive market.

CHRYSLER PLANT—Rows of houses of the automotive workers in Detroit sprawl beside the factory where the 1927 Chryslers were built.

Important Price Reductions
Many Improvements
and Record Sales for 1926

Approximately 340,000 Dodge Brothers Motor Cars sold in 1926—an increase of more than 30% over 1925. . . . .

More improvements made than during any previous year—a number of these improvements of a very far-reaching and fundamental nature. . . .

Prices materially reduced as increases in production and sales made these reductions possible. . . .

That, at the year's end, is Dodge Brothers record. Fair dealing and progressive engineering have again received the reward they so richly deserve.

Special Sedan $945—De Luxe Sedan $1075
f. o. b. Detroit

DODGE BROTHERS, INC. DETROIT
DODGE BROTHERS (CANADA) LIMITED
TORONTO, ONTARIO

DODGE BROTHERS
MOTOR CARS

DODGE BROTHERS' CARS—The Dodges were in the same price range as the intermediate Chrysler models.

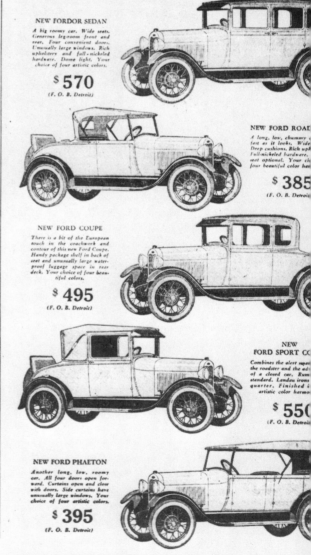

$495
(F. O. B. Detroit)

irst Pictures of the New Ford Ca

Get
plete
tails

TODAY
Ford salesrooms

eral years we have been working
ew Ford car. For weeks and
ou have been hearing rumors
For the past few days you have
ing some of the details of it in
apers.

ver you do today, take at least
utes to get the full story of this
mobile.

ill realize then that it is an
ew and different Ford car, de-
created to meet modern condi-
ar that brings you more beauty,
t, comfort, safety, economy and
an you ever thought possible
rice car.

obile history will be made today,
Ford is not only new in appear-
performance . . . it is new in
design. Many features of it
ive Ford developments. Some
new in automobile practice.
e is a reflection of manufactur-
ements and economies that are
aking as the car itself.

years of experience in building
automobiles are behind the
car and have counted in its
Resources unmatched in the
industry are its heritage and
t.

policy of owning the source
rials, of making virtually every
ing business at a small profit
cut many dollars off the price
ordinarily have to pay for a
.

ay to you—learn about this
car today. Compare it with
car in the light-car field
of line—for comfort—for
quick acceleration—for flex-
affic . . . for steadiness at all
for power on the hills . .

for economy and low cost of up-keep . . .
for its sturdy ability to stand up under
countless thousands of miles of service.

Then you will know why today will be
remembered as one of the greatest days
in the entire history of the automobile
industry. . . . Then you will know why
the new Ford car will be *your* car.

NOTE THESE FEATURES

Beautiful new low body lines

Choice of four colors

55 to 65 miles an hour

Remarkable acceleration

40 horse-power

Four-wheel brakes

Standard, selective gear shift

Hydraulic shock absorbers

*20 to 30 miles per gallon of
gasoline*

Theft-proof coincidental lock

*Typical Ford economy and
reliability*

STANDARD EQUIPMENT ON
ALL NEW FORD CARS

Starter
Five steel-spoke
  wheels
Windshield wiper
Speedometer
Gasoline gauge

Dashlight
Mirror
Rear and **stop**
  light
Oil gauge
Tools

Pressure grease gun lubrication

NEW FORDOR SEDAN
*A big roomy car. Wide seats.
Generous leg-room front and
rear. Four convenient doors.
Unusually large windows. Rich
upholstery and full-nickeled
hardware. Dome light. Your
choice of four artistic colors.*

$570
(F. O. B. Detroit)

NEW FORD ROAD
*A long, low, chummy
fast as it looks. Wide
Deep cushions. Rich up
Full-nickeled hardware.
seat optional. Your ch
four beautiful color*

$ 385
(F. O. B. Detroit)

NEW FORD COUPE
*There is a bit of the European
touch in the coachwork and
contour of this new Ford Coupe.
Handy package shelf in back of
seat and unusually large water-
proof luggage space in rear
deck. Your choice of four beautiful colors.*

$ 495
(F. O. B. Detroit)

NEW
FORD SPORT CO
*Combines the alert
the roadster and the ad
of a closed car. Run
standard. Landau irons
quarter. Finished i
artistic color harmo*

$ 550
(F. O. B. Detroit)

NEW FORD PHAETON
*Another long, low, roomy
car. All four doors open forward. Curtains open and close
with doors. Side curtains have
unusually large windows. Your
choice of four artistic colors.*

$ 395
(F. O. B. Detroit)

FORD MOTOR COMPANY
Detroit, Michigan

© 1927, Ford

"A" UNVEILING—This is one of the ads announcing the new Ford line.

"A" SEDAN—The four-passenger Ford enjoyed much more sales volume than the sporty coupes with their rumble seats. This was the $495 Tudor Sedan.

COMPETITIVE AD DEVICE—This ad showing the evolution of the "T" notes how Fords already dominated the roads prior to the introduction of the "A."

INSTITUTIONAL AD—The U.S. Borax Company started using its famous 20-mule-team picture for promotion of its products in 1927. From 1883 to 1889 the teams hauled borax out of Death Valley over the steep Panamint Mountains and across 165 miles of California desert to the nearest railroad junction at Mojave.

BUSINESS AND INVENTOR LINEUP OF THE CENTURY—These nine controlled and contributed more to the era than any other ensemble.

H.Firestone   J.Rosenwald   Thomas Edison   Sir Thomas Lipton   Chas.Schwab   HenryFord   W.P.Chrysler   Geo.Eastman   T.A.Wilson

BACK TO THE MAIL, FOR A MOMENT—Col. Charles Lindbergh made an airmail flight run for Maddux Air Lines from San Diego to Inglewood. Will Rogers peers out the plane window along with Lindbergh on September 22, 1927.

percentages maintained that 80 percent of the population received only 52 percent of the income. His figures noted that the average income was $2,550, and it took $2,432.39 for a family of five to live in a city. Still, he said, there was reason for "thanksgiving," but the country certainly was not unanimous in its prosperity.

While one of the nation's great financiers was en route to his winter home in Florida in early December, reporters interviewed him when his train stopped in Savannah, Georgia. Old and gaunt, 88-year-old John D. Rockefeller seemed to be refreshed by the newspapermen. He talked with them for ten minutes and gave them a copy of his prayer, which he read at least once daily, he said.

The journalists were not moved. Some could remember when the powerful businessman was breaking the backs of many big businesses and was wiping out competitive corporations with ruthless coldness in his highest world of high finances. The prayer read:

> Heavenly Father, we thank Thee for the glad and wholesome contagion of cheerfulness. If frowns and distempers are contagious, we thank Thee that smiles are not less so. The smile goes forth from face to face. By the stranger law of increase, gladness begets gladness. Remembering then that no frown ever made a heart glad, help us go forth to meet the day with high hope and smiling face, and even though it has not been easy to smile, let us rejoice if so we have been able to add to the sum of human happiness and make burdens lighter.

Two other men of great wealth made notable human-interest statements that year. Manhattan multimillionaire Charles R. Flint, one of the foremost trust assemblers of the early 1900s, shook up the establishment by declaring, "Greed is the reason for a man's wanting to swell his wad million after million." In Chicago, Julius ("Sears, Roebuck") Rosenwald, who had a $115 million "wad," said on his 65th birthday in September, "With rare exceptions, the man who accumulates wealth displays no more genius than the prize winner in any lottery."

Playboy millionaire Tommy Manville, heir to the Johns-Manville asbestos building-materials corporation, was married to his second wife in '25 and divorced her in '30. The asbestos heir started his marriage marathon in 1911 and wed his eleventh wife in 1960. Throughout the

20s he lived, as always, in baronial splendor. He was fond of pretty blondes and good brandy. Manville said he liked to keep money in circulation, although he once had to sell some property when his millions were in the low numbers. Chrome-plated trash cans and Rolls Royces were among his flamboyant trademarks.

There were a few subtle forecasts of the crash two years away. In September the National Shoe Retailers' Association met in New York City. It predicted higher footwear prices—15–20 percent higher—were coming. It attacked vegetarians as the culprits who would be responsible for the increased costs. The accusation was made on the basis of the less beef eaten, the fewer cattle killed. The less slaughtered, the higher the cost of leather, the shoe group explained. Bernarr Macfadden, the *Graphic* publisher, one of the foremost meatless food fiends in the country, had no comment.

The business world almost had an authentic advertising first that year. The American Tobacco Company broke a precedent, then had to withdraw it. Diva Madame Ernestine Schumann-Heink was quoted in an ad as saying that she smoked Lucky Strikes. Until then no cigarette maker dared to declare that women thought of smoking. In Atlanta the great singer refuted the testimonial and said she didn't even approve of her sons' smoking in her presence. The company attributed the error to an overzealous ad man.

The surging monies flowing through the wild bull market that year attracted very few official remarks. Secretary of the Treasury Mellon had made $300 million in oil and aluminum. Several times during the year the Federal Reserve Board was on the verge of commenting on Wall Street speculation, but while it was clearing its throat, Coolidge issued a statement saying the year would be healthy and prosperous. Mellon added, "The stock market seems to be going along in an orderly fashion, and I see no evidence of overspeculation." While Coolidge was in the Black Hills, he repeated his assurances on soundness. The market immediately jumped 26 points.

Advertising was becoming formalized. Bruce Barton had founded his agency after World War 1. On 45th Street, not Madison Avenue. Major advertising agencies handled billings in the tens of millions of dollars. The account executive was as much a part of the scene as the customer's man on Wall Street. Copywriters earned more than bank

presidents. But everybody was making money—or so it seemed.

There was so much free money around that the surge appeared to be frighteningly muscular. Broker loans increased from $3 billion in January to $4.5 billion by December. Stock market shares rose from a volume of 451 million at the beginning of the year to 577 million at the end of it. The hoppers still appeared to be running freely with no money congestion in sight by the speculators. Fortunes were spent on stock market tips.

Rural America shared in the money harvest. Farmers and villagers were prosperous enough to drive almost as many new cars as their urban counterparts. They were tuned in on radios. They were purchasing the clever new appliances that were making life on the farm easier than it had been since the invention of the plow. Some farm wives even had power-driven washing machines. They went to the talkies when the theaters were converted, and they still went to vaudeville. They still had their flying circuses. Those who were leaving the farms for city jobs came back to tell how the big-town speakeasies compared with the local mash joints. And they came back in Niagara Blue Ford roadsters or Arabian Sand phaetons.

President Coolidge felt the farmers were doing all right without additional legislation. He opposed every farm bill for almost four years, vetoing even the McNary-Haugen bill for farm surplus purchases. The farms produced more than the people in the nation could eat, wear, or otherwise use or waste, and there was a farm surplus for sale in competition with foreign-produced crops. The U.S. already was protecting most of its manufactured products by tariff. Farmers felt they must buy their clothes, labor, building materials, and toiletries and other things from a protected market and sell in an unprotected market. Many farmers were making enough money and didn't want any government aid or subsidies.

The big mystery that marked all, including the state of the economy, was why Silent Cal would not run again. He calmly ignored the frantic blandishments of the politicians of his own party, who knew that the next administration would gallop in with a business momentum such as no new President had ever had. The First Lady, in her sweet bluntness, explained why her husband may have given up the presidency: "Poppa says there's a depression coming."

1 9 2 7

CHAPTER 13

The Greatest Knockout
Year in Sports

SWEAT girdled his cap, turning the felt a darker color. Pressure furrowed lines in his brow. Patches of wetness flared from under each arm. He hunched into position and set his foot on the rubber. The signal was the only one. Washington Senator lefty Tom Zachary looked at the winning run on third for the Yankees. It was the bottom of the eighth. He stretched, kicked, and delivered a low inside fast ball to the plate.

George Herman "Babe" Ruth drove the ball into the right field bleachers. Clapping and bellowing on that day, October 1, 1927, blended into the wildest ovation ever accorded a man on the diamond. The barrel-chested man who could eat two dozen hot dogs in one afternoon had hit his 60th homer of the season. He played 151 games that season. The record stood until 1961, when another Yankee, Roger Maris, hit 61 home runs in a season of 162 games. Due to the differences in the game totals for the seasons, the records are logged separately in the statistics.

Yankee fans in particular and baseball fanatics in general like to argue about which is the greatest team in history. The '27 Yankees are

inevitably one of the contestants. They won by 17 games that year. The outfielders were Combs, Ruth, and Meusel; the infielders were Gehrig, Lazzeri, Koenig, and Dugan. Pat Collins and Benny Bengough were behind the plate. The mound cast included Hoyt, Pipgras, and Pennock.

Babe hit 17 homers in September and ended the season with 60 and a .356 average. Iron Man Gehrig hit 47 and batted .373. The power down the rest of the lineup hit 50 more homers. The club totaled 157 homers that season, almost three times as many as the second-place Athletics. The series with Pittsburgh was an invasion with no resistance. The Pirates succumbed in four straight.

World Series fans who arrived at Forbes Field a couple of hours before the first game started saw an exhibition that several of the sports writers said was a psychological nightmare. The Pirates also saw the Yankee batting practice that day. The Bambino and Horse sent a barrage of balls over the fences, and the other players were booming them out also. A few seasons later Gehrig would be the first man of this century to hit four homers in one game. His fifth time up he bounced one off the scoreboard for an automatic double.

In the final game of the Series the Pirates were fighting for survival. The score was 3–3 in the ninth when the Steel City relief pitcher Johny Miljus walked Combs and Koenig beat out a sacrifice bunt. Ruth stepped to the plate, and a wild pitch advanced the two runners. Pirate Manager Donie Bush ordered the Babe to be passed intentionally to load the bases. Miljus bore down and struck out Gehrig and Meusel. Yankee Manager Miller Huggins, one of the great dugout sages, called the ending.

"He's bearing down too hard," Miller said. "He'll throw that ball away." Lazzeri stepped to the plate, and the first pitch was too high and too hard. Catcher Johnny Gooch came out of his crouch and went into the air for it, but it was far out of reach. The winning run was scored by Combs, who didn't even have to slide.

The Golden Age was poetry in motion and drama in muscles in '27. During the jazz age it was said that Harry Heilmann used to lead the American League in batting in the odd-numbered years. He did so in '21, '23, '25, and '27. The averages for the six-foot, 200-pound Detroit Tiger were .394, .403, .393, and .398, respectively. He hit a niggardly

.344 in '29 and was sold to Cincinnati. Menacing Harry usually fought for the last percentage points right down to the final game. Tris Speaker seemed to have the record cinched in '25 when Harry picked up almost 50 points in September. During the final game, a double-header, the fiercely competitive Heilmann went three for six in the first game, moving him a couple of points ahead of the Gray Eagle.

"Don't play the second game, Harry," his teammates encouraged. "You're in now. Don't take any chances."

"Don't worry," Heilmann grinned. He hit three for three in the nightcap to beat Speaker .393 to .389.

In '27 he was much more dramatic. Al Simmons was his foe for the crown. Again the Tigers had a doubleheader to end the season while the Athletics were playing only a single game. Simmons got two for five to give him a .392 for the season. Due to the time-belt difference, Harry knew what Al had done. He knew how many hits he had to have. Two doubles and a single resulted from his first four tries at the plate. This was during the first game. His friends urged him to quit since he was then ahead and had the batting championship again. He persisted and walked to the plate the fifth time and knocked a homer.

Despite the pleas of his fellow players and the law of averages being against him, Harry took his black bat—he liked the somber color since it made him appear even more gruesome to pitchers—to the plate his four scheduled times during the second game. He hit three for four, a homer, a double, and a single. Harry's .398 beat Simmons by six points. That afternoon he hit safely seven times in nine trips to the plate, getting an unbelievable total of 16 bases.

Scores of other great players were active in '27, some near the end of their careers, others just starting them. Ty Cobb was 41 years old, had just been sold to Philadelphia, and would retire the coming year. Mel Ott was 18 years old and starting his second season with the Giants. Jimmie Foxx was 20 and would play another 18 years in the major leagues. He hit .323 for Philadelphia the year the City of Brotherly Love gave Lindbergh one of his biggest receptions. Rogers Hornsby was in the middle of his 26-year career and hit .361 for the New York Giants, who had just bought him that season from St. Louis. It was the climax year of the Golden Age of Sports.

During the fall, football fervor was as wild as the noisy attention

sports fans had been bestowing on baseball. The supreme decade of
sports champions already seethed with more skill and stories than it
could sanely hold. On the campus fields Notre Dame was undefeated
in '20 when George Gipp was at his best. From 1923 to 1925 Red
Grange was the most talked about All-American halfback in the nation. Pittsburgh, Illinois, and Yale were considered to be the best
teams that year, according to the chroniclers of the era. In the South,
football was getting more balance and much stronger. The University
of Tennessee was unbeaten that year.

Sports enthusiasm was so overwhelming that the 1920s became the
age of stadium building. Dozens of huge concrete structures were
constructed to replace the aging wooden stands. Parking lots were
jammed with almost every one of the 620 different models available
that year. Raccoon coats were functional as well as fashionable as they
hid hip flasks easily, could envelop Betty Coeds or flappers into their
folds with their men, and keep out the frost. Going behind the stadium
to take a drink became tradition during Prohibition. Alabama, Duke,
and Georgia were among the many football dynasties working on new
fields in '27.

Professional football gained prosperity and popularity during the
flashy sports decade. Although pro football had been around since
1895, it was a very minor sport in attendance and attention. Then interest began to pick up as franchises increased in value. The National
Football League had been founded only the year before. Red Grange
became a big gate attraction. He was not as spectacular among the pro
players as he had been with the college men, but he was still good box
office. The Galloping Ghost for the University of Illinois had become
the Roaring Redhead of the Chicago Bears. The game was becoming
quicker and more streamlined because passing was becoming an important part of it.

Johnny Blood is one of the classic tales of the Prohibition years. His
real name was McNally. In the early 20s he played with any pro team
that would accept him. Rules were not so severe, and regulations were
rather scarce. So the son from a wealthy family would play ball on
some Sundays. Just for fun. He needed a pseudonym to protect his last
name. While he and a friend whom he played with on the Green Bay
Packers were watching the Valentino movie *Blood and Sand*, McNally

said, "You be Sand, and I'll be Blood." Johnny Blood was born to go with the body of the 195-pound Apollo. His exploits as a halfback are still clubhouse legends and were then good colorful sports news. He played for 15 seasons in the NFL, most of them with Green Bay.

Notre Dame was the best-advertised college team in the land in the time between the great wars. The reason was Knute K. Rockne, who started coaching at the university in 1919. His record to 1927 was 64 games won, 6 lost, and 2 tied. He was regarded by many as the greatest coach of all time. In his tenser moments he could bark orders and complaints like an infuriated bulldog. His locker-room talks are legends. His team won seven, tied one, and lost one the year the Sultan of Swat hit 60 homers. The next year during a losing season he asked his players to win one for George Gipp, one of the most outstanding players the university has ever had.

The 175-pound quarterback died his senior year from a throat ailment. On his deathbed, he talked to the coach whom he loved.

"I've got to go, Rock," he whispered. "It's all right. I'm not afraid. Sometime, Rock, when the team is up against it, when things go wrong and the breaks are beating the boys, tell them to go in there with all they've got and win just one for Gipp. I don't know where I'll be then, Rock. But I'll know about it and be happy."

The message is one of the most inspirational ever made by man, an athlete or not. Perhaps this drama had something to do with the great coaches, players, and teams that dominated the years of the champions. The one won for the Gipp was the biggest upset of the next season, a 12–6 defeat of Army.

Diamonds, furs, and leather. Big-time hoods in tailored suits, men of riches and bearing, and locker-room sweat. Molls and flappers at ringside and the finely tuned specimens with the taped hands offering mayhem and sex appeal. Boxing became more than big business in the decade. Those men inside the ropes were children of and for the times. The appeal of the profession was its stark ferocity in an age when everything else glittered. The swirling giddiness of the years became excitedly sober between the gongs. Ring carnage was one of the hangover cures for Prohibition. And there was the compelling allure of the gloves on the greatest fighters the world has ever seen.

The times did something to fists, strength, and instinct. There have

been men with equal power, equal finesse on the finest points of the sport, but no group so exalted in pugilistic history. The contest that had once been an outcast became accepted culture. Some of the most influential names in the nation became associated with the sport. A few invested fortunes in the clash between two highly developed boxers. No other period has ever had such savagery.

Dempsey, Tunney, Leonard, Firpo, Carpentier, Tendler, Greb, Gibbons, Walker, Loughran, Delaney, Canzoneri, Flowers, Wilde, Sharkey, McTigue, Berlenbach, Risko, Stribling, Slattery, Dundee, Mandell, Kilbane, Villa, Schmeling, and Criqui were among the superlative punchers. The mighty crowds were enthusiastic over all weight divisions. From fly to heavyweight, there were men of great merit. Boxing was really All-American: a blend of sportsmanship, superb physical conditioning and a contest of man's ability to defeat another. Boxing was no longer the exclusive club for the few, a plaything for a select coterie; it was the entertainment of the masses.

Jack Dempsey and Tex Rickard gave the fight game its tremendous affluence in the most challenging years of all sports. Each led revolutionary changes in the boxing world. As a team, they have the unanimous decision over any other fight-mating popularity in ring history. The Manassa Mauler ushered in the Golden Age of Sports on the Fourth of July in 1919. Under a relentless sun, the six-foot 187-pound Dempsey butchered the six-foot-seven 245-pound Jess Willard for the World Championship.

For the next seven years he pounded some very outstanding boxers to helplessness. No other man has so methodically wrecked a list of fighters. Although some of his opponents gave him some devastating punishment, they could not stop his vicious blows. He came back, sometimes so wildly many thought he would kill the men. He became popular primarily because of his fighting ability. His personality was not a big part of his image. Fans went to see one of the most awesome sluggers, not a character.

William Harrison Dempsey went to work right after leaving grammar school in Salt Lake City. In his teens he did hard labor. His great strength came from some of the brutish jobs he held in mines, lumber camps, on railroads, and in shipyards. He was also a drifter and had that strain of toughness to go along with an innate contempt for conse-

quences. He fought out of a crouch, curling in his power, then unleash-
ing paralyzing blows. He had mastodonic strength and a desire to win.
The press dubbed him a "killer of killers." He hit with killing power.
He punched faces out of shape until they were bruised blobs that
seemed to have no bones. They didn't stop fights in those days until
the towel came in.

On September 24, 1926, in Philadelphia, Gene Tunney unequivo-
cally whipped Dempsey. The ex-marine and former steamship clerk
did everything to the ferocious brawler but knock him out. The killer
of the century was helpless before the superb boxer. If Tunney had
been as strong as the man he deftly punched hundreds of times that
night, he would have knocked him out. Dempsey pursued the enigma
of the ring to every corner, flailing at him from his crouch only to have
the handsome boxer left-jab him in barrages, then shake him with
right crosses to the head and face.

Dempsey didn't know it, but the genteel fighter, who frowned on
the image of the profession, had been planning to whip him for years.
The characters with shady and questionable reputations who infested
the sport bothered him. He was also far superior in intellect to other
fighters. Although he had little formal education, he was a friend of
professors and writers. He knew literature and could quote Shake-
speare. These traits were enough to make him seem more than odd to
those who made their living with their fists. His modesty and brilliance
did not enhance his popularity. He ranks as one of the most unpopular
champions.

Tunney analyzed his opponents in minute detail. Nothing they did
came as a surprise to him. He was thoroughly familiar with their assets
and liabilities. He studied the moving pictures made of Dempsey's
fights. From the Firpo bout he decided Dempsey was an open target
for him despite the crouch and his speed. The Carpentier fight proved
to him the deadly Tiger Killer could be hurt. His fight with Brennan
said he didn't have nearly as much boxing skill as he had.

On July 21, 1927, ex-champ Dempsey fought Jack Sharkey. It was
an elimination bout, and the winner would fight Tunney. Heavy-faced
at the age of 32, Dempsey weighed 194½ pounds when he met the
handsome 25-year-old ex-sailor who was a pound and a half heavier.
Eighty thousand people crowded Yankee Stadium that night. Sailor

Jack threw many blows, but Dempsey seemed to be hitting harder. Millions listened to the blow-by-blow account on radio.

In the seventh round a series of blows by Dempsey ended the fight, but where they landed started a debate. Perhaps it was the prelude to the coming controversy.

"There is no question about the punch on Sharkey's left leg by Dempsey's right," Referee Jack O'Sullivan said after the fight. "It was a sweeping blow which glanced off the leg, and it was followed by Dempsey's left to the solar plexus, which was the decisive blow as I saw it. Before the solar plexus blow was delivered and after the right landed on Sharkey's left leg, I was stepping in toward the men, saying, 'Watch your punches, Jack.' Then, realizing there were two Jacks, I said, 'I mean you, Dempsey.' Then Dempsey hit the solar plexus blow. Sharkey dropped his right hand and Dempsey hit him a left on the jaw."

The rough sailor fell. O'Sullivan counted off the ten seconds and declared Dempsey the winner. Sharkey complained, naturally enough, after regaining consciousness, but he made no formal protest. Sports writers at ringside quickly polled themselves. There was a variety of opinions on what had just happened. New York City Mayor Jimmy Walker and Champion Gene Tunney said there had been "no foul." Renowned sports writer Grantland Rice said, "Dempsey struck Sharkey two fouls blows."

The gate pulled a few dollars less than a million. The fight receipts were distributed:

Federal Taxes	$ 98,502
New York State Tax	49,251
Dempsey	352,000
Sharkey	210,426
Promoter Rickard	273,350

Dempsey and Tunney signed to fight on September 22 in Chicago's Soldiers' Field. The ex-champ chose to train at a race track in Crete, Illinois. The more suave Tunney located his conditioning camp at a country club in Lake Villa, Illinois. The press reported almost every rope skip and sparring blow as the two prepared for what was billed as

SULTAN OF SWAT LOOKS AT ANOTHER—Peering into the heavens, Babe again watches the ball riding high over the fence.

BAMBINO WITH PRACTICE BAT—Babe Ruth's barrel chest and big belly made his legs seem spindly by comparison.

60TH HOMER—Lou Gehrig congratulates Babe on a record 60 trippers in 154 games, which record still stands.

IRON HORSE—Powerful Lou Gehrig hit behind Babe with almost equal ability.

GREATEST YANKEES EVER?—Many authorities say this '27 team was the best of all time.

ATHLETICS POWER HITTER—Bull-necked Jimmy Foxx kept Philadelphia in pennant contention during most of the decade.

FRECKLED AND AGGRESSIVE—Harry Heilmann led the American League in hitting in '27, as he did many other years.

FORMER GASHOUSE GANG PLAYER—St. Louis sold Rogers Hornsby to the Giants in '27 after 11 years with the Cardinals; Hornsby returned to Cards in '33 after seasons with Boston and Chicago.

WHITE SOX LYONS—Although Chicago was a fifth-place team in '27, Ted Lyons won 22 and lost 14.

SHIFTED TO FIRST BASE—Tris Speaker was on first 'as well as in the outfield in '27, his next to last year in the majors, but he still hit .327 for Washington, just 17 points shy of his lifetime batting average.

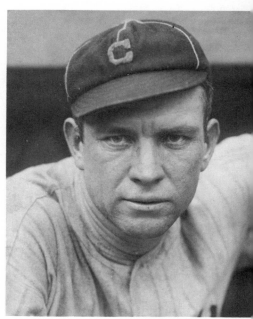

FLASHING SPIKES—Base-running star Ty Cobb was making his last slides in '27 as his diamond career ended.

GALLOPING GHOST COULD JUMP—Halfback Red Grange became an All-American celebrity at the University of Illinois for three years of the 20s before playing pro ball for Chicago during the rest of the decade. *Pro Football Hall of Fame*

MOST FAMED COLLEGE COACHES—Pop Warner and Knute Rockne of Notre Dame were among the best-known names of the Golden Age of Sports.

RING CONFUSION STILL CONTINUES—Referee Barry raises Tunney's hand ending the controversial "long count" fight.

1927 INDY WINNER—George Sounders sits at the wheel of his Duesenberg Special at the Indianapolis Speedway.

KENTUCKY DERBY WINNER—In '27 Whiskery with 126-pound L. McAtee up in the coveted circle after clocking 2:06, which won $51,000.

PACE CAR—W. P. Chrysler, right, and a track official pose with this Imperial roadster which started the 1927 Indy "500."

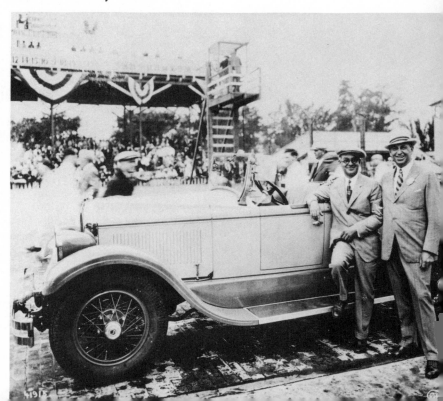

COURT JESTERS STARTED IN '27—Current whiz Meadowlark Lemon seemingly has six hands in this trick shot.

"the fight of the century." Promoter Rickard, former gambler, rancher, lumberjack, and gold prospector before becoming the greatest sports impresario of the century, was swamped with demands for tickets.

The day before the bout Chicago was jammed with boxing fans. Every hotel and motel room in the city was rented. Bookies weren't doing much business. They figured it even, then moved it to 9 to 10 for Tunney to win. The square-featured Dempsey had the bulk of the crowd sympathy that always rides with the deposed champ. Almost 3,000 policemen were there to insure the 163,000 fans—those in the choice seats paid $40 for them—did not get unruly. Men filled the aisles and clung to the girders like stalactites. Thousands of radio stations were ready to announce the battle. Around 50 million people were tuned to the spectacle. Graham McNamee, the most popular radio announcer in the country, was at the microphone.

For the first six rounds, the fight was a replay of the Philadelphia encounter. Dempsey stalked the agile Tunney, jabbing wildly from his hunched squat, hitting with grueling power. The fair-skinned pinkness of Tunney was splotched with red from the punches. Dempsey, black-browed and tanned of body, showed the blows he had been taking were fast and many only by taking smelling salts in his corner between rounds.

During the one-minute break between the fifth and sixth rounds, the first friction developed. Dempsey's managers started smearing Vaseline on his face, which would have made the blows glance off and cause less damage. Tunney alertly caught the action. Dempsey was ordered to remove the grease. The huge arms of the former champ seemed to be even more like pistons the next round, but it was still easy for Tunney to move away from him, then move in again, tattooing him with volleys from both hands.

In the seventh, Dempsey hit the World War I vet hard for the first time in a vital spot. As he came out of his crouch, he smacked Tunney with a long left hook, which put him back against the ropes. Before he could recover his balance and his perception, the Mauler from Manassa, Kansas, was on him viciously. He bashed his face and head with almost berserk blows. Tunney went down. Referee Dave Barry stepped to the side of the prostrate man under the glare of the 44 one-

thousand-watt lamps over the ring, to begin his count. Paul Beeler, the knockdown timekeeper, rose across the ring to watch the seconds on the watch clutched in his hand. Dempsey stood tensely against the ropes with his arms resting on their top.

Barry's arm came down, and he yelled "one" as he motioned Dempsey to the opposite neutral corner. Four more seconds lapsed before Dempsey heeded the referee's order to follow the rules and go to the farthest neutral corner. Barry began counting again: one, two, three, four, five, six, seven, eight, nine . . . Tunney came up and back-pedaled away as he set himself. The veteran killed motioned the faster man toward him, wanting to exchange blows. Dempsey could not hit him solidly, so elusive was the big man who had risen with super-human effort.

In the eighth Tunney brought the dark-complexioned crowd-pleaser to one knee with a right to the jaw. The former champ's eyes were getting ugly. He appeared to the announcer to be getting very, very tired as the fight ended. The terrifying power and savagery of Dempsey and the quickness and dazzle of Tunney were too much for some who were listening on radio. A man in Iowa and one in Pennsylvania died during the terrific suspense when their sets failed to deliver the announcement of the decision. One wire service reported that 11 died during the bloody drama from strokes and heart attacks.

Pandemonium erupted over the decision that matured into the greatest "controversy" boxing has ever known. Tunney maintained he was in control of his faculties as soon as he hit the floor. He said he started to get up at "four," but his handlers motioned him to stay down for a few more seconds' rest. That is the reason, his camp and followers maintained, he waited until "nine." Dempsey and his crew protested to the Boxing Commission. They said the champ was down for fourteen seconds, four over the allotted number to constitute a win.

Timekeeper Beeler was looking at his watch tolling off the time. He said he looked up to see the referee trying to push and wave Dempsey to a neutral corner. The referee started counting as Beeler called "five." Instead of calling "six" on the second swing of Barry's arm, he took up the count with him and called "two." They counted to nine together. According to the official clock, he said Tunney was on the canvas for

13 seconds. Boxing fans are still counting on whichever clock they think should be correct. Dempsey's career was over. He picked up a check for $884,500 and retired.

Tunney collected $990,445, a little shy of the million he had been guaranteed. Rickard got the rest of the $2,658,660 after incidentals. Naturally, there were many nasty stories circulated after the epic clash, just as there had been following their first fight. But it was an age of miraculous stories. There were too many true ones to trifle long with the unfounded.

Language on the links hasn't improved any, but the scores have. The whip and torsion of the hickory shafts were variables that almost couldn't be matched in a set. Cracked shafts were common; the steel shaft didn't make its appearance until the early 30s. The books record some notable rounds in the jazz age. Pros of the period prided themselves on having acquired outfits with no whip or torsion. Only a few years later technology made it possible for anyone to buy an excellent set for modest prices. Unlike today, very few stars of other sports played golf. Maybe the gilded years were times of great specialization, too. Bobby Jones was 25 years old when he won at St. Andrews in 1927. Over 20,000 walked the fairways as the man from Atlanta amazed the galleries. Scotland's cradle of golf had highlanders, pipers, distillers and clergymen straining for a view of the Georgia boy.

The inwardly tense, wavy-haired wizard sauntered into St. Andrews' loop—a deceptive area where the holes zig-zag through shrubbery and greenery. He took twelve shots to play four holes, finishing the round in 68 to tie the course record. The next round totaled 72. In a third round he had a par 73 and finished with another 72. He ended the tournament six strokes ahead of the previous record there.

Then tension finally hit the Southern boy, though, as an attack of nausea climaxed his day. "To be a champion at St. Andrews is quite too much for me," Jones said. His putter high over his head, Jones was paraded on the shoulders of his admiring crowd.

In other sports action, the U.S. fought gallantly for the Davis Cup at the tennis finals in Philadelphia. Veteran American champs were matched against a younger French team that hadn't previously shown much class, comparatively. William T. Tilden was the unrivaled colossus, a world champion without apparent effort, and a strutting ego-

ist. The tall, gaunt showman who loved lawn tennis and the limelight
was a supreme strategist. America had one of the most renowned
quartets in the history of tennis: Tilden, Little Bill Johnston, Vincent
Richards, and R. Norris Williams. The confident French team had the
immortal Four Musketeers: Rene Lacoste, Henri Cochet, Jean Borotra,
and Jacques Brugnon.

No non-English-speaking country had ever taken the coveted Cup.
When Cochet met Little Bill Johnston in the final match, the partisan
crowd was a little edgy. Lacoste had defeated Tilden, the American
champ, to tie the series. Despite the emotional crowd, Cochet defeated
Johnston 6–4, 4–6, 6–2, 6–4, and the Davis Cup went to the Land of
Lafayette. Tilden was deposed from his Olympian perch temporarily,
but he came back two years later to win again. He was always a
winner in a decade that saw the most brilliant strokes and spins by the
most memorable terrors of tennis.

Polo was much more popular in the 20s than it is now. The immense
sums required to run a stable of ponies were available. Horses were
still part of the scene. Gentlemen learned to ride before they could
walk. Flawless riding, the ability to take physical contact, a deft touch,
sheer, zany courage—the requirements of polo—were not that rare.
Tommy Hitchcock had them all. He was the best player in America
from 1919 to 1944. The broad-shouldered man with the powerful arms
raced across the polo fields of the world winning for America. Unruly
brown hair gave him a mussed appearance. He was a superbly con-
ditioned man who loved the game so much it shadowed his other
exploits. Hollywood moguls also took up the sport and the director
dressed in whipcord and boots became a cliché. Will Rogers was one
of the best polo players.

Pool hustlers were part of the dazzling incandescence of the Demp-
sey-Ruth-Grange period. Billiards in the jazz age ran the gamut from
the scarred tables in Harlem to the plush felt in some of the speakeasies. The incomparable Willie Hoppe was the world champion. Prohibition to Willie was just shooting under different lighting. He started
in the Gaslight days in 1906 and was still winning tournaments in 1936.

In 1927 Willie stepped back into the balkline to defeat Hagen-
lacher. The game was shot in the grand ballroom of the Hotel Pennsylvania. The lead changed four times during the tense match until

Willie ran off the final 41 billiards for a 1,500 to 1,387. It was his accustomed dominance of 18.2.

Basketball in the 20s was somewhat a local sport. Teams ran into problems on the road. What was legal on one court sometimes bordered on assault and battery another 50 miles away. The New York Celtics were the most talked about big team from 1920 to 1930. College net play was more consistent in its regulations. Leagues started to mature during those years.

Slapstick basketball started in '27. Abe Saperstein took dribbling and the goals out of Chicago's Savoy Ballroom and put in roller skating. The Harlem Globetrotters were born. The court jesters have been on the road with their routine of skill and comedy ever since. In 1970 they played their 10,000th game. At that time their record included 9,678 wins!

Automobile racing has become the world's biggest spectator sport. Early tracks were crushed stone covered with tar, and the first engines made more noise than power. The sport not only has allowed man to seek how fast he can travel on the surface of the earth, but also has added immeasurably to the development of the automotive industry. Better motors, more advanced designs, and many safety features have been produced from the desire to drive in speed meets.

The Indianapolis Motor Speedway was opened in 1909, and the first 500-mile race was held two years later. In 1927 Captain Eddie Rickenbacker, the World War I flying ace, bought the famed track with the backing of some associates. He headed the Speedway through the coming financial crash and until the advent of World War II caused the temporary suspension of the sport. George Souders won the famed "500" in '27 at an average speed of 97.545. Tens of thousands watched his tube-shaped Duesenberg Special hit speeds over 100 miles per hour on the two-and-a-half-mile oval.

Johnny Weissmuller and Gertrude Ederle were the most memorable names in natatorial history. The water twins made almost all the swimming achievements in the 20s. Weissmuller set the world's record for the 100-yard free style in 1927 at 0:51 seconds. It stood 16 years. Long before his record was eclipsed by .4 of a second, he was playing Tarzan, Burrough's jungle hero, in movies.

Ederle swam her way to fame when she crossed the English Channel

in 1926. She was not only the first woman to conquer the grueling tide and cold water; she also smashed the existing men's records. She made it from the Battery to Sandy Hook in 14 hours and 30 minutes. The best male record then was 16 hours and 23 minutes, set by Sebastian Tiraboschi of Argentina. Her mark for *femme* swimmers still stands. Her competitiveness was stressed when she appeared to be tiring badly a mile from shore. Margaret, her sister and also a swimming ace, goaded her. "Get going," she said from the boat, "you're loafing."

"For that I'll make it if it kills me," Gertrude said indignantly. She finished with strength. In November 1927, she met President Coolidge, who said, "I am amazed that a girl of your small stature could swim the English Channel."

Water carnivals were staged often during the hectic years. In January 1927, 96 male and female swimmers thrashed about in the cold and sharky water off Catalina Island. Chewing gum tycoon William Wrigley, Jr., conceived the marathon race of swimming 22 miles to the California mainland to promote a real-estate development on the island that is a part of Los Angeles County. Some wore rubber suits, some regular bathing suits, many wore goggles, and at least one girl and one man refused to wear anything.

As dark came, the boats staying alongside their sponsored swimmers indicated with a red flare when their entry had dropped out of the race. Doggedly, slowly, the rest splashed on into the night. Henry F. Sullivan, who swam the Channel four years earlier, was among the athletes. The strong current was too much for him. He was pulled aboard. Exhaustion forced them out of the water, including the nudes, who had aroused the ire of prissy clerics. Three or four miles from shore only two were left. A 17-year-old Canadian, George Young, was too tired to finish. A big Chicagoan, Norman Ross, swam ashore alone to collect the $25,000 prize. He lost 25 pounds during the 15 hours, 44 minutes, and 33 seconds of swimming the stretch of Pacific.

The Sport of Kings during the jazz age was a paradox. It was an outdoor poolroom, an open-air roulette wheel, a cultural outing for the sophisticates of society, and, most of all, a track for all those who are addicted to seeing the colors and the rhythmic hooves. Man o' War brought the sport and honor of the thoroughbred to the nation. Some 4,000 horses were racing when the gusty stallion came out of the

chutes at the opening of the decade. Double that number were running at the end of it. Stake money also doubled, from less than a million and a half to over three. The big horse ran 22 times and went to the winning ring every time but once, and came in second the one miss. Some of the Hollywood silver screen stars dropped fortunes during the seasons.

The profits from the Noble Experiment allowed some of the most notorious characters of the Capone administration to get into horse racing. Once-humble hoodlums bought and controlled tracks and stables. The stuffy turf families weren't always overjoyed at having the gangsters grace their exclusive clubs. Notorious Arnold Rothstein of New York City mob fame made one of the biggest betting coups. He put hundreds of thousands of dollars on one fine animal named Sidereal.

Zev was one of the name horses in the early years of the decade. When the Teapot Dome oil scandal broke, it also got Harry F. Sinclair mentioned prominently on the sports pages. It seems Sinclair owned Zev, who was named after a famous attorney whom the oil man employed. Earle Sande rode the big horse to the flower circle at Belmont once for the $80,000 first prize. The fiery jockey became one of the most renowned riders and trainers during the late 20s. John E. Madden, the most famous horse breeder of the day, died in 1927. The wealthy, the unsavory, and the obscure rendezvoused at the races, while other fans chomped hot dogs and watched the Bambino swing with such power that he often went sprawling when he missed the ball.

1 9 2 7

CHAPTER 14

Miscellany of the
Maddest Montage of All

REGARDLESS of the synonyms for the 1920s, they were susceptible
to games, fads, and crazes. They slammed into the playful period, and
then graced no other decade. Mah Jong was introduced in '23. A
Standard Oil representative had become interested in the Chinese
game. A San Francisco lumber dealer imported $50,000 worth of the
sets. Then the American game producers started making sets.

"Pung" and "chow" and talking fluently about bamboo, Red Dragon,
and South Wind became common to millions of Americans. For a good
part of the Torrid Age, women played the tile-arranging game instead
of bridge. Ivory and bamboo tiles were arranged on green-baize tables
at formal parties. The ritzy players used $500 sets, but the local dime
stores stocked them also.

A French psychotherapist, Émile Coué, came up with a premise that
helped reduce the thrill of the Oriental title word game. He advocated
that the power of the mind can conquer all. His book, *Self-Mastery
Through Conscious Auto-Suggestion,* sold over a million copies within
months. It was a decade that was thinking and doing like no other, and
it liked the essence of his doctrine.

Those who didn't dig his therapy were doing crossword puzzles. In '27 a young man named Richard Simon was talking with his aunt about one of their relatives who happened to be a puzzle fiend. Newspapers had been carrying them for years, but there were no others available. Simon convinced his partner, Schuster, that they might print a book of crossword puzzles since they had just established a small publishing venture. The book with a pencil attached to it became a bestseller. Puzzle addiction was so intense throughout the decade that almost anyone could tell you the name of the Aztec rain god or give you a ten-letter word for swimming. Dictionary sales bounded to new heights.

Dance marathons were dying by '27 because some of the dancers were literally waltzing themselves to death. The dance games were a dreary ballroom promotional device. One of the first dance endurances was in March 1923, when Miss Alma Cummings danced for 27 straight hours, wearing out six men and some shoes. Then a girl in East Port Chester, Connecticut, became champ with 69 hours of nonstop foot work. She was on the move in other ways, too. Her swinging tootsies danced in three states during the ordeal because she was hoofing in a moving van most of the time.

Although the usual rules allowed 15 minutes out of the end of each hour to rest, the ordeals were still agony. Partners kicked each other to keep going. But the blows weren't enough, and couples fell to the grimy floors. Contests started with zest but ended disgustingly. Cigarette butts and bottles littered the floors. Attractive damsels became wretches. Stockings plummeted to their ankles, their hair surrendered to sweat, and they shuffled around as if they were in great misery; and they were. After a young man had completed 87 hours of dancing and was walking from the floor, he fell dead. Heart failure was listed as the cause. Some wondered why almost all the endurance dance records were won by women. Critics said girls just naturally had more staying power when it came to long periods of work. Others said dames simply drooped on the men most of the time and didn't have to tote their own weight.

"Of all the crazy competitions ever invented," the New York *Evening World* said, "the dancing marathon wins by a considerable margin

of lunacy." Police banned the dances in some cities, especially those on the West Coast.

The dancing sensation became a sickness because of the great interest in the swing bands of the time. The Charleston—a Harlem version of the knock-kneed, heel-kicking dance from South Carolina—was the first of the famed steps introduced during Prohibition. As the hip-swinging and hopping dance continued into the late 20s, it grew more hypnotic and often intimate. The suggestiveness was so demanding that generally the girls were more pooped than passionate when the music ended.

The fanny-slapping Black Bottom evolved from Negro jazz dancing, as did the Charleston. The name of the dance supposedly referred to the muddy bottom of the Suwannee River, but not many were gullible enough to accept the polite interpretation of the title. In England it was called "The Black Base" and sometimes "The Black Bed." The latter nickname didn't need any definition. The uninhibited dances helped usher in the big public ballrooms, and dime-a-dance parlors sprang up. The "taxi-dancers" began dancing with the lonely who couldn't find companionship anywhere else. And there was always the fox trot.

There were other records to break off the dance floor. St. Louis flagpole sitter Alvin "Shipwreck" Kelly was one of the most famous figures of the decade. He would sit on a rubber-covered seat, eight inches in diameter, that was strapped to the top of the flagpole ball on top. The daring acrobat was well paid for his living for days and nights perched high over a building. Usually, he was doing it as a publicity stunt for promotion of a hotel or some other business interest.

While Shipwreck was sitting atop the pole of a Dallas hotel in '26, he got word that an admirer of his was in one of the hotel's elevators. A shapely redhead had slapped a man who said, "Is that damn fool still up there?" The sitter was impressed and had her hoisted by ropes up to his level, over a hundred feet above the street. They held hands and conversed. Shortly after descending the pole, he married the 18-year-old lass.

His flapper bride became his assistant. She supervised his bucket deliveries of food and cigarettes while he perched on a pole. He also

had a character to wake him up when he fell asleep for more than ten to twenty minutes at a time. He jammed his thumbs down holes bored in his tiny platform so he wouldn't fall off when he dozed. A sleet storm got him one winter, and he had to have a hatchet to chop the ice from his legs and body.

Television antennas were around in the 20s, but Shipwreck couldn't sit on them. Very few people knew what a TV set was. Dr. Vladimir Zworykin patented his iconoscope camera tube in '25. The Russian inventor came to the U.S. and made other refinements in transmission and reception of pictures by electronics. Research into the medium had been going on almost half a century.

In the Manhattan auditorium of the Bell Telephone Laboratories in April 1927, Walter S. Gifford, the president of the American Telephone & Telegraph Company, talked to his vice president, General J. J. Carty, who was in Washington, D.C. He also watched him on a special television circuit.

"Hello, General, you're looking fine," the AT & T boss said. "I see you have your glasses on."

"Does, it, ah, does it flatter me?" the veep asked of his picture on the yellow framed glass before him. "Yes, I think it's an improvement," the president said.

Secretary of Commerce Herbert Hoover stepped to the television camera next. Small circles of light raced across the tube, casting a bluish light on his round face. The apparatus for sending and receiving was expensive and bulky. The screen size was only a fraction over two inches square. But the detail was very good.

On January 13, 1928, the day after Ruth Snyder died in the electric chair, Mr. Earl Shaub, who has been quoted previously, covered one of the first television demonstrations in America. After witnessing her death, along with some other reporters, and writing the execution story for his newspaper, the day and night were gone. It was 6:00 A.M. when he got home following the hours of horror, tension, and work. He remembered he had to cover a story in Schenectady that afternoon.

"I looked through a contraption similar to the back of a camera with a black focusing cloth over my head," Shaub says in his autobiography *All in a Day's Work*, "like an old fashioned photographer used, and I saw several executives of General Electric Co. moving about in an-

other room. The picture was quite foggy, but it was something new. May I add for the benefit of the industry, which is being criticized in so many quarters today, that TV has improved some since that day.

"Anyway, I was impressed then and wrote the following lead on my story: Schenectady, N.Y.—Men looked around corners and through stone walls here today."

Television was already a topic of the science-fiction writers of the period, and a German film director had already incorporated a set into one of his movie scenes. Unfortunately, almost no one realized the entertainment and education potential of television then. As soon as the sound films were introduced in '27, some of the inventors who had been perfecting talkies began working on television. A year later the first intercontinental picture was transmitted. Dr. John Baird, an Englishman, sent a picture of a woman from London to Hartsdale, New York. The following year he worked out more logistics and succeeded in sending color pictures. Just how television would have influenced the jazz age conjures up some wild premises. If it had been available to the masses, would the era have been emancipated even more? Would there have been speakeasy variety shows?

Out on the deserts of the Southwest, Dr. Robert Goddard was pulling rockets behind cars in '27, as he had in other years. The pioneer space scientist was looking far into the future along with the most brilliant researchers. Television and rocketry were amazingly advanced, but research money was scarce. Some interest was being exercised by business, but the collapse of the economy staved off any assistance to the refinement of these areas of technology for too many years.

It was the ingenious ventilation system developed by Ole Singstad that allowed the construction of New York's Holland Tunnel in '27. The master tunnel builder from Norway devised so efficient a method of sucking out the deadly exhaust fumes with fans that it is still used the world over. He also built New York's Lincoln and Brooklyn Battery Tunnels, as well as the two-mile Baltimore Harbor Tunnel.

The death of Hudson Maxim in May was a major loss to both science and the military. The inventor of deadly explosives died at the age of 74 at Lake Hopatcong, New Jersey. The lively man who worked with bombs lost his left hand during one of his experiments; he also lost some aides over the years. The inventor of smokeless powder and

MANHATTAN TOUR—These pretty flappers perched on a sight-seeing bus wave for the promotional photographer.

SANTE FE'S CALIFORNIA LIMITED—Seven sections of the famous train getting ready to leave Los Angeles for points east.

FORD ASSEMBLY LINE?—No, the first Orange Blossom Special from New York City to Miami has just arrived on January 8, 1927. This is the crowd assembled at the Seaboard Air Line Railway Station to welcome the more than 500 passengers in this celebration of the rail connection from New York City to the Florida east coast.

CHIEFS LEAD IN FIRST ORANGE BLOSSOM SPECIAL—Bringing the train down the ties are Seminole Chief Tony Tommy and Seaboard President S. Davies Warfield. Florida Governor John W. Martin walks behind Warfield, and Hialeah Mayor John P. Grether follows the tribal leader.

BOXY BUSES—This Chicago fleet is typical of the transportation companies that solved the metropolitan commuter problem.

CAMPY, YES—This bus design of the Age of Wonderful Nonsense was stylish then and much later.

NO, NOT THE LUFTWAFFE!—This is a '27 brigade of the "and leave the driving to us" bus drivers in their military uniforms and Sam Browne belts. Youngsters envied the uniforms of the Greyhound corps.

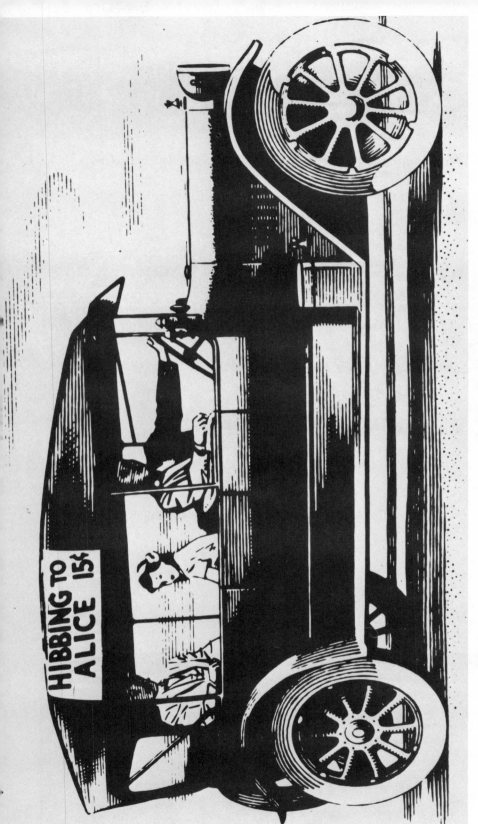

CHEAP TO ALICE—Greyhound graduated from his one-Hupmobile enterprise in 1914. Hibbing, incidentally, was a mining town of 10,000 on the Mesabi Range, which was soon to become the world's largest open pit iron operation, and Alice was a tiny village two miles away where many miners lived. Even so, 15 cents was fair fare to Alice.

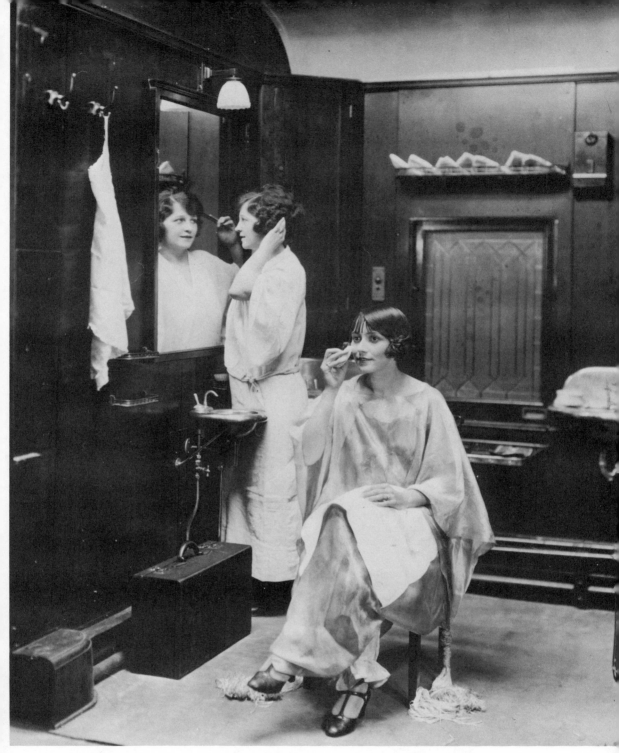

CATERING TO FLAPPERS—Lounges and dressing rooms in sleeping cars were well appointed to appeal to the ladies.

PRINCE AT THROTTLE—The Prince of Wales sits in a CP locomotive.

ROYALTY ARRIVING FOR TRAIN TOUR—This party of the Prince of Wales poses on the bridge of the liner *Empress* of Australia on its arrival in Canada, July 30, 1927. They are (l. to r.) Captain Jock Latta; Prime Minister Stanley Baldwin; Mrs. Baldwin; Edward, the Prince of Wales; Prince George (later Duke of Kent); and Captain R. N. Stuart.

SMALL-TOWN STATION'S DAY OF GLORY—If you wanted to travel in style, you took a train. This Louisville & Nashville train is loading in Bay St. Louis, Mississippi.

MASSIVE WILDS ABOVE THE BORDER—Snow on the mountains and stiletto-like pines bracket this Canadian Pacific express, and many Americans took the scenic trip to Montreal and Quebec.

STEAMING INTO BEND—This Pennsylvania Railroad express pulls around a horseshoe curve; note the warning marker in rock in the left foreground.

POTOMAC RIVER VALLEY—The B & O Capitol Limited races by with a wisp of steam coursing above the shiny engine.

PLUSH UPHOLSTERY—During the 20s, the more luxury the railroads could provide the better their business and prestige.

ILLINOIS CENTRAL BEHEMOTH—The line that Casey Jones rode to immortality was one of the main carriers from Chicago to New Orleans.

FIRST TV TELEPHONE—Commerce Secretary Herbert Hoover talks from Washington to New York during the first intercity TV broadcast. AT & T Vice President J. J. Carty (to Hoover's left), Chesapeake and Potomac Telephone President A. E. Berry, and Judge Stephen Davis, a Commerce Department employee, witness this television first.

INSIDE TUNNEL—The tiled tube under the river was a great boost to the traffic flow in New York that year.

HOLLAND TUNNEL OPENS—On November 12, 1927, this crowd was hearing the dedication ceremonies opening the road under the Hudson River.

nitroglycerin used to shock his guests during the booming 20s by walking out on his back porch and showing his party friends a little vial with a few drops of clear water-like stuff in it. He would heave it toward the brush and watch the astonishment of his guests as his concoction blew a big hole in the ground.

Muscular Billy Sunday was the foremost evangelist who claimed to be trying to save the lost generation from the fate of Sodom. The former prize fighter had the attention of the media if not all the masses during his strenuous revivals. The wavy-haired, handsome reverend was as blunt as he was stirring. His excellent enunciation projected and penetrated, especially to the more emotional in his audiences. Some of his world-renowned popularity was undoubtedly due to his sermons and commentaries on the news and morals of the decade.

"Give 'em the juice," Sunday bellowed from his pulpit concerning Sacco and Vanzetti. "Burn them, if they're guilty. That's the way to handle it. I'm tired of hearing these foreigners, these radicals, coming over here and telling us what to do." When Prohibition became the law of the land, he had John Barleycorn, the patron saint of the bottle, ceremoniously buried. He happened to be preaching in Norfolk, Virginia, on the occasion and had a pine box borne through the streets as he put liquor to what he said was its final rest. "Hell is now open for rent," the preacher declared.

Sunday's most spectacular opposition, competition, or fellow evangelist was Aimee Semple McPherson. She was an attractive woman who could have passed for a pretty flapper if her dresses had been more brazen in the fashion of the era. (Catty commentators said her legs were too heavy for short skirts.) She became one of the best-known radio performers, airing her sermons more often than any other major religious worker of the day. Her metaphors and similes were graphic.

"A church without the Holy Ghost is like an automobile without gasoline," Aimee said in a Manhattan sermon. "Oh, Lord, let there be an outpouring of the Holy Ghost. When I come into a meeting sometimes I feel just like a sponge, dripping with honey and milk. I just give everything I've got. I'm weak when I come out. But I go and pray to Jesus and get all charged up like a battery."

That same week in February 1927 revivalist Sunday spoke in At-

lanta. His interpretations of the Scriptures were icily practical. He did not hold the new views of the Bible too highly. With his powerful fists slamming the pulpit, he would denounce those who dared to offer new theories concerning "old-time religion." He lashed a local congregation of "modernists" shortly after his arrival in the Georgia capital.

"The pack of pretentious, pliable, mental perverts are dedicated to the destruction of religion and one and all are liars, so labeled by the authority of Almighty God," the onetime boxer said. Sunday didn't have the angelic rhetoric of Aimee, but he had other devices just as moving. He liked to use the audience to make a point. When he hit the rough areas like the Appalachian coal-mining section, he was prone to use gimmicks that they could grasp with impact.

During a meeting attended mostly by miners and mountaineers near Big Stone Gap, Virginia, in the late 20s, he told all the women in the big tent to cross their legs. "More holes of sin have been covered up just now than have been closed in years around here," the husky preacher said. He used similar suggestiveness when he deemed it effective.

Religion in the Golden Age was colorfully combatant. It had to be to cope with the bathtub gin parties, the unusual sins of the era, and the pace was either sinful or holy. Sunday and Aimee are names that still register immediately in millions of American households today.

There was love, all kinds, all depths, but there was a romance with the times that added more to every affection. The year is a beautiful flapper with spit curls and a cloche hat. Tubular frocks didn't indent or protrude the curves, but they were bouncingly there. The birth rate continued to climb. The slick elegance of male and female dress had a prop-room glamour. Fumes from Prohibition booze and the gangster guns polluted the air with happy criminality.

Phenomena? *The year* didn't have any of that false virginal innocence to inhibit it. It came in with the impact of marines making an assault landing in Nicaragua, whirred with the endurance of new motors making it over oceans for the first time, and went out with a floor show of drama and technological advancement that has never been approached by any other year. The ingredients and achievements

of 1927 are a heady, explosive mixture. Even today, almost a half-century later, we can still feel the shock waves of the year's accomplishments and extravagances, its frantic jazz tempo, its exuberant neon-tinted boldness, and its youth. Especially its youth.

1 9 2 7

Some of the Songs They Were Singing in 1927

AT SUNDOWN. Words and music by Walter Donaldson. This ballad sold over 2 million records. It was a Ruth Etting favorite. In the 30s, both Jimmy and Tommy Dorsey recorded it.

THE BEST THINGS IN LIFE ARE FREE. Words by DeSylva and Brown; music by Ray Henderson. It was sung in the musical, *Good News*. It was also the title song of the 1956 movie based on the lives of DeSylva, Brown and Henderson.

BILL. Words by P. G. Wodehouse; music by Jerome Kern. Introduced by Helen Morgan in *Show Boat*, where it was an interpolated number. Originally written in 1918, this is the only song in *Show Boat* with lyrics not written by Oscar Hammerstein II.

BLUE SKIES. Words and music by Irving Berlin. This was introduced a year earlier by Belle Baker in the musical, *Betsy*.

CAN'T HELP LOVIN' DAT MAN. Words by Oscar Hammerstein II; music by Jerome Kern. It was sung in a fast dance tempo in *Show Boat,* but Miss Morgan sang it as a torch song in her night club act.

HALLELUJAH. Words by Leo Robin and Clifford Grey; music by Vincent Youmans. Heard in *Hit the Deck.* It was the song that started Vincent Youmans on a musical career. Long a navy favorite, it was featured by bandmaster John Philip Sousa in his concerts.

I'M LOOKING OVER A FOUR LEAF CLOVER. Words by Mort Dixon; music by Harry Woods. Twenty-one years after its introduction, it became a national hit again when Art Mooney recorded it in 1948.

LET A SMILE BE YOUR UMBRELLA ON A RAINY DAY. Words by Irving Kahal and Francis Wheeler; music by Sammy Fain. Sung in the 1929 movie, *It's a Great Life.*

ME AND MY SHADOW. Words by Billy Rose; music by Dave Dreyer and Al Jolson. Written for entertainer Frank Fay, who sang it in the revue, *Harry Delmar's Revels.* It was popularized by Jolson and by bandleader Ted Lewis.

MY BLUE HEAVEN. Words by George Whiting; music by Walter Donaldson. Eddie Cantor sang it in the *Ziegfeld Follies of 1927,* adding some lines about his five daughters to the original lyrics. Gene Austin's various recordings of this song sold over 12 million copies.

MY HEART STOOD STILL. Words by Lorenz Hart; music by Richard Rodgers. Written for the Charles B. Cochran London show, *One Dam Thing After Another,* then used in *A Connecticut Yankee.* The song, incidentally, became an international hit after the Prince of Wales sang it for a night club orchestra that didn't know it.

OL' MAN RIVER. Words by Oscar Hammerstein II; music by Jerome Kern. This classic was, of course, first heard in *Show Boat*. Of this song, Hammerstein wrote that it was "a song of resignation with a protest implied, sung by a character who is a rugged and untutored philosopher." Many people believe it to be a folk song, so forcefully has it become part of our musical heritage.

RAMONA. Words by L. Wolfe Gilbert; music by Mabel Wayne. Dolores Del Rio had made a movie by this name and a song was commissioned to promote the flick. The movie is forgotten but the melody lingers on. (It was played by Paul Whiteman's orchestra on a coast-to-coast radio hookup. The orchestra was in New York and the singer, Miss Del Rio, was in California. Another radio first!)

SAM, THE OLD ACCORDION MAN. Words and music by Walter Donaldson. Another Ruth Etting favorite.

SIDE BY SIDE. Words and music by Harry Woods. Kay Starr revived this old vaudeville standby in the 1950s.

SOMETIMES I'M HAPPY. Words by Irving Caesar; music by Vincent Youmans. Introduced in *Hit the Deck*. It was the first hit record of Bunny Berrigan's.

'S WONDERFUL. Words by Ira Gershwin; music by George Gershwin. Introduced by Adele Astaire and Allen Kearns in *Funny Face*.

THOU SWELL. Words by Lorenz Hart; music by Richard Rodgers. Bill Gaxton and Constance Carpenter sang this in *A Connecticut Yankee*.

THE VARSITY DRAG. Words by Buddy DeSylva and Lew Brown; music by Ray Henderson. One of the most appealing souvenirs of the year 1927. It was sung by Zelma O'Neal in *Good News*.

WHY DO I LOVE YOU? Words by Oscar Hammerstein II; music by Jerome Kern. Sung by Charles Winninger, Edna May Oliver, Howard Marsh and Norma Terris in *Show Boat*.

Other songs of 1927: *Ain't She Sweet*, by Ager and Yellen; *Among My Souvenirs*, by Nichols and Leslie; *Broken Hearted*, by DeSylva, Brown and Henderson; *Chloe*, Gus Kahn and Neil Moret; *Girl of My Dreams*, by Sunny Clapp.

1 9 2 7

Some of the Shows They Were Seeing in 1927

[This was Broadway's biggest and best year ever. There were 268 productions offered the theatergoing public in 1927—a record never equaled since.]

A CONNECTICUT YANKEE. With William Gaxton

ALLEZ OOP. With Victor Moore and Charles Butterworth

AND SO TO BED. With Emlyn Williams, Yvonne Arnaud and Wallace Eddinger

AN ENEMY OF THE PEOPLE. With Walter Hampden

A NIGHT IN SPAIN. With Helen Kane, Phil Baker, Ted Healy and Grace Hayes

ARTISTS AND MODELS. With Ted Lewis and Jack Pearl

BABY MINE. With Roscoe Arbuckle

THE BARKER. With Walter Huston, Claudette Colbert and Norman Foster

BEHOLD THE BRIDEGROOM. With Judith Anderson

BEHOLD THIS DREAMER. With Glenn Hunter

THE BROTHERS KARAMAZOV. With Alfred Lunt, Edward G. Robinson and Morris Carnovsky

BURLESQUE. With Hal Skelly and Barbara Stanwyck

THE COMMAND TO LOVE. With Mary Nash and Basil Rathbone

COQUETTE. With Helen Hayes

CRIME. With Sylvia Sidney, Douglass Montgomery, Chester Morris and James Rennie

THE DOCTOR'S DILEMMA. With Alfred Lunt and Lynn Fontanne.

DRACULA. With Bela Lugosi

ESCAPE. With Leslie Howard

EXCESS BAGGAGE. With Miriam Hopkins, Frank McHugh and Morton Downey

FALLEN ANGELS. With Fay Bainter

FOUR WALLS. With Paul Muni

FUNNY FACE. With Fred and Adele Astaire

GOOD NEWS. With Zelma O'Neal and Gus Shy

HER CARDBOARD LOVER. With Jeanne Eagels and Leslie Howard

HIT THE DECK. With Stella Mayhew and Charles King

INTERFERENCE. With A. E. Matthews

THE IVORY DOOR. With Henry Hull

THE LETTER. With Katharine Cornell

MANHATTAN MARY. With Ed Wynn

THE MARQUISE. With Billie Burke

THE MERRY MALONES. With George M. Cohan

PADLOCKS OF 1927. With Texas Guinan

PARIS BOUND. With Madge Kennedy

THE PLOUGH AND THE STARS. With Sara Allgood

PORGY. With Frank Wilson, Percey Verwayne and Evelyn Ellis

RIGHT YOU ARE IF YOU THINK YOU ARE. With Edward G. Robinson and Beryle Mercer

THE ROAD TO ROME. With Jane Cowl

THE ROYAL FAMILY. With Otto Kruger, Haidee Wright and Ann Andrews

SATURDAY'S CHILDREN. With Ruth Gordon

THE SECOND MAN. With Alfred Lunt and Lynn Fontanne

THE SHANNONS OF BROADWAY. With James Gleason and Lucille Webster

SHOW BOAT. With Charles Winninger, Edna May Oliver and Helen Morgan

SIDEWALKS OF NEW YORK. With Ruby Keeler and Ray Dooley

THE SPIDER. With John Halliday

THAT FRENCH LADY. With Louis Mann and Clara Lipman

TRELAWNEY OF THE WELLS. With John Drew, Estelle Winwood, Otto Kruger and Helen Gahagan

THE TRIAL OF MARY DUGAN. With Ann Harding

WOMEN GO ON FOREVER. With Mary Boland (James Cagney appeared in a small role)

YES, YES, YVETTE. With Jeanette MacDonald and Jack Whiting

YOURS TRULY. With Leon Errol

1 9 2 7

Some of the Movies They Were Watching in 1927

AFRAID TO LOVE. With Clive Brook and Florence Vidor

THE CAT AND THE CANARY. With Creighton Hale and Laura La Plante

FLESH AND THE DEVIL. With John Gilbert and Greta Garbo

THE GAUCHO. With Douglas Fairbanks

THE GENERAL. With Buster Keaton

IT. With Clara Bow

THE JAZZ SINGER. With Al Jolson

THE KING OF KINGS. With H. B. Warner

LADY IN ERMINE. With Francis X. Bushman and Corinne Griffith

LOVE. With Greta Garbo and John Gilbert

MY BEST GIRL. With Mary Pickford, Lucien Littlefield and Buddy Rogers

NIGHT OF LOVE. With Vilma Banky and Ronald Colman

SEVENTH HEAVEN. With Janet Gaynor and Charles Farrell

SOFT CUSHIONS. With Sue Carol and Douglas MacLean

SPECIAL DELIVERY. With Eddie Cantor

THE STUDENT PRINCE. With Norma Shearer and Ramon Novarro

SUNRISE. With Janet Gaynor and George O'Brien

TWELVE MILES OUT. With Joan Crawford and John Gilbert

UNDERWORLD. With Clive Brook and Evelyn Brent

THE WAY OF ALL FLESH. With Emil Jannings

WINGS. With Buddy Rogers, Clara Bow, Gary Cooper and Richard Arlen

1 9 2 7

APPENDIX IV

Some of the Books They Were Reading in 1927

FICTION

* Sinclair Lewis. *Elmer Gantry*. This study of an amoral evangelist sold 200,000 copies in its first 10 weeks in print.

Willa Cather. *Death Comes to the Archbishop*. Critical reception was mixed. The Boston *Transcript* praised it as "one of the most superb pieces of literary endeavor this reviewer has ever read. It is a piece of work that everyone may read with reverence and respect." *The Bookman* dismissed it as "a formless sort of novel," and the New York *Post* complained: "I feel Miss Cather has cluttered up her story and her mind with facts and with anecdotes."

Agatha Christie. *Mysterious Affair at Styles*. This was the first Agatha Christie novel, and it was greeted by the *Literary Review* thus: "The reader is ingeniously confused."

James Weldon Johnson. *God's Trombones*. "There is sensitivity, artistic judgment, and a sustained emotional beauty in his work. If the old negro preachers discoursed and chanted in this fashion, they were poets indeed."—New York *Herald Tribune*

* Booth Tarkington. *The Plutocrat*. Tarkington found writing difficult, and said of this book—a story of a self-made man traveling abroad—that it was "a very painful job, worse than having the measles."

* Mazo de la Roche. *Jalna*. This novel won the Atlantic Monthly prize for 1927. *Jalna* was the first book in the White Oak saga, which eventually became twelve volumes. "Overnight she has revealed herself a novelist to be reckoned with."—New York *Herald Tribune*

* Louis Bromfield. *A Good Woman*. The critics were courteous to Mr. Bromfield, hardly more. "A good book. As reading matter it is entertaining and moving. It is filled with finely concerted action."—New York *Times*

* Warwick Deeping. *Doomsday*. Deeping, an English writer, struck it rich with this book and another, *Sorrell and Son*. Both were on the American bestseller list for 1927. Both were made into movies, with *Sorrell and Son* being filmed twice—in 1927 and in 1934.

Robert Benchley. *Early Worm*. "Benchley can hardly write a line which has not in it a joyous spirit of fun."—*Outlook*

Sir Arthur Conan Doyle. *Case Book of Sherlock Holmes*. Gilbert Seldes in *The Bookman* reflected the majority opinion: "Sir Arthur is obviously weary of his detective and weary of writing."

William Faulkner. *Mosquitoes*. "Much ability is apparent."—Boston *Transcript*

Samuel Hopkins Adams. *Revelry*. This novel about the crooked Harding administration was greeted with perplexity. "The picture of the President who was too small for his job is done with genuine sympathy."—*Saturday Review*

Michael Arlen. *Young Men in Love*. The author of *The Green Hat* struck out. The Boston *Transcript* said: "Like yesterday's beer, than which there is nothing flatter."

* Anne Douglas Sedgwick. *The Old Countess*. This tragedy, contrasting French and English standards, received respectful reviews. "The real skill of the story is to be found in the bold artistry with which the semi-tragic background is painted in."—*Literary Review*

Other fiction published in 1927 included: *Tomorrow Morning** by Anne Parish, Mary Roberts Rinehart's *Lost Ecstasy**, and Edith Wharton's *Twilight Sleep*.

NONFICTION

* Emil Ludwig. *Napoleon*. A fast-moving, unscholarly biography of the Corsican who became emperor.

* Charles A. Lindbergh. *We*. Over 550,000 copies of Lindbergh's own story of his epochal flight were sold.

* George A. Dorsey. *Why We Behave Like Human Beings*. Dorsey, an expert on American Indians, wrote learned works, and for relaxation turned out popular books on self-help and psychology.

Luther Burbank. *Harvest of the Years*. This autobiography of the famous horticulturist disappointed reviewers. The *Herald Tribune* commented,

"There are flashes of insight; but also low deserts of bleak sentimentality and didactic primary school lessons."

George Arliss. *Up the Years from Bloomsbury: An Autobiography*. "A delightful book to read, and which strips away in the most agreeable manner a good deal of bunk from acting."—*North American Review*

Ray Stannard Baker. *Life and Letters of Woodrow Wilson*. "Something almost as intimate as a diary, and infinitely better and more honest than an autobiography."—*Saturday Review*

Charles Beard and Mary Beard. *Rise of American Civilization*. "It is appallingly learned, stirringly enlightened, and movingly human."—Carl Van Doren, New York *Herald Tribune*

* Will Durant. *The Story of Philosophy*. Over 1,500,000 copies have been sold since the publication of this popular introduction in 1927. Most of the copies have been sold through the Book-of-the-Month Club.
[Book club note: 1927 saw the debut of the Book-of-the-Month Club's arch-rival, the Literary Guild.]

Stuart Chase. *Your Money's Worth*. "The high purpose of the puritan has been charged with the sparkling flippancies of a Mencken to make a literary drink of exceptional taste and stimulation."—New York *Times*

* T. E. Lawrence. *Revolt in the Desert*. Lawrence of Arabia, whose career as a British agent in the Arabian Desert during World War I had been glamorized by Lowell Thomas, was an intriguing blend of mysticism, mystery, and myth. *Vanity Fair* nominated him for its Hall of Fame in 1927, calling him the "truest adventurer of our day," and his book, "one of the most talked-of books of the year."

* Alfred A. Horn and Ethelred Lewis. *Trader Horn: Volume One*. The adventures of Alfred Horn amazed most reviewers and readers, but there

were those who didn't buy the story. "I continue in the impression that this volume represents an authentic, clever, convincing swindle."—*Independent*

* Richard Halliburton. *The Glorious Adventure.* This and the author's *The Royal Road to Romance* were on the bestseller list for 1927. "There is probably less of actual information about the Greek lands in this book than in anyone of an average of dozen volumes."—*Saturday Review*

* Bestseller

1 9 2 7

Calvin Coolidge's Cabinet

Vice President: Charles G. Dawes

Secretary of State: Charles E. Hughes
                    Frank B. Kellogg

Secretary of Treasury: Andrew W. Mellon

Secretary of War: John W. Weeks
                 Dwight F. Davis

Attorney General: H. M. Daugherty
                 Harlan F. Stone
                 John G. Sargent

Secretary of Commerce: Herbert C. Hoover

Secretary of the Navy: Edwin Denby
                 Curtis D. Wilbur

Secretary of the Interior: Hubert Work
                    Roy O. West

Postmaster General: Harry S. New

1 9 2 7

Prizes and Awards in 1927

OSCARS
For Best Production: *Wings,* Paramount
For Best Actor: Emil Jannings, for *The Way of All Flesh* and *The Last Command*
For Best Actress: Janet Gaynor, for *Seventh Heaven, Street Angel,* and *Sunrise*
For Best Direction: Frank Borzage, *Seventh Heaven*
Other Oscars went to Lewis Milestone, for best comedy direction, Ben Hecht, for the best original story (*Underworld*), and a special award went to Warner Brothers, for its production of *The Jazz Singer,* and Charles Chaplin, for *The Circus.*

PULITZER PRIZES
Fiction: Louis Bromfield, *Early Autumn*
Drama: Paul Green, *In Abraham's Bosom*
History: Samuel Flagg Bemis, *Pinckney's Treaty*
Biography: Emory Holloway, *Whitman: An Interpretation in Narrative*
Poetry: Leonora Speyer, *Fiddler's Farewell*

Editorial Writing: Boston *Herald,* F. Lauriston Bullard
Cartoon: Nelson Harding, Brooklyn *Eagle*
Meritorious Public Service: Canton, Ohio, *Daily News*
Reporting: John T. Roberts, St. Louis *Post-Dispatch*

NOBEL PRIZES
Literature: Henri Bergson, France
Peace: Ferdinand Edouard Buisson, France, and Ludwig Quidde, Austria
Physics: Arthur H. Compton, U.S.A., and Charles T. R. Wilson, Great Britain
Chemistry: Heinrich Wieland, Germany
Medicine and Physiology: J. Wagner-Jauregg, Austria

1 9 2 7

Sports Champions in 1927

Baseball

The New York Yankees beat the Pittsburgh Pirates in 4 straight games to take the World Series.

AMERICAN LEAGUE

Home Run Champion:
Babe Ruth, New York 60
Runs Batted in Leader:
Lou Gehrig, New York 175
Batting Champion:
Harry Heilmann, Detroit .398
Pitcher with Best Won and Lost
Percentage (15-game minimum):
Waite Hoyt, New York
Won 22   Lost 7   Percentage .759

NATIONAL LEAGUE

Home Run Champion:
Hack Wilson, Chicago 30
Cy Williams, Philadelphia 30
Runs Batted in Leader:
Paul Waner, Pittsburgh 131
Batting Champion:
Paul Waner, Pittsburgh .380
Pitcher with Best Won and Lost
Percentage (15-game minimum):
Larry Benton, New York
Won 17   Lost 7   Percentage .708

Football
ROSE BOWL:
Alabama 7 Stanford 7
NATIONAL COLLEGE FOOTBALL CHAMPS:
Illinois

Boxing
Division Crowns:

Heavyweight	Gene Tunney
Light Heavyweight	Mike McTigue
Middleweight	Mickey Walker
Welterweight	Joe Dundee
Lightweight	Sammy Mandell
Featherweight	Benny Bass

Tennis
Davis Cup: France
Wightman Cup: U.S.A.

U.S. Men's Singles: Rene Lacoste, France
U.S. Women's Singles: Helen Wills, U.S.A.

Golf
PGA: Walter Haven
USGA: Robert T. Jones, Jr.
USGA Open: Tommy Armour and Harry Cooper tied
at 301. The playoff was won by Armour, 76–79

Women's Amateur Golf: Miriam Burns Horn

Horseracing
Kentucky Derby: Whiskery
Preakness Stakes: Bostonian
Belmont Stakes: Chance Shot
Leading money-winning horse: Anita Peabody, $111,905

Autoracing
George Souders won the Indianapolis 500
driving a Duesenberg. His time: 5:07:33:08

Chess
World Chess Champions: Jose R. Capablanca
Alexandr A. Alekhine

U.S. Chess Champion: Frank J. Marshall

1 9 2 7

APPENDIX VIII

Disasters in 1927

Apr. 12. Tornado killed 74 in Rocksprings, Texas
Apr. 30. 97 dead in coal mine explosion, Everettville, West Virginia
May 9.   Tornado kills 92 in Poplar Bluff, Mo.
Aug. 25. Two Japanese destroyers collide. 129 lost
Sept. 29· Tornado kills 72 in St. Louis, Mo.
Oct. 25. The Italian ship *Principessa Mafalda* sinks, with a loss of 314 people
Dec. 17. The American submarine *S-4* sinks, with a loss of 40

1 9 2 7

Average Retail Food Prices in 1927

	1927	1968
10 lbs. wheat flour	55¢	1.17
lb. rice	11¢	19¢
lb. white bread	9¢	22¢
lb. round steak	39¢	1.14
lb. rib roast	35¢	99¢
lb. chuck roast	25¢	64¢
lb. pork chops	37¢	1.03
lb. sliced bacon	48¢	81¢
1 qt. milk (delivered)	14¢	30¢
lb. butter	56¢	84¢
lb. cheese	39¢	89¢
15 lbs. potatoes	57¢	1.15
lb. sugar	7¢	12¢
doz. eggs	49¢	53¢
lb. coffee	47¢	76¢

Index